PENGUIN BOOKS

OVERCOMING AGORAPHOBIA

Alan Goldstein, Ph.D., is a psychologist and professor in the department of psychiatry at Temple University in Philadelphia. In 1977, after treating agoraphobics for five years, he founded the Agoraphobia and Anxiety Program at Temple. The methods Dr. Goldstein developed are now used as a model for treatment programs across the country.

Dr. Goldstein coedited *The Handbook of Behavioral Interventions* and *Agoraphobia: Multiple Perspectives on Theory and Treatment*. He lives in Philadelphia.

Berry Stainback has cowritten several books, including Earl Weaver's *It's What You Learn After You Know It All That Counts* and Ken Stabler's *Snake*.

Overcoming Agoraphobia

Conquering Fear of the Outside World

DR. ALAN GOLDSTEIN
and BERRY STAINBACK

PENGUIN BOOKS

PENGUIN BOOKS
Published by the Penguin Group
Viking Penguin Inc., 40 West 23rd Street,
New York, New York 10010, U.S.A.
Penguin Books Ltd, 27 Wrights Lane, London W8 5TZ, England
Penguin Books Australia Ltd, Ringwood,
Victoria, Australia
Penguin Books Canada Ltd, 2801 John Street,
Markham, Ontario, Canada L3R 1B4
Penguin Books (N.Z.) Ltd, 182–190 Wairau Road,
Auckland 10, New Zealand

Penguin Books Ltd, Registered Offices:
Harmondsworth, Middlesex, England

First published in the United States of America by Viking Penguin Inc. 1987
Published in Penguin Books 1988

Grateful acknowledgment is made for permission to reprint excerpts from the
following copyrighted material:

"I Want to Live," by John Denver. © Copyright 1977, 1978 Cherry Lane Music
Publishing Co., Inc. All rights reserved. International copyright secured.
Used by permission.

"Agoraphobia," by Laraine C. Abbey, R.N., M.S., from *The Journal of Orthomolecular Psychiatry*, Volume 11, No. 4. Copyright 1982 by the Canadian
Schizophrenia Foundation. Reprinted by permission of the Journal of Orthomolecular Psychiatry, Regina, Saskatchewan, Canada.

LIBRARY OF CONGRESS CATALOGING IN PUBLICATION DATA
Goldstein, Alan J., 1933–
Overcoming agoraphobia.
Includes index.
1. Agoraphobia—Popular works.   2. Agoraphobia—
Case studies.   3. Agoraphobia—Treatment—Directories.
I. Stainback, Berry.   II. Title.
RC552.A44G65   1987b   616.85'225   87-29255
ISBN 0 14 00.9468 7

Printed in the United States of America by
R. R. Donnelley & Sons Company, Harrisonburg, Virginia
Set in Bembo

Acknowledgments

*M*y very special thanks go to Dianne Chambless with whom I have collaborated over many years. She has provided encouragement, support and keen intelligence every step of the way. Without her effort we would not have the scientific base for our program, which she has created through her role as our research director. No amount of praise is sufficient, so please just accept my heartfelt thanks, Dianne.

And to Linda Welsh, thank you for your warmth and untiring support of me personally, and for your dedication to the staff and to the welfare of the program. You have always been there to bolster us individually and to anticipate any foreseeable problems and to correct those that were not. You have truly been the backbone of our clinical program.

To B. J. Foster, our warm-hearted and hard-headed administrator, thank you for keeping us on track and organized in such a humanistic style—a rare quality among effective administrators.

To Zelma Kennedy, my appreciation for being on the front line as secretary, receptionist, and kind-hearted, caring intermediary since our program began.

Thanks, too, to Sophia Baginski, who has volunteered so much of her time and caring for the welfare of those who call in and need an understanding ear, and who is always willing to fill in where needed.

Throughout the many years of development of the Agoraphobia and Anxiety Program, I have had the extraordinary good fortune to be surrounded by talented and dedicated people. The program as it is today reflects the input of these people and no doubt owes its success to the blending and integrating of the ideas and experiences of these exceptional people. I would like to acknowledge your "authorship" of this book by thanking all of you: Barbara Shoulson, Georgia Sloan, Alex Tullis, Julie Weiss, David Ramirez, Takako Suzuki, Gerald O'Brien, Diane Coia, Timothy Dickens, Susan Jasin, Lisa Yasui, Ulla Horsten-Watter, David Cordier, Sylvia Elias, Joan Heacock, Simone Gorko, Bonnie Simon, Priscilla Bright, Steven Scale, Ellen Lack, Gail Zitin, Madeleine Richardson, David Schotte, Joseph Canevello, Blanche Freund, Nazareth Pantaloni, Edward Gracely, Craig Caputo, Diane DeMarco, Ben Cohen, Michael Zelson, Beth McAllister, Bethanne Littlefield, Christine Williams and Diane Zimmerman.

Last, I would like to express my appreciation to our editor, Nan Graham. Throughout this process, she has been an enthusiastic supporter of this project, a valuable contributor and a superb editor.

—A. G.

C H A P T E R

Contents

Overcoming
Agoraphobia

Defining the Disorder and Developing a Treatment Program That Works

*A*goraphobia is the most terrifying, debilitating and all-consuming of the phobias. Its sufferers, the vast majority of whom are women, are suddenly and out of nowhere seized by panic attacks that may last for a few minutes to many hours. Typically, a woman is doing nothing more fear-provoking than standing in the checkout line at a supermarket, her wagon full of groceries, when her stomach abruptly feels queasy, her knees turn weak, she begins to tremble, beads of sweat pop out on her brow and on the palms of her hands, she grows dizzy and her heart starts pounding faster and faster until she fears it will burst through her chest. She wants to cry out, to scream, but she's gasping for breath, her throat is constricted and her mouth is dry. Blood drains from her face, she runs from the store, staggers to her car in the parking lot, climbs in and lowers her head onto the steering wheel until the panic finally passes. She drives home slowly, shaken and exhausted by the experience. She is scared, and with each subsequent attack her anxiety intensifies.

Wherever an attack strikes thereafter—driving over a bridge, riding in an elevator or sitting in a restaurant—she avoids from then on in fear of a recurrence. She may no longer do the banking or the grocery shopping for her family (more lines she's afraid to wait in) or she may be unable to return to her job. Soon she is too frightened to drive a car and so she can't drive her children to their Little League games or to visit their cousins across town, and she can't consult their teachers at school. Next, fearing she'll have an attack while socializing with friends, she begins making excuses about why she can't get together with them. Her anxiety is now with her constantly, panics gripping her several times a day. Her disorder places an enormous burden on the rest of the family, and she feels guilty and depressed about not doing her share. All of the family's activities revolve around her symptoms, and in time her husband and children will often grow resentful, annoyed, even angry, which intensifies her anxiety. Now the slightest change in her body sensations can trigger anxiety or even a panic attack. A headache becomes a potential brain tumor, a fluttery pulse suggests an imminent heart attack. The agoraphobic can find no relief, feel comfortable virtually nowhere as the anxiety clicks away in her mind like a manically timed charge.

This very brief description of a typical case of agoraphobia includes its key ingredients: panics, avoidance of the places where attacks occurred, chronic anxiety, depression and the distressing impact the disorder has on the agoraphobic family. (As most agoraphobics are female—85 percent of those who have been treated at the Agoraphobia and Anxiety Program* over the last dozen years—all case references will be to females unless otherwise stated.) The panics are spearheaded by a variety of fears, as reported by clients when they first seek help. Each attack is keyed by an overwhelming dread that something catastrophic is about to happen to them, such as a heart attack. Others say, "I can't breathe—I feel like I'll faint!" Or, "Oh, my God, I think

---

*The Agoraphobia and Anxiety Program is a satellite clinic of Temple University Medical School, Department of Psychiatry, and is located at 112 Bala Avenue in Bala Cynwyd, Pennsylvania 19004.

I'm going crazy!" Or, "I feel like my head's about to ex-
plode!" Or, "I'm going blind; it gets darker and darker
until I can barely see!" Or, "Everything around me becomes unreal and the sidewalk starts to come up at me. Then
I begin to fade away, and I feel like I'm going over the edge
and never coming back!"

AVOIDANCE, OR WHY YOU FLEE

Under this kind of siege, the only thing people can think
about is flight, getting away from the awful place where the
panic is snapping at them, to a safe area. Often this is home,
sometimes it is a hospital, a trusted friend's residence or perhaps a spouse's place of business. But the fear of further
panic attacks is so horrendous that it begins to dominate
one's existence. The agoraphobic avoids not only the places
and circumstances where panics took hold, but all similar
places and circumstances. Thus a panic on a particular elevator may lead to avoidance of all elevators. Tunnels, bridges
and major highways are all common sites of panic, as are
crowded areas such as shopping centers or ball parks. Any
place from which there is no easy escape to safety—such as
a dark theater, a rear table in a restaurant, a seat on an airplane or other public transportation—can make an agoraphobic feel trapped and produce panic.

Some of our clients come to us after their first or second
panic attack, though most consult their family doctor and
psychotherapist for a time and suffer from agoraphobia
(which until recently was often not properly diagnosed) for
years before we see them. Typical of the latter client is this
thirty-year-old woman from our files who reported:

I've been like this for over two years, but it's gotten worse.
Now I just can't go anywhere. I know that any time I leave
the house sooner or later panic will hit me. It always does.
Last week my uncle died and for days I dreaded the funeral. I

knew I had to go because I was close to him. I went to the service at church and sat in the back, but my heart started pounding. I had to slip out of the church. Once I was in the fresh air, I felt a little better. I stayed out awhile, then tried to go back in. But my heart started in again and I thought I'd die if I didn't get back outside. I just waited there until everyone came out. I couldn't even go to the cemetery. I had my husband take me home.

This woman was not totally housebound. The most severely avoidant cases never leave their dwelling place, and some won't even leave their bedroom except to use the toilet. Then there are mildly avoidant agoraphobics whose mobility is limited to their own city or to within several hundred miles of home. Some may not fly, some may avoid skyscraper elevators and some may avoid driving on expressways.

A MILDLY AVOIDANT CLIENT

One recent case involved a male high school teacher in his late thirties who said he'd begun having panics three years ago when his marriage broke up. Soon he found himself feeling anxious about entering a classroom. Next he grew anxious about joining his friends in their weekly night out. They usually met at a bar with a pool table where they played for quarters and sipped beer all evening. "But suddenly I was apprehensive and I didn't know quite why," the teacher reported. "One thing was I didn't want to drink, because alcohol was making me feel out of control all of a sudden. I usually only had four or five beers in as many hours while out. But I had two beers at home one night and felt really spacy, anxious, kind of scared. What would my buddies think if they saw me get shaky shooting pool? They'd think I was weird, so I stopped joining them."

He forced himself to enter the classroom and keep teaching because he was putting his daughter through college and he wasn't going to let her down. He kept pushing himself, and in a month or so rejoined his friends on their night out. As long as he continued to push himself he felt fairly comfortable most of the time. The reason he sought help was his desire to overcome a fear of flying. His daughter was in school in Wisconsin and he wanted to visit her. "But being locked in a plane for six hours, I know I'd go bananas," he said. Recently he had bought a plane ticket to Wisconsin and driven to the airport. En route he heard of an air disaster on the radio, and he turned right around and went home. So this man had learned to manage his fears and to do pretty much what he wanted to, except fly. We worked on that and in a month he was aloft.

CHRONIC ANXIETY

Most agoraphobics are beset by too much unremitting anxiety to manage their fears. In addition to fearing places and circumstances where panics strike, many fear that they will lose control of themselves in public and be humiliated or look foolish bolting from, say, a restaurant in mid-meal or from a movie. They are afraid people will think they're crazy, and they themselves suspect they're crazy. Other agoraphobics have a persistent fear that they will suffer so severe an attack in public that they will faint, an ambulance will be summoned and they'll be hauled off to a hospital. There, they fantasize, it will be determined that there is nothing physically wrong with them; they have a mental problem and need to be locked up in a mental institution. In truth it is not place or circumstance that brings on panic but the *anticipated* fear of an attack—the fear of fear itself. The panic strikes, rises and subsides, but the fear of the next attack is always there.

A typical comment on chronic anxiety from our case files: "Life is always miserable. I'm feeling anxious *all* the time, even at home, even when things are going smoothly. It seems like it never goes away. If I avoid certain places where I feel trapped, I don't have full-blown panic attacks. But the anxiety just doesn't let up. I wake up in the morning anxious and I go to bed anxious. It just gnaws away at me."

Other clients report that they have tension headaches, are irritable and short-tempered. "I can't stand any sudden loud noise around the house. I mean, even the doorbell ringing can send my heart into my mouth. I'm always on edge."

ANTICIPATORY ANXIETY

In addition to this background of steady anxiety there is periodic anticipatory anxiety to deal with. "Whenever I learn that I'm going to have to go someplace, almost anything that takes me out of the house," said one client, "the anxiety starts to climb. And every day as that date draws closer, the more anxious I become. For instance, I was supposed to attend my sister's graduation last month. I told her I'd be there, I wanted to see her receive the diploma she worked so hard for, and I really tried. I bought a new dress. But the day came, and I just couldn't go. Next week my son's graduating from sixth grade and . . . well, just thinking about sitting in a big auditorium among all those people scares me so much I begin to tremble. I do." The woman paused, choking back tears. "I don't know what I'm gonna do on graduation day. But the fear gets worse every day and I don't see how I'll ever be able to go. And what can I say to my son?" She sobbed. "Jimmy won't understand. I know it, damn it!"

Worry about the things that they don't do helps maintain the anxiety felt by agoraphobics. Wives and mothers feel they should be doing the shopping chores that they've turned over to their husbands, they feel they should be doing more for their children, particularly away from home, and they worry about limiting both husbands and children in terms of vacations and other family excursions. Because of their agoraphobia, family picnics and trips to the lake or to relatives in other towns have virtually ceased. Guilt-triggered anxiety is inevitable. Women who are in school or working feel guilty about not being as productive as they feel they should be.

Though these facts emerge in therapy sessions, the majority of agoraphobics cannot understand why they are always anxious. "Even when nothing seems to be wrong I'm anxious," they say. It's perfectly understandable, I tell them, and offer this analogy: "If you live in a city and have a fear of snakes, you feel comfortable because you are confident that you won't come across one. But if you're fearful of dogs you are more anxious because the city's full of dogs. Step out of your home and a dog may turn the corner and come at you. So you spend a lot of time planning ways to avoid running into a dog and this produces anticipatory anxiety. However, at least when at home, in restaurants and stores, with the door closed, there is safety, so that it's possible to get relief. But people who have panic attacks and are naturally fearful about their recurring can never feel safe because they often report the attacks 'come out of the blue.' So you are always on guard, always anxious about a potential panic attack—just as you would be if you feared a canine attack while on the street. Your fear is completely understandable. Your anxiety is a normal response to an unpredictable occurrence: panic."

BESET BY DEPRESSION

As if panics, avoidant behavior and chronic anxiety are not burdens enough, agoraphobics are also beset by depression. There are numerous signs of this in client descriptions of their current existence. They say they just don't enjoy anything in life anymore, even activities they once found great pleasure in. They no longer enjoy playing with their children, visiting friends or having them over, attending family gatherings or having sex. We have heard many agoraphobics say, "That was something that used to be really good between me and my husband. But now I'm always so tired I have no interest in sex. I just don't have the energy for anything."

Exhaustion is universal among agoraphobics, because they are troubled sleepers. Some retire early, sleep late in the morning, arise and return to bed for a nap before noon. Others have a hard time going to sleep and then they toss and turn, things just rattling around in their heads, not complete thoughts, but a kind of cacophony of activity. Still others suffer from broken sleep, regularly waking in the middle of the night and finding it difficult to fall asleep again.

While some keep themselves constantly busy with homework so they "don't have to think," many are listless and say things like, "I can't seem to get started on anything anymore. I'm a freelance writer and I used to like to spend two hours writing each morning before going out to research a story . . . and I don't do any of that anymore. I started an article months ago and I've only done four pages. I know I should be doing things, but I just can't seem to. It's so depressing."

While some agoraphobics are too agitated to eat, and lose weight, many tend to gain weight. Others let their appearance go completely, no longer putting on makeup. One client says: "I always seem to have something in my mouth. Cookies, potato chips, doughnuts, and I've always loved Pepsi-Cola. I can drink four or five bottles a day. It's ridiculous, because I used to worry about how I looked. I never left the house without making up my face. Now, of course, I seldom leave the house. I've gained over twenty pounds. I've stopped weighing myself. What for?"

The depression and anxiety of agoraphobics are sustained and multiplied by the fact that they are cut off from all pleasurable activities, so they experience no relief from the everyday stresses of life. As the stresses fester, they cause more anxiety and depression. It is all relentlessly grim.

REDUCED TO HOPELESSNESS

The worst of agoraphobia is that most sufferers are absolutely convinced that their case is hopeless, that they will never get better. Even those who continue to fight and hope live with constant frustration. Most first see a family physician who may put them through a number of tests to rule out diseases that might cause similar symptoms. Since agoraphobia is not a medical disorder, these tests will be negative and the doctor will probably prescribe tranquilizers for anxiety. Many of those beset by agoraphobia go on to consult a psychiatrist or psychologist doing traditional therapy; they, too, prove to be of little help. In fact, many agoraphobics find their symptoms worsening in such therapy because there is insufficient focus on teaching the agoraphobic how to cope with everyday anxiety, panic and avoidance, which are the immediate sources of severe distress. When these skills are not learned, the agoraphobic becomes progressively more discouraged and out of control.

When people first come to the Agoraphobia and Anxiety Program for treatment they have often been to a number of professionals, and their faces reflect a simmering fear and sorrow and an overwhelming incomprehension. Without a word they seem to be saying, "Why am I suffering? Why doesn't anyone understand? Why can't someone help me? It's hopeless." This attitude is reflected in intake interviews with the vast majority of our clients.

Jane R. was a typical client of ours. A young woman who had been married less than a year, Jane said she was too frightened to shop unless accompanied by her husband and that he was talking about a separation unless she returned to "normal." "I couldn't bear to be separated from Bill." Here is an excerpt from her intake interview:

T (therapist)—Do you have panic attacks when you shop alone?

J (Jane)—Yes. Any place that's crowded.

T—So you try to avoid places that are so crowded you feel like you can't get out of them quickly?

J—You know, I never thought of it that way before but crowded stores make me feel trapped. I get this horrible feeling that I'm going to pass out, or my heart beats so hard I think it's going to burst. It's like I'm about to have a heart attack.

T—Can you recall when you first had these panics?

J—On my job, just before my marriage. Twice I had to run home from work. A third time I went to my doctor. He said my problem was nerves and gave me the tranquilizer Valium.

T—What were you nervous about?

J—My wedding. [She looked down at her lap and twisted the handkerchief in her hands.]

T—You weren't sure you wanted to marry Bill?

J—I . . . I wanted to marry Bill. My mother didn't want me to. I love Bill. He's been good about my problem, my attacks.

T—Even though he's talked about a separation?

J—(Looking tearful) Yes. He . . . he says he doesn't want to spend all his free time shopping. Bill works hard, lots of nights.

T—Does that bother you?

J—Sometimes. Lots of times. I don't like being alone.

T—You feel better when Bill's around?

J—I went to a psychiatrist for three visits and he said it's because I'm like a child and don't want to grow up. I think I understand more about how growing up in my family made me feel so insecure, but my panics haven't let up and I can do less by myself than I could a year ago.

T—I'm sure there are times when you feel like a child, as most of us do when we're frightened. Do you think you'd feel all right driving around the city with me?

J—I think I would. You're a doctor. You'd know what to do if anything happened to me.

T—Such as?

J—If I started to pass out or go crazy or have a heart attack.

T—When you're with someone you trust to take care of you if you have a panic attack, you can go places you don't go alone?

J—Yes, I could always go shopping with Bill until two months ago. Now I'm even afraid to do that.

T—I'm getting the feeling that if we could control your fear of panic attacks—I call it fear of fear—you wouldn't need to have your husband with you so much.

J—That's why I came here. When I read about the program in a newspaper story, I knew I had agoraphobia, which my own doctor and that psychiatrist hadn't even told me.

T—Because effective treatment is highly specialized and has been available only recently, there are a lot of therapists who can't yet diagnose agoraphobia. But you *can* learn to handle these panic attacks and be able to shop on your own again.

J—You mean you think you really *can help* me? [Tears welled in her eyes.]

T—I think if we work hard together we can be successful. What do you think?

J—I *want* to get better. I really do.

T—I believe you. I think you just don't know how to go about getting better, but we will help you with that.

People can get over agoraphobia, as we will see. In Chapter Two we will show how the disorder developed in

Jane, presenting her background from childhood until the onset of agoraphobia, and in Chapter Three we will examine in depth the treatment program at Temple that brought about her recovery.

CHAPTER 2

The Roots of Agoraphobia

Children need loving, dependable, competent parents as role models, a secure base from which to go out into the world and cope with life independently. Without solid guidance and the opportunity to develop the skills needed to solve the inevitable problems that arise, people tend to become fearful and rather than face stressful situations they avoid them. What kind of childhood experiences make people so anxious that they, unconsciously, assume an avoidant lifestyle that can ultimately lead to the onset of agoraphobia?

Interviews with hundreds of clients over the years reveal that sufferers from agoraphobia have backgrounds that break down into six general categories. Most of them were reared in at least one—and some more than one—of the following circumstances: (1) Their parents overprotected them. (2) Too much responsibility was thrust on them because they had to take care of a mother or father who was chronically ill, alcoholic or agoraphobic. (3) Their parents' behavior was unpredictable because they were alcoholic, agoraphobic or psychotic. (4) Their parents were perceived to be overcritical, often impossible to please. (5) The youngsters either felt threatened by or were actually subjected to the premature loss of or separation from one or both parents. (6) The youngsters were sexually abused, usually by an adult male in the family. Often the abuser was intoxicated.

The very briefly summarized cases that follow present the sequence of events in childhood that we believe produces the insecurity and anxiety that can erupt in panic attacks in adulthood. Please note that the examples included here are almost all extremes because they best illustrate the category cited. But many of our clients initially reported on entering treatment that they came from model families. It was only after they had spent some time in therapy that they began to recognize the subtle yet very powerful influences in their family system.

THE OVERPROTECTED CHILD

Charlotte was an only child. During her childhood, her father was forced to spend most of his time at his marginally profitable business; her mother was frightened by the city in which they lived. Though Charlotte's school was just a few blocks from their apartment, her mother escorted her in the morning and met her after classes until the child was ten. The mother did everything for Charlotte, from laying out her clothes early on to selecting her friends into the girl's teens. Charlotte was seldom permitted to sleep over at girlfriends' homes and was not allowed to begin dating when her peers did at age sixteen. Her mother was so plagued by her own insecurities that she could not bring herself to allow Charlotte, at age seventeen, to take a job after school at a nearby luncheonette. As her mother seemed so fearful, Charlotte told her therapist that she invariably hurried home from school, worried that if she tarried something bad might happen to her mother.

As a result of her experience Charlotte felt that home was the only safe place. She lacked a solid base for dealing with the world, because she had not explored it as young people need to if they are to gain confidence. Her father's absence caused her to feel abandoned and it also failed to counterbalance her mother's fearfulness, which Charlotte unknowingly absorbed. She reached adulthood without acquiring sufficient coping abilities, and without feeling capable of functioning on her own.

TOO MUCH RESPONSIBILITY

a) *The Child as Caretaker of a Chronically Ill Parent*

Nancy was the oldest of four children and her mother was ill as far back as the child could recall. Nancy became her mother's helper with each of the other children, changing them, feeding them, entertaining them, watching over them. She felt close to her mother and rather enjoyed the feelings of importance that emanated from her role as little mother. But when Nancy was nine her mother developed a degenerative nerve disease that grew progressively worse over the next five years. Nancy became both mother and nurse through that period. She did much of the cleaning and all of the cooking, personally serving her mother in bed right up until her death when Nancy was fourteen. Her father tried to lift Nancy's burdens by hiring a part-time housekeeper-cook, but within six months the father's business declined sharply and he had to let the housekeeper go. In addition he had to work longer hours and could provide even less emotional support for his family. Nancy saw how this grieved him and she felt for her dad. But she also was saddened by her lack of a social life. While her girlfriends were going out together or dating, Nancy was home caring for her younger brother and sisters. She developed a tremendous resentment of the fact that she herself had never been taken care of, never been parented. And she had been so isolated in the house that she grew anxious whenever she was out of it, for she had learned little about dealing with the world at large. Home was Nancy's haven and her prison.

b) *Caretaker of an Agoraphobic Parent*

Though undiagnosed at the time, Clara's mother was agoraphobic and would not leave the house unless accompanied by her husband or daughter. Clara was even called out of school on occasion by her mother, who was having panic attacks and could not control her fears. The girl became convinced that if she was not present to support her mother, one day she would come home and find her mother seriously ill. Clara also felt she had to protect her mother from her father, who was overwhelmed by trying to do everything for his family. Periodically he'd crack under the pressure and yell at his wife, saying things like, "You can't do anything by yourself, dammit." Once he slapped his wife in front of Clara. As a teenager Clara dated sparingly because she was afraid to leave her mother. One summer her mother said she was feeling better and agreed that it would be nice for Clara to spend two weeks with an aunt in the country. Three days after Clara arrived in the country her mother phoned and begged her to come home, saying, "I'll just die if you're not here tomorrow!" Clara dutifully headed home. Later she shelved her plans to attend college, her life now dominated by concern about her mother.

c) Caretaker of an Alcoholic Parent

Margaret's mother was the family breadwinner, a woman who worked as a waitress from noon until 10 P.M. six days a week. Margaret looked after her alcoholic father, who could not keep a job. He sat home drinking in front of the television set except when his wife had her day off. She would complain and he'd take his bottle to the park. But Margaret usually found her father drunk when she came home from school. She'd prepare something to eat and clean up any mess he'd made. If he had passed out, she would help him to bed. Margaret was too embarrassed by her father to have friends over, and she had virtually no social life. She just stayed home, caring for her father, cooking, cleaning and doing the laundry. Margaret seldom saw her mother, who didn't get home until after 11 P.M. and who was still sleeping when the girl went off to school in the morning. Essentially Margaret grew up without having had any support from her parents, and she was left with no sense of security in the world.

UNPREDICTABILITY

a) Alcoholic Parent

Jenny never knew what to expect from either of her parents. Her alcoholic father could be warm, amusing and very loving when he wasn't inebriated, even at times when he was drinking. He would thank her for caring so much for him, hug her and tell her he didn't know what he would do without her. But the very next day he might shout at her, charging that she didn't give a damn about him. As the family breadwinner, Jenny's mother was usually exhausted and often gruff with her. Yet the mother could also be tender and loving on occasion. Like the father, she was the tease of a good parent. To feel secure and safe, a child needs to perceive consistency and dependability in his or her parents. When one cannot anticipate what to expect from parents, insecurity and anxiety result.

b) Psychotic Parent

Diane's mother was psychotic and often angry and abusive, many times losing her rationality and accusing Diane of errors she had not committed. "I told you to clean your room, Diane, and you didn't do it!" the mother would yell. "Mom, you didn't tell me. Besides, I cleaned my room two days ago." "You did not! It's filthy!" Diane's mother was under extreme financial and emotional stress. When she was taking medication and her psychosis was in remission, she was calm and caring, often to the point of over-protectiveness. The mother's personality would be totally different from week to week. Sometimes she would be withdrawn and silent for days. Diane would have to remind her that it was time to go to bed, time to get up in the morning, time to leave the table when she'd finished eating. Diane was only three when her father left the family and cut off all contact with his wife and daughter, who felt abandoned by him.

c) *Agoraphobic Parent*

Jack's father was a disciplinarian whom the boy seldom seemed to please. Often the father came home from long hours at a job which drained and frustrated him. He would issue some complaint: "You didn't cut the grass!" "Your homework's not done!" "If I've told you once I've told you a thousand times—take your elbow off the table!" Jack became attached to his mother, who was kind to him and enjoyed playing games with him. But she was agoraphobic and as a result of the disorder she often disappointed him. He just didn't know what was the matter with her. When he was a second grader he was to appear in a school play and he was very excited about it. When he told his mother, she was also enthusiastic, proud of him. Yet when the curtain rose on the play, Jack looked out into the audience from the stage and his mother wasn't there. He couldn't understand that. Some years later as a member of the track team, Jack had his mother drive him to meets. Inexplicably, though, sometimes she refused to do so. "I don't feel well," she would tell him, while looking fine to Jack. He never knew when he could count on his mother, who periodically just seemed to reject him. At other times she was concerned, loving, pleased to do anything she could for him. It was all very confusing to Jack.

OVERCRITICAL PARENTS

Beverly had two older sisters who were excellent students without having to study a great deal, and their father praised them endlessly. Wanting the same acclaim, Beverly worked very hard in school and usually excelled. But when she brought home a report card with a B in one subject, compared to her sisters' straight A's, her father smiled and said, "Maybe you're just not the student your sisters are. That's okay, we can't all be perfect." But Beverly kept trying to be. She was a bit overweight and was always dieting, because her father kept commenting on her appearance. "Don't you think you're a little too heavy to wear that tight sweater, Bev?" he'd say. "Your sisters look good in sweaters, but I'm afraid you'll have to drop a few pounds before you can wear form-fitting clothes." Any time her performance or appearance did not win approval, Beverly felt as if her father was withdrawing his love. He had plenty to give her sisters, who kept telling her to relax and not be so uptight, "That's just Dad's way." But Beverly was never secure in the relationship with her father.

FEAR OF LOSS

a) *Threat of Separation from Parents*

When she was very young Janet remembered that her parents used threats to get her to do their bidding. At first they said, "If you don't behave we'll send you to live with Aunt Silvia," who was a rather grouchy older woman. Later, when Janet started school, she remembered their saying, "We'll send you away to boarding school if you don't stop crying." Terrified, Janet would stop crying immediately and go to her room. Even pleasurable things were sometimes used as threats, such as, "If you don't straighten up, Janet, we'll send you away to camp for the entire summer!" Always fearful of being sent away by her parents, Janet began to cling to them. She felt a need to be with one of them all the time. As she grew older her parents stopped threatening her and began attacking each other. Several times she heard her father swear he was going to leave the home. "Damn you, I'll just pack my bags and go!" he would say. Janet would beg her mother not to let her dad leave, and her mother tried to comfort her, saying, "It's all right, he won't go because he loves us too much." But Janet was never sure, she felt so little security in her parents while growing up.

b) Separation from Parent(s)

Until his sixth year, Bill had been very close to his father, a large outgoing man who loved taking him to the park, the zoo, the beach, ballgames. Then the father, his business in decline, returned to his former profession of ship's captain. He commanded oil tankers and went on cruises that kept him at sea for a year or more at a stretch. He would come home for a month or two, then sail off again. And each time Bill felt as if his father was deserting him, that this man he loved dearly wanted to get away from him and his mother. The mother was herself distressed by her husband's absence and was unable to show Bill much affection. That came only from his father, who regularly took it away for, it seemed to Bill, interminable periods.

c) Loss of Parent(s)

Frank was twelve when he came home from school one day and found his mother lying on the kitchen floor unconscious. Horrified, tears streaming down his face, he ran for help next door and neighbors called for an ambulance. His mother had suffered a massive coronary and was rushed to the hospital. She never regained consciousness. Three days later Frank hurried from school to the hospital and found his father weeping by his mother's bed. The sheet had been drawn over her face. "She's gone, Frankie, your mom's gone!" his father cried, embracing the boy. Frank joined him in tears, but his father quickly composed himself and said, "Don't cry, son, you've got to be a big boy now." Frank wiped his cheeks. Later when he broke down again at home, he realized that caused his father to begin sobbing, too. So Frank held himself in check, refusing to cry. He did not shed a tear at the wake or funeral service for his mother, even when her casket was lowered into the earth. The result was that Frank shoved aside his grief and never mourned the loss of his mother.

SEXUAL ABUSE

Joan was the only child of a father who co-owned a dry cleaning plant and a mother who had a dressmaking shop and did a lot of sewing at home as well. Joan could not remember any feelings of emotional warmth in the family. Her mother would arrive home from her shop about 5 P.M., prepare dinner, swiftly clean up afterward and then go upstairs to her sewing room and work until she retired about 10:30. After eating the father would move to his newspaper and television in the den, rising from his easy chair only to refill his martini glass. Most evenings he had several.

Joan remembers her father entering her bedroom late at night when she was ten years old and quietly slipping into bed beside her. He didn't say a word and she was so frightened she pretended she was asleep. He would caress her body and place her hand on his genitals, staying for what seemed to her like hours. Joan was too fearful and confused to tell anyone and she suffered through almost a year of these weekly terrorizing nocturnal visits. They abruptly ceased, but she was left with the feeling that she was somehow "bad" and that her body was somehow "dirty." Joan did not speak of these episodes until she entered therapy at age thirty-one.

THE EFFECTS OF CHILDHOOD EXPERIENCES ON ADULTHOOD

All of the aforementioned experiences were quite overwhelming to the young people cited. In the absence of supportive adults, there was no way the children could cope with or change those formative experiences. What one does in such a situation is deny that it exists by suppressing the painful feelings that arise and avoiding them at all costs. Feelings deliver information for us to act upon. If we are upset, that tells us we need to address whatever is upsetting and resolve the problem.

But none of the children described here had the power to resolve what was troubling them. They could not make a father stop drinking, or cause an overcritical parent to relax, or cure a phobic mother. So they learned to deny not only the problem but also the fact that they felt bad. As a consequence of suppressing their feelings, they could no longer identify what they felt.

AVOIDANT LIFESTYLE

Because people who suffer from agoraphobia have not learned how to resolve stressful situations, they begin to avoid them. Their method of coping with stress is avoidance even when the problem might be solvable. Constant denial and avoidance of problems make them chronically anxious. They are not aware of the cause of their anxiety, but they know that anxiety has always been with them, gnawing away, an unceasing fearfulness. And many people who are chronically anxious eventually respond to stress by having panic attacks, which leads to agoraphobia.

Some personality characteristics of agoraphobics are almost always present. They tend to lack self-sufficiency, are nonassertive, have trouble functioning independently and fear that they will be left alone in the world to fend for themselves. In addition, many agoraphobics who had to care for parents while growing up have an exaggerated sense of their own destructive powers. Almost all agoraphobics have a sense of being isolated. They feel alone even when in a relationship and fear that they will end up utterly alone. Fear of becoming a "bag lady" for example is common.

Lack of self-sufficiency: Being anxious children made it hard for them to learn the skills to cope with life and they had little opportunity to go out and test themselves in the world, which appears to them to be a very scary place. So they tend to be frightened of separation from anyone who has been caring for them, whether that relationship is satisfying or not.

Nonassertiveness: Due to their lack of self-sufficiency, these people also have great difficulty asserting themselves. They haven't learned to deal with others, not only when there is a disagreement or any unpleasantness involved, but also when expression of warm feelings might leave them feeling too vulnerable. They move away from confrontation, don't argue, protest or make scenes and are rarely able to feel a connection with others through honest expression of affection. Seeing the world as a scary place, they don't want to make it more frightening by upsetting people or leaving themselves open to rejection.

Trouble functioning independently: When people lack self-sufficiency and are nonassertive, there is virtually no way they can bring themselves to act independently. They feel the need to be guided by and to lean on others, and this is why they are beset by fear of being left alone to fend for themselves. All of these personality characteristics fill the same scary package that agoraphobics carry around.

An exaggerated sense of their own destructive powers: Agoraphobics often say things like, "If I had ever told my mother how I *really* felt, she would've had a heart attack and died." That may be what the parent told the child when the latter said anything upsetting, or the child may have assumed it by observing the parent's behavior. Often, though, an agoraphobic remembers expressing some feeling that so upset a parent that the child learned to cut off her feelings, or at least keep them to herself.

Both the overprotective and overcritical parent can destroy assertiveness by punishing a child for making an appropriate expression, though neither mother may realize what she is doing. For example, when a child is angry for a legitimate reason and the mother says, "*Nice* girls don't act like that," the child soon stops showing anger. And if you are the child of parents who threaten to send you away or to take off themselves every time you cry, eventually you no longer shed tears.

INABILITY TO HANDLE CONFLICT

As agoraphobics tend to be nonassertive, don't express feelings and have trouble functioning independently, they also often have difficulties in their personal relationships. Their main problem is that they never learned how to deal with conflict and therefore avoid it at all cost, as if by avoiding it they can make the conflict disappear. Not only does the conflict refuse to disappear, it is also soon accompanied by heavy stress. For example, if a woman is resentful about being treated unfairly by her husband and she does not confront him by expressing her feelings, then ultimately she will find herself harboring anger and feeling trapped in her marriage. Most pre-agoraphobics (people who have not yet suffered their first panic) are enmeshed in a period of profound stress prior to the onset of panic attacks, and fully 50 percent are threatened by the dissolution of a relationship at that time.

Generally the onset of agoraphobia occurs either in a woman's late teens to early twenties or in her late twenties to early thirties. Among those in both groups the underlying conflict often centers on a fear of separation from or loss of a prime provider of security such as a parent, spouse or lover, or the separation from a primary place of security such as a home environment. Late adolescence, when people begin to think about leaving home to carve out a place in the world for themselves, is a difficult time for almost everyone. But for those who have grave doubts about their ability to function on their own beyond the protection of a familiar environment—even an unhappy one—separation can be very frightening.

Many agoraphobics move directly from their families into marriages. But chronically anxious people seldom choose ideal partners. Most tend to choose strong, dominant, unemotional individuals whom they feel they can depend upon for all things. People who lacked security in childhood may look for a surrogate parent, because they never had one who was able to fill their needs. And the spouse they choose may exhibit many of the same characteristics the unfulfilling parent displayed. When the pre-agoraphobic realizes that the marriage is not working out, the ongoing conflict leads to anxiety and panic.

ANOTHER STRESSOR: SOCIAL ANXIETY

Ultimately the avoidant style of dealing with stress, combined with lack of self-sufficiency, unassertiveness and chronic anxiety, leads to social anxiety. Agoraphobics are not comfortable in social situations because they feel a total lack of control. When someone criticizes you and you are unable to respond, you feel helpless. When someone makes you angry and you can't handle it, you withdraw. In a sense agoraphobics are at everyone's mercy, so it's not surprising that they become afraid to mingle with other people. This causes them to give up the things they once enjoyed doing socially, and the resultant abject isolation is just one more link in the growing chain of heightening anxiety.

REVIEWING THE DEVELOPMENT OF AGORAPHOBIA

ONGOING CONFLICT (which remains unresolvable because of Fears of Aloneness, Lack of Self-Sufficiency and Unassertiveness) leads to CHRONIC ANXIETY AND DEPRESSION which

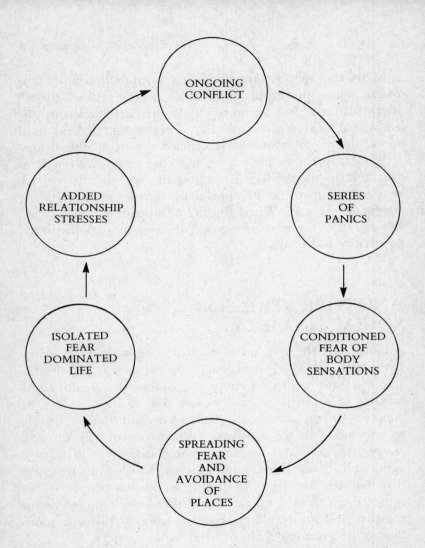

produces a SERIES OF PANICS, etc. (and because of the Avoidant Style of Dealing with Stress makes the agoraphobic unable to see that the cause lies in her personal relationships) which leads to CONDITIONED FEARS OF BODY SENSATIONS, and Obsessive Focusing on Symptoms Feeds the Spread of Fears which leads to CATASTROPHIC THOUGHTS, SPREADING AVOIDANCE and SECONDARY CONDITIONED FEAR OF PLACES which results in an ISOLATED, DISTORTED, FEAR-DOMINATED LIFESTYLE which leads to INCREASED STRESS IN RELATIONSHIPS which increases the ongoing CHRONIC ANXIETY AND DEPRESSION, the whole process becoming circular, feeding on itself.

THE ROOTS OF AGORAPHOBIA IN A TYPICAL CASE, FROM CHILDHOOD TO ONSET

Jane was twenty-three when she first appeared at the Program. A tall, slender woman with fear in her eyes and hands that nervously patted her tightly curled dark hair, she came to us fearing that if she did not gain control of her anxiety, her husband would divorce her. She had grown up as the daughter of an undiagnosed agoraphobic mother who was also overcritical and somewhat overprotective. Jane's brother, Len, was four years older and spent as little time as possible at home. Jane was close to her mother, accompanying her on all shopping excursions, as well as helping with the household chores.

As we talked, Jane remembered having a disconcerting problem with her mother in early childhood. One day when she was about four, Jane got very angry, stamping her foot and crying. Her mother clamped a hand to her chest and cried out, "Oh, my heart! I can't take this, Jane! You're killing me! I've got to lie down!" Then she plopped down on the sofa and covered her eyes with a hand. The scene was repeated whenever Jane acted out in anger. All young children have occasional temper tantrums, but Jane soon ceased having them. She would get angry and not show it, afraid to upset her mother. She did not want to be responsible for the death of her mother, whom she loved.

Jane got on well with her father, who pampered her and liked to bring her surprise gifts. But he was a salesman who covered four states and he was usually away on business. Jane missed him and could barely contain herself when he was due to come home to her with a big hug, kiss and a present.

Jane's family had moved so many times by her thirteenth year that she had attended six different schools. She always felt like an outsider and had trouble making friends. Then, too, her mother had never permitted her to linger after classes as her peers did, saying, "It's not safe, Jane. There are too many molesters out there. You come right home and don't talk to *anyone*." So Jane was virtually always home, and she was reluctant to invite classmates over because her mother regularly criticized her and it was embarrassing.

After her brother left to join the service, Jane was usually alone with her mother. When it came time to begin dating and having a social life, Jane was made to feel inferior by her mother. She said things like: "Jane, you know you're not as pretty as most of the other girls. You have your father's nose, which, Lord knows, is anything but feminine." And: "I'm sorry you don't have more clothes, Jane, but do you have to keep wearing that awful plaid skirt? It looks terrible on you." And: "Why are you going to that party? You never seem to have a good time, Jane. Besides, you know I need you home with me; I just don't feel well."

Jane had earned good grades in high school and thought about going to college, perhaps to become a teacher. But her mother said, "Are you serious, Jane? College work is much, much harder than high school. And you really should learn how to take care of yourself right now. Go to secretarial school. Then you can get a job that offers security for someone like you."

In secretarial school Jane was shy, silent, anxious and couldn't seem to make friends. Whenever an instructor or fellow student said anything that she took as critical of her performance or appearance, Jane could not express herself in rejoinder. And if anyone became the least bit angry with her, Jane was terrified.

Still, she completed the course of work, became proficient at shorthand and an excellent typist. She got a good job, opened a charge account and bought a new wardrobe. She also had her hair styled, began using makeup and, despite her mother's opinion, became a very attractive young woman. Just before her twenty-second birthday she began dating a tall, blond-haired salesman for her firm who was from a well-to-do family. Jane kept thinking, "I can't believe this. What in the world can Bill possibly see in me?"

But Bill was smitten, taking her out two or three times each week. Jane's mother was agitated and complained almost every time she came home from a date. Then, several months into the relationship, Bill asked Jane to marry him. Her mother heard the news and got upset, saying she felt ill. Jane became very anxious about going to work. She not only felt unworthy of Bill, she was very fearful that if she married him something dreadful would happen to her mother. Adding to the tension was the fact that Bill wanted to be wed in the Catholic Church. Although Jane had no objection to this, her mother—a nonpracticing Protestant—used Bill's faith as an excuse to oppose the idea vehemently.

Jane was being pulled apart on all levels, but she proceeded to take instructions in Catholicism. Her mother was angry and critical, and periodically withdrew to bed "with my heart." Jane was now chronically anxious, and after an evening's scolding from her mother, she suffered her first panic attack the following morning at work. She hyperventilated, her fingertips started tingling and she began sweating profusely. "Oh, my God," she thought, "I'm going to pass out!" This signaled the onset of agoraphobia.

Once the attack peaked and passed, Jane told her boss she was ill and hurried home. The next morning at work she suffered another panic attack and again raced home, where she immediately felt better. On the third morning the panic struck moments after she arrived at her office and saw Bill. This time Jane's heart felt as if it would pound through her chest and she thought she would die.

She went to see her family doctor and described her

symptoms. The doctor said, "It's all in your head, Jane, just nerves," and prescribed Valium "to calm you." She had the prescription filled, took five milligrams of the medication and did feel somewhat calmer. But not for long. She kept thinking of the doctor's words, "It's all in your head." That was what she had suspected and feared during the panic attack—that she was crazy. Each time she thought she was on the very edge of completely losing control, that she would collapse, an ambulance would be summoned and she would be hauled away to "a mental institution" where she would be locked in a back ward forever.

So Jane quit her job. Somehow she felt safer at home, even though she suffered occasional panics there when her mother berated her. Meanwhile Bill continued to pursue Jane, to take her out, to see her extensively on weekends and to go forward with the wedding plans. Jane's mother continued to rail against the marriage. Yet Jane could not address her ongoing conflict. By this time she was totally immersed in her "illness," which she in no way connected to the stress in her life.

Jane went ahead with the wedding but throughout the time leading up to the wedding, the wedding day and thereafter she was confused and highly anxious. Not long thereafter she began to be obsessive about her disorder, the agoraphobia advancing from fear of having panics to *fear of her own body sensations*. Before Jane could ignore a slight flutter of the heart, the kind of sensation everyone experiences on occasion. Now the mildest flutter told Jane she was having a heart attack, and her anxiety would trigger panic. Jane would hyperventilate, grow dizzy and feel that she was about to faint.

Now she was constantly worried that she was going to have a heart attack, lose control, faint or go crazy. She became afraid to do anything that might set off an attack. Even after the wedding the conflict with her mother persisted. Her mother phoned her to complain almost daily, and Jane became fearful whenever the phone rang.

Thanks to Bill's income, Jane did not have to return to work and so could hide behind the role of housewife. When they first settled into their home she was able to do all the shopping on her own despite her anxieties. Then she suffered a panic attack in a supermarket and, fearful of a recurrence, would not do the grocery shopping without Bill at her side. Later she was struck by panic while in line at the bank; then she had an attack in a department store. Soon she was afraid to go any place alone because she was afraid she might panic and feel trapped. She would leave her house only when accompanied by Bill, the one person she trusted to take care of her.

Jane persistently prepared herself for the worst, thinking, "What if I panic in a store and can't get out? What if I panic and can't reach Bill on the phone—what will happen to me? Oh, God!" Such thoughts maintained her anxiety at a high level and increased the likelihood that she would panic. Her anxieties were now unremitting, and they placed a tremendous strain on the marriage. She wanted to know where she could reach Bill every moment of the day, which was patently impossible with a salesman who kept moving around. If he had to work late at the office or needed to make an evening sales call, Jane became very upset. Finally she could no longer go shopping even with him, and he had to do it all himself.

Bill cared for his wife. But, unable to understand what was happening to her, unable to meet her demands no matter how hard he tried, he grew more and more frustrated and angry. Finally he hollered, "Dammit, Jane, you have to stop this nonsense. I can't work all week and spend most of my weekends shopping. You've got to contribute to this marriage. Either you get yourself together or I'm going to think about a separation!"

The threat of losing her husband sent Jane to seek treatment for her disorder. The thought of being left alone was too frightening for her to bear. She saw a psychiatrist briefly, was dissatisfied, then came to the Agoraphobia and Anxiety Program.

Jane's story is quite typical of those told by agoraphobics. While the particulars differ, the common elements are the difficult childhood, the lack of self-sufficiency and assertiveness, and the unresolvable conflict. Due to lack of self-sufficiency and her inability to overcome her guilt and act assertively, Jane was in conflict between her mother and her marriage. This led to chronic anxiety and depression, followed by a series of panic attacks. And because Jane had developed an avoidant style of dealing with stress she was unable to see that the conflict was the cause of her panics. After her marriage the panic attacks increased in frequency.

Next Jane began focusing on her own body sensations and interpreted the slightest tremors as sure signs of terminal illness or burgeoning insanity. These concerns further removed her from trying to resolve her conflicts.

This tendency to become frightened of body sensations is a normal consequence of having panics. Through the process of conditioning, anything that accompanies panics such as a pounding heart can come to produce fear in and of itself. Just climbing a flight of stairs may make the heart pound enough to cause fear that—if fueled by catastrophic thoughts—may spiral into panic.

All people experience extreme fear when they find themselves in a life-threatening situation. Then the preservation mechanism clicks on and helps them deal with the crisis, whether that means steering a skidding car back into line or jumping out of the path of a careening car as a pedestrian. But when people are afraid of something *inside* themselves— something that is undefined and totally unpredictable—they may see no effective way to deal with the fear. This is the anguish that agoraphobics endure. Then unknown sources of fears are persistent and can be totally debilitating.

Jane's pattern is typical of people with agoraphobia. Their lives revolve around fears of a recurrence of their symptoms. They plot every move of every day in an effort to avoid situations that might trigger panic. All of a family's activities are distorted by such planning. Soon everyone in the family is under stress, and the agoraphobic person feels guilty about not living up to his or her responsibilities to family members and the demands of work. All of this increases stress and keeps the agoraphobic highly anxious and depressed. Jane ended up afraid to leave her residence without her husband and became isolated, her existence completely distorted by her disorder, her life dominated by overwhelming fear.

No one who has not experienced the crushing impact of agoraphobia can fully understand the depth of fears visited upon its sufferers.

Effective Treatment— a Detailed Case

*D*eveloping an effective program for agoraphobia stumped therapists for almost one hundred years. Freud described agoraphobia as a "romance of prostitution" and said it stemmed from forbidden impulses, usually sexual, that are attempting to come to the surface. The awareness and acting out of the impulses are seen as being avoided by the development of that fear of stores, crowds, etc., keeping the sufferer off the street and away from temptation. This was the theory Freud used to explain almost every symptom and he lumped all phobias together. The treatments prescribed were psychoanalysis, which is typically five fifty-minute sessions of therapy per week for several years, or psychoanalytic psychotherapy, which tends to be one or two fifty-minute therapy sessions per week. In both the aim is to uncover the hidden impulse, and when that insight is gained the symptoms supposedly disappear. This is the treatment given by many psychotherapists because they are trained almost exclusively in psychoanalytic theory. Agoraphobics who have received such treatment report their therapists showed scant interest in their phobias and concentrated on drawing out their childhood experiences while offering little feedback. The client sits and talks and the therapist rarely gives any kind of instructive help or explanation. This has proved to be ineffective in treatment of agoraphobia as it doesn't deal with the conditioned fears, and under psychoanalytic psychotherapy often the avoidance and fear just worsen.

Often agoraphobics report having seen professionals who provided warmth and support in getting them through daily life, as well as help in other ways. For example, the therapy may have led to an understanding of how marital discord, conflict with parents or certain early traumas such as incestual sexual abuse was contributing to the client's anxieties. But there was no consistently followed treatment that was appropriate for agoraphobia. Still other agoraphobics report seeing therapists who were formal and did not provide the warmth they desired. Sometimes therapists could be destructive with interpretations such as, "If you really wanted to, you could do the things you avoid," or "When are you going to grow up?" These statements tend to add to the load of guilt already carried by agoraphobics.

Another theory of agoraphobia assumes that all the symptoms are the result of disease. Either there is a genetic fault or a biological process at work—a hormonal or chemical imbalance. Practitioners of this theory share the assumption that the task is to find the disease and correct it with drugs. Many psychiatrists are trained in the use of medication to treat agoraphobia and will prescribe drugs appropriately. Along with medication, clients are likely to receive what is called supportive therapy wherein they discuss the events of the week and possibly hear suggestions from the doctor which can be helpful. But there is usually no clear goal to resolve the agoraphobic's problem except by changing the amount or type of medication prescribed. The drugs prescribed may sometimes have been helpful in cutting down on symptoms and in reducing panics. But more often people report that drugs were not helpful and often in fact proved harmful as they became physically or psychologically addicted to them. I have never seen anyone who was able to change his or her self-perception of "sick" to "well" while on drugs.

The problems with drugs are many and will be dealt with

at length in Chapter Nine. But suffice it here to say that though the minor tranquilizers tend to take the edge off anxiety, people can quickly become psychologically addicted to them. Clients feel they can't do anything without the drugs, and that undermines their self-esteem—which is low in agoraphobics from the start. Any advances they make in therapy they attribute to the drugs, not to themselves. And while certain antidepressants can lower depression and even reduce panics in some agoraphobics, most relapse when they go off the drugs.

In the mid-sixties behavioral therapy was introduced in the treatment of agoraphobia. The assumption was that agoraphobia was a fear of external situations, like other phobias. Behavioral therapy worked very well with some victims of simple phobias, such as fear of dogs, fear of flying, fear of crossing bridges—any of those things one becomes afraid of after a bad experience. One learns to be afraid of dogs after having been bitten by a dog. Such conditioned fears can be readily cured by what is known as systematic desensitization. Clients are trained to imagine themselves in the situation they fear (while in a state of relaxation) until they grow comfortable with this image; their lack of fear in the imagined situation then helps make them comfortable in the real situation.

When systematic desensitization was used with agoraphobic clients, many gradually improved after several months of work. But they often relapsed following their first new panic attack and were right back where they started. The panics were again produced by conflict situations that were not addressed, and the client still felt helpless in the face of panic because she had never learned skills for dealing with it. Behavioral therapies that later adopted exposure (repeatedly taking people out into situations that they feared) resulted in moderate but reliable long-lasting reduction in fears of certain places. But agoraphobics remained basically anxiety-ridden.

So, by the late sixties, it became apparent to me that none

of the theories on treating agoraphobia—psychotherapy, chemotherapy, behavioral therapy—worked. I put aside all the theories and began listening to what the people with the disorder had to say about it. There were very striking consistencies in the kind of conditions at home during childhood, in the circumstances in which the first panics occurred, in the sequence and symptoms of development.

A review of these consistencies shows how they all fit together to give us a coherent understanding of agoraphobia. The consistencies were a difficult childhood, lack of self-sufficiency and assertiveness, inability to function independently and adoption of an avoidant lifestyle.

The overriding comment that people made about their fear was that it was not external but something inside them they feared—that they were going to panic and lose control. Their overwhelming fear was fear of the next attack.

FEAR OF FEAR CENTERS THE PHOBIA

With the realization that *fear of fear* was the central phobic element of agoraphobia, we began teaching people techniques for coping with anticipatory anxiety and panics. We used "exposure therapy." We began accompanying our clients out to the sites of previous panics and had them face, rather than avoid, the fear of an attack. We gave them lots of reassurance that they were not going to lose control. Once people stopped running from an attack, they realized that they were not going to faint, have a heart attack, go crazy or suffer any of the other catastrophes their fears had conjured. Repeatedly facing the sheer terror gradually lessened it. Still, most people continued to be dominated by anxiety. The question was why?

As I went out with clients on exposure exercises, visited them in their homes, spoke with their parents, spouses or lovers, I soon discovered a consistent pattern among agoraphobics. Most avoided dealing with some important conflict in their lives; they had acquired few skills for dealing with stressful interpersonal situations (so they withdrew from stressful situations); and they had tremendous difficulty identifying—much less expressing—their feelings. Whether they were feeling scared, mad, sad or even glad, clients rarely said they experienced anything except anxiety.

It was not unusual for a client to arrive for a therapy session looking shaken and say, "I just had a panic attack driving here."

"What might have caused it?" I'd ask her.

"I don't know," she'd say. "Nothing happened. It just came on me out of the blue."

I'd ask her to tell me what happened since she woke up that morning, searching for the cause of panic.

"Nothing unusual. I made breakfast as I always do, and my husband yelled about the eggs. Then he went off to work, I cleaned up and came here."

Over subsequent sessions it turned out that every time her husband screamed at her, she would later suffer a panic attack. I asked her to recall the most recent scene in which her husband had yelled. The woman thought a moment, her face clenched and she cried, obviously remembering: "I'm starting to have a panic attack!"

INHIBITED FEELINGS PRODUCE ANXIETY

She was asked to explain what it was like, when she was feeling panic. Soon she realized that when she panicked she was feeling anger. It turned out she was angry with her over-critical husband and in denying her true feelings had become anxious. Suppressing her anger produced anxiety that led to panic. When the first glimmerings of panic appeared, her struggles to ward off a full-blown attack actually increased the chances of having one.

It was about this time that I was fortunate to be joined by

a psychologist colleague, Dianne Chambless, who was equally interested in finding a way to cure agoraphobia. Over the years of working together, we evolved the fully developed program of cure outlined here.

GESTALT WORK TO OPEN TO FEELINGS

As agoraphobics have difficulty identifying their feelings we began using Gestalt therapy with them. In Gestalt work, the client is assisted in staying with his or her feelings until there is understanding of where they come from and what must be done to resolve the issues causing the feelings. Most often, without this help agoraphobics are so frightened of feelings that they unconsciously do something to "turn them off" or interpret them as anxiety, so they do not reach resolution and relief. Gestalt therapy proved to be very effective in combination with the exposure work that gave people some control over the fear of fear and reduced the conditioned fears.

ADD PSYCHOTHERAPY TO REACH UNDERLYING PROBLEMS OF AGORAPHOBIA

The third part of our multilevel treatment program is psychotherapy, which is useful in getting to the underlying problems of most agoraphobics. The overall program is designed to deal not only with conditioned fear of fear and avoidance behavior, but anxiety-provoking thoughts and attitudes, inappropriate styles of coping with stress, dependence on others and the inability to resolve conflict. The latter usually revolves around such earlier events in a client's life as unresolved grief and unresolved parental issues, as well as, most significantly, overwhelming dread of isolation. Even though the results of agoraphobia may place agoraphobics in isolation from friends, they will cling desperately to the one or more people whom they identify as saving them from utter aloneness. There is an anxious overattachment to these people who are usually spouse or parent, sometimes a child. It's not surprising that dependent people who have developed few skills for coping with the world would dread being alone in the world.

Marital maladjustment—and the threat of separation—are the most common stressors preceding panics among adult agoraphobic women. We therefore added couples therapy to the Temple program. Agoraphobics and their spouses tend to interact in child-parent fashion, so the work here is aimed at enabling the couple to relate as two autonomous adults with good open communication.

Perhaps the most productive addition to the Temple treatment package was the Two-Week Intensive Program that was introduced in the spring of 1979. Six to eight clients undergo therapy from 9:30 A.M. to 4:00 P.M. for ten days. Members of the group become "family" almost immediately. "I'm so happy to know I'm not the only one who has this awful problem," they say. "I thought I was alone!" They help one another to face their fears, to work hard in regaining mobility, and to be strong and open in revealing suppressed feelings. Most are no longer significantly avoidant by the end of the two weeks and panics are much less frequent. To recover from agoraphobia, though, usually takes from six months to a year.

Let us pick up with Jane's story in order to illustrate how these components are put together for a particular person with agoraphobia.

In planning treatment for Jane, the young woman we met in Chapters One and Two, we reviewed the problems she presented. She was afraid to go any place where she might feel trapped unless her husband Bill was at her side. She engaged in a great deal of catastrophic thinking. She was also afraid of her own body sensations; she interpreted heart flutters as an oncoming heart attack and frequently hyperventilated. Jane at best was moderately anxious. She was experiencing typical signs of depression, such as disturbed sleep, lack of energy, an inability to perceive pleasure in life and an overriding sense of hopelessness.

Jane's self-esteem, never soaring, had plummeted. Like most agoraphobics she could not see or appreciate her considerable talents, intelligence or physical attractiveness. She could not understand why Bill married her.

It was clear that Jane was frightened of angry scenes and was afraid to recognize her feelings of annoyance with Bill. She interpreted as anxiety her anger at her mother, with whom she was particularly unassertive. Her relationship with both husband and mother was strained. Jane's attention was totally focused on relieving her anxiety and avoiding panic. She wanted desperately to do the things that others did easily, such as shopping alone and returning to work. Treatment had to start with Jane's chronic anxiety because so long as she was debilitated by the panics and fears it would be impossible for her to deal with the deep-seated issues in her life. Not paying attention to the conditioned fears has led many therapists astray and kept their agoraphobic clients in unsuccessful therapy far too long. Until the chronic anxiety can be managed, the focus is on it unremittingly. Once some progress has been made in coping with the panic and avoidance, hope builds in clients, who tend to develop real resolve to push themselves toward recovery.

THE NEED TO FACE HER FEARS

At her initial evaluation we told Jane that many of her symptoms were perfectly natural, given her constant state of anxiety, and she was assured that she would not go crazy, have a heart attack or suffer any of the other dire fates she feared. She would be taught ways to face her chronic fears—which is perhaps the hardest task agoraphobics will ever have to do. But it is only by facing fears that people can see that they will not lose control. We also told Jane that she would not be asked to do anything that she could not do, that she would make advances at her own pace with the help of therapists.

With Jane's permission I met with her husband, Bill, and explained what her symptoms meant and briefly described the treatment we would follow. Bill was most appreciative, saying the psychiatrist that Jane had consulted on several occasions had refused to see him.

THE IMPORTANCE OF PROPER BREATHING IN MAINTAINING CONTROL

Next I met privately with Jane and told her about the strategies she would be using to control panic when we went out to the sites of her earlier attacks and she faced the fears that were sure to arise. We talked about the importance of proper breathing in maintaining control, pointing out that when people are anxious or frightened they take rapid, shallow breaths and often hold their breath. Agoraphobics and others with constant high levels of anxiety breathe like this all the time, using only the upper chest and drawing in and out through the mouth, in contrast to relaxed breathing from the diaphragm, which entails taking slow, rhythmic breaths from the diaphragm, in and out the nose. These different ways of breathing are closely associated with the way we feel—shallow-fast equaling anxiety, slow-diaphragmic equaling calmness—and we can actually change the way we feel by consciously controlling our breathing.

"All right, Jane, I would like to show you how to breathe slowly with the diaphragm if you'll follow my instructions," I said. "Try lying down on the carpet on your stomach, as that position makes diaphragmatic breathing automatic. Rest your head on the back of your hands and feel what it's like to breathe in calmly. Notice how your abdomen expands as you breathe in and how it lifts from the floor as you breathe out. Be aware of the pace of your breathing, and draw in slowly through your nostrils and all the way down to your stomach. Imagine you are blowing up a balloon in your stomach on the inhale and emptying it on the exhale. In a few minutes you should feel calmer."

"I do," she said, then repeated the exercise for five more minutes.

Next Jane practiced proper breathing in the sitting position. She did well until she lost her concentration and speeded up, breathing only from the chest. I reminded her to think about filling and emptying a balloon in her stomach, and she regained the pace. But once she began practicing in the standing position—which is most difficult for almost everyone—Jane began breathing rapidly in her accustomed fashion.

"Slowly, Jane."

"I am breathing slowly," she said.

"You may think you are," I said, "but you're not getting the air down into your diaphragm."

"I'm trying."

"I know you are and this is not easy to learn after years of breathing with only the chest," I said. "Let's try a count, say six, for each inhale and exhale. You count and see if that's comfortable."

Jane completed her in-and-out breath within a count of three. She kept practicing until she settled on a count of six, and I told her to practice on her own at home four times a day. "It usually takes people several weeks to get this, but it's a great calming coping skill," I said.

USING A RUBBER BAND TO SNAP AWAY CATASTROPHIC THOUGHTS

I also told Jane about another useful coping tool that's sometimes easier to remember. "From what you've told me it's apparent that you engage in lots of catastrophic thinking," I said. "Such as, 'Oh, God, I'm going to have a heart attack!'"

"Well, not all the time, I don't think," she said, like many people with agoraphobia, unaware of her thought processes.

"What I'd like you to do is slip this rubber band onto your wrist. If you have a catastrophic thought I want you to snap the rubber band to break the thought. Just snap it once or twice and it doesn't have to be hard. Don't hurt yourself with it. I'd also like you to say, either aloud or to yourself, 'STOP!' and imagine a big red stop sign in your mind's eye."

"Okay, that seems easier than the breathing."

"Good. Let's try an exercise. You told me you had suffered a panic attack while in line at your bank. Now I'd like you to imagine yourself standing in that line, and to remember your rubber band and stop sign if you need them."

The moment Jane put herself into the scene her eyes grew wide with fright, she gasped and stopped breathing. "Oh, God!" she said.

"Snap your rubber band and break the thought! And breathe!"

She snapped and her expression relaxed. "It works!" she said, amazed. "I was actually getting panicky just thinking about being in line at the bank."

"That was the result of catastrophic thinking," I said. "I would guess you were thinking things like, 'What if I panic while in line? What if I can't get out of the bank? What if I can't get enough air and faint?'"

"Yes, and I'd be embarrassed for people to see how upset I was."

"It's those kinds of catastrophic thoughts that cause your anxiety to increase. You then begin to hyperventilate, which brings on additional symptoms. So it's important for you to learn yet another coping strategy to counter the destructive thoughts."

FOCUSING ON THE PRESENT

I pointed out that castastrophic thoughts always focused on the future or on frightening memories—never on the present. "A good way to stay in the present is to focus on what we call the here and now," I said. "That means you focus on what your senses—sight, hearing, touch and smell—are telling you *at this very instant*. So sit quietly for a moment, Jane, and see what you are aware of. This exercise will give you another excellent tool when we begin our travel work."

Jane's eyes wandered about the room for a minute or more, then seemed to settle on nothing. I asked what she was thinking. "Uh, I don't know . . . I guess my mind wandered."

"You look a little worried."

"Well . . . to be honest I was worrying about where we'd be going."

"If it's all right with you, I thought we'd go to a supermarket since you had problems there. But for now I want you to be aware of the present through your perceptual senses—your eyes, ears, sense of touch, taste, smell, your own body sensations. For example, feel the texture of the upholstery in that sofa you're sitting on. Look around and note the colors in this room, the shape of that table lamp. Don't think about what you touch or see, just be aware of those things." When she had focused on the room and its appointments for about ten seconds, I asked Jane how she was feeling. To her surprise she reported that she felt rather calm.

I asked her to try an experiment. "Think about going with me to a supermarket tomorrow." After a few seconds I asked how she was feeling.

"Anxious. I'm getting a little anxious. Maybe more than a little."

"Okay, now come back to your senses! Be aware of the colors in this room, the sounds you hear, the feeling of your feet on the floor!" Again after a few seconds I asked how she felt.

"Calmer," Jane said.

SWITCHING FROM THOUGHTS TO SENSATIONS

This exercise of switching back and forth from thoughts to sensations was practiced over and over again until Jane readily gained control of rising anxiety by tuning in her senses and tuning out thoughts. Jane now had three new means of managing anxiety—proper breathing, using her rubber band to snap back to the present, and using her senses to focus on the here and now—and we asked her about her medication intake. She said she was taking four five-milligram Valium tablets each day.

"If you continue to take that much, Jane, I have to tell you that it could interfere with what we call 'transfer of learning.' By that I mean if you go out to a place where you've been having difficulty, use your coping skills and feel better, we count on that experience transferring to the next time you go out. But large doses of Valium tend to block that transfer from occurring, as you'll feel the drug and not yourself accounted for your successes. In addition, there is evidence that many drugs may physiologically prevent the breakdown of the association between a place and a fear. So if you're on lots of medication even after we have done lots of exposure work, you're likely to go back to that place where you felt better and find yourself feeling anxious again."

Jane was introduced to the Program's psychiatric consultant who explained that she would have to reduce her Valium intake slowly as going off the drug quickly can cause a number of serious reactions. He suggested that she cut her daily dosage by two and one-half milligrams and wait four days, then cut another two and one-half milligrams and hold there until her session next week. This plan would cut her present dosage of twenty milligrams to fifteen milligrams over seven days, and she was told to contact the psychiatric consultant if she had any difficulty with this.

"Be assured, Jane, that within three months you'll be feeling quite well without *any* medication," I said.

"I think I'd like that," Jane said, "because the Valium is one reason I feel I'm so tired all the time."

"It certainly doesn't help your energy level, and it can add to your depression. As we work and your depression lifts, you'll begin to feel much less tired."

GETTING OUT AND FACING FEARS

The next week Jane arrived at the Program offices looking apprehensive, but said she was resolved to go with me to a nearby supermarket. Although she had begun going to market with her husband, she said she was still anxious in the store. The memory of the panic attack she had suffered in a supermarket remained very strong.

"Well, we won't have to go all the way in today," I said. "But do you think you can stand just inside the door for a few minutes?"

"I don't see why not as long as you're with me," she said.

As we left the Program offices and headed for the supermarket several blocks away, I said, "As we walk, Jane, I want you to be aware of everything that's going on in your head. And I want you to tell me if you begin to feel agitated." She nodded and everything was fine until we turned a corner and the supermarket came into view across the street.

Jane stopped and cried, "I can't go in there! I'm starting to panic! What if I get trapped in there and can't get out? I know I'll faint!"

"You are catastrophizing. I want you to snap your rubber band to stop the thoughts and bring yourself back to the present. Look around; you're in no danger. Check out the street light here, the stop sign, the clouds in the sky. Feel the sidewalk under you. That's it. Are you back in the here and now?"

Jane, tension dissolving from her face, said, "I'm . . . I'm beginning to feel calmer."

Three more times before we reached the store Jane was able to dispel panicky thoughts by switching to the present and focusing on her surroundings. Then, when we were just outside the entrance—despite her struggles to bring herself back to the present—Jane panicked. "I have to get away from here!" she cried, sweat popping out on her brow. "I can't stand to be here!"

It is counterproductive for an agoraphobic to run because that simply continues the avoidant behavior that is so destructive, so I said, "I'm glad you feel like that because it gives us a perfect opportunity to find out what you do on the verge of panic. Even if you do panic, you need to learn that panic has a life of its own whether you run or not. Panic approaches, rises, peaks—and then it descends and goes away. That's the important thing you have to learn. Panic peaks and goes away. So just stay with your feelings, Jane, and let's see what happens."

The panic was very powerful. "I feel faint!" Jane cried. "I want to go! I have to get away from here!"

"Stay with it," I said, taking her hands in mine to reassure her. "That's the only way you're going to see that you won't faint, that you won't lose control, that none of those things you fear will actually happen."

Jane stood there, her hands slightly trembling, and in about five minutes the attack passed. She let out a huge breath, gulped and dabbed a handkerchief on her damp forehead.

"See, you didn't faint, did you?"

Jane shook her head and muttered, "No."

"All right, now breathe from the diaphragm. I want you to understand that all those fears you have about facing the panic are based on the times you felt afraid and ran. Superstitious beliefs, we call them, because they have no basis in fact. There is no way you can know that until you stick out the panic a number of times instead of running from it. To hold your ground in the face of panic is very, very difficult, and you should be proud of yourself. Remember, when you can do it on your own your panics will start to fade away."

Jane forced a small smile. "I feel drained."

"Of course. But the more you stay with the panic, the more you'll see that nothing happens, that you really have nothing to fear—and soon the fears and the panics will disappear."

"Are we going back to the office?" she asked.

"Not until we complete our assignment." I nodded at the supermarket entrance.

Jane stopped smiling, but she stepped into the store and stood tensely just inside the door. Her anxiety level rose rapidly but she stood firm for several minutes. "We never want to leave a situation when you're feeling uncomfortable," I told her, "because that is avoiding."

Once Jane felt all right, we returned to the office and she said, "It didn't kill me after all! That's wonderful. I haven't felt this good in six months, since before my wedding."

FOLLOWING UP ON TRAVEL WORK

I asked if she would follow up on the work we had done, and when she agreed to I said, "Could you do so on your own, without me present?"

"I think I could stand in front of a supermarket as long as my husband goes with me," Jane said. "I'm sure he will."

"Then I'd like you to stand in front of a store three times this week for not less than five minutes. Never leave if you're the least bit panicky. Stick it out and use the coping skills we learned today. Stop those catastrophic thoughts. Bring yourself back to the present and see exactly where you are, that there is no danger. Then be aware of your breathing pattern."

Jane's husband Bill was very excited about her progress and happy to help with her homework. On the first night after some anticipatory worry about what might happen to her, Jane went back to the store and felt little discomfort while she stood outside. The second night her anxiety level leaped up several times, but each time she called on her coping skills and calmed down. Yet at her next therapy session Jane reported that on night three she hadn't wanted to go out at all and had been anxious throughout the assignment. "I was very apprehensive about the whole thing," Jane said.

Questioned about what had happened prior to going out on the last assignment, and about when she first began to feel apprehensive about it, Jane answered, "After the second night out, Bill was really excited. 'You did so well tonight, why don't we go in the store next time,' he said to me."

Jane hadn't understood why she was uncomfortable until I pointed out that her husband's words were reason for her to be apprehensive. "Spouses of agoraphobics see them accomplish something and often try to push them to do more. This is not helpful. You felt pressured and didn't tell Bill."

THE NEED TO BE ASSERTIVE

This opened an opportunity to work on Jane's need to be more assertive and express herself to Bill. She could have simply told him, "No, I'm not ready to enter the store with you yet," just as she could have been more assertive with her mother. Jane's style was to say nothing that could create animosity. She was still in conflict with her mother and feeling guilty over having "deserted" her by marrying Bill. She was also feeling guilty about not pleasing her husband sufficiently. I pointed out that she was not dealing with these issues and that there was an interaction between her personal conflict and the anxiety she felt about doing things like going to the grocery store.

"It's important for you to note such connections," I said, "particularly as they occur. One way for you to do that is to start keeping a record of the times you feel uneasy or have panics. Write down the circumstances and what you're feeling. Bring in your notes and we'll examine them to see if there is a pattern to your discomfort. Even though you may not be aware of them, there are consistencies in the circumstances of your panics. Your early entries may say, 'I'm at home and I'm starting to feel uncomfortable and I don't know why.' But once you add the circumstances of your day, we'll find out that things happening in your life are leading you to feel anxious."

Jane and I then decided what we would do on her travel work. This time we would enter the supermarket and walk around it for at least three minutes, but we would not get in line to purchase anything. Jane said she wasn't ready for that. The panic attack that caused her to avoid the market had occurred while she was in the checkout line.

We set out and I soon noticed that Jane looked tense, so I asked what she was thinking.

"What if I have another attack in the store and I'm not able to control it?" she said. "That'll be terribly embarrassing. My God, Alan, except for that few minutes with you, I haven't been in a supermarket in two months! Not even with Bill!"

"Jane, you're catastrophizing again, imagining all the awful things that could happen. As I've said, all catastrophic thinking concerns the future, so bring yourself back to the here and now. Stop and tell me what you notice as you look around."

CONNECTING WHAT YOU THINK AND HOW YOU FEEL

She did and I listened to her comments on the surroundings until she sounded composed. "Jane, I'd like you to pay close attention to what you think because there is a connection between what you *think* and how you *feel*."

We set off again and within minutes Jane appeared to be anxious once more. I had her return to the present and pointed out that it was perfectly understandable that she fell into the same old habits of thought. "You're not going to change those habits easily or quickly. You'll have to practice changing again and again. Your habits are very strong, and that's not at all surprising, given how frightened you've been. But the habits just don't work for you, so let's keep making every effort to change them."

When we arrived at the store, Jane boldly opened the door, walked in and headed down an aisle. Halfway down it she stopped abruptly. Her eyes darted about, her hands squeezed her purse. "What are you thinking about?" I asked.

"What if I panic way back here? The store is crowded. What if I can't get to the door? People keep coming in. I could never get out of here without fainting. Everyone will see me and think I'm crazy."

"Stop. You're catastrophizing again. Get back to the present." Checking my watch, I said, "We decided we'd stay here three minutes, so you have two minutes left. But if you feel uncomfortable, we'll stay until you feel better."

"I'm not sure I want to do that now," Jane said, agitated.

"That's like telling me to jump off the Walt Whitman Bridge and insisting I'll be all right."

"In fact it will be all right to stay here, Jane, and the only way you can find that out is to stand fast. I'm right here with you."

Jane was still a bit tense several minutes later, but the feelings of imminent panic had passed. She had demonstrated her determination to make changes, to gain control of her conditioned fears. As noted, in some ways dealing with the all-consuming conditioned fears is the hardest part of the treatment, and Jane had gotten herself to perform admirably. She had taken a major step on her road to recovery.

PRACTICING EXPRESSING HERSELF

We discussed her homework and Jane wanted to repeat last week's travel with her husband. In addition I asked her to tell Bill how she felt about the pressure he'd put on her in a way that he would understand. "I'll play the part of Bill, Jane, and you speak to me as you would to him."

"Bill, you really shouldn't push me when you know I've been sick," she said. "Maybe you didn't mean it, but I don't want you to do that kind of thing to me anymore."

"That's a start, Jane, except that it might be better to express yourself in a way he'll *hear* and one that doesn't leave him feeling bad about himself. So let's try to stick to *your* feelings. A good way to do that is to stay with 'I' statements about the way you feel. For example: 'When you asked me to go in the store last week I felt pressure as if I had to meet your expectations, Bill. And what I need from you, Bill, is to let *me* set the pace. Because when I'm doing that, I feel like I'm in control; when I'm not doing that I feel out of control.' "

In the beginning it was very hard for Jane to speak out. She had never before expressed herself, never announced *her own feelings*, even to herself. But she kept working at it until, after several weeks, she began to feel more comfortable expressing her feelings to Bill, although she often forgot and slipped back.

Over the next month we accelerated Jane's travel homework and I spent more time with her at the sites of her previous panics. I also examined the notes in which she recorded the circumstances of her discomfort. It turned out that any time Jane was feeling angry, she was likely to experience anxiety and avoidance. *Her inability to express her anger* with her mother caused her to become more anxious and led to panic. Mrs. R. phoned almost daily and was critical of Jane. Whenever the phone rang Jane grew anxious in fear that it was her mother. Twice after calls from her mother, Jane suffered panic attacks.

In my office sessions with her, I assumed the role of Mrs. R. and encouraged Jane to express herself, to say that she felt angry when her mother phoned to criticize her. I would repeat the kind of statements Mrs. R. would make to Jane: "You don't love me. You're just like your father. He was always away and now you've deserted me. You know I have a bad heart, but you don't care. You don't care what happens to me. Some day you're gonna come over here and find me dead. Then I guess you'll be satisfied."

At first even as Jane practiced expressing herself in role-playing, trying to tell her mother exactly what she was feeling, she had trouble. She feared that if she expressed any of her annoyance or anger to Mrs. R., it would physically harm her mother, perhaps fatally. Though gradually, over a period of weeks, Jane made progress in stating her anger in practice sessions, she could barely hint at her annoyance when she was face to face or on the telephone with her mother.

"I resent the fact that my mother demands that I visit her at least once a week, or that she just walks in on me unannounced," Jane said. "But I just can't seem to tell her that I resent her demands and intrusions."

Jane continued to give in to her mother, continued to hold in her true feelings, and continued to be anxious whenever she met with or spoke with her mother on the phone. "Sometimes, when I know that my mother's coming over or that I have to visit her," Jane said, "I get so anxious that I almost feel like I'm going to panic. If I didn't have my rubber band and my other coping tools, I'm sure I would panic. Last night she called just to berate me for marrying Bill and leaving her alone. For the first time in my life I yelled at her. I said, 'I can't stand it!' and hung up the phone."

SPEAKING OUT AND FEELING GOOD

"How did you feel?" I asked.

"I felt good. I really did. Then the phone rang and I told Bill to answer it. I knew it was my mother, and I told him I didn't want to talk to her. I didn't. But then I felt guilty, as if she was right and I was deserting her."

Except for this one important issue, her relationship with her mother, Jane had made remarkable progress in six months of treatment, usually one session a week of travel work and another devoted to psychotherapy. She had started by shopping again accompanied by Bill, and in the last few weeks had begun to do all of the shopping on her own. She had overcome her fears of bank lines and department stores and had even returned to her former office where her earliest panic attacks had taken place; she experienced no anxiety. As she resumed her role of complete housewife during the months ahead, her guilt feelings with Bill over her previous inactivity slowly vanished. Her depression lifted steadily and she began to sleep soundly most nights. She had more energy and was beginning to feel better about herself. There was hope where before there had been only hopelessness. She had taken just one Valium tablet in the past thirty days, after a scene with her mother. "It didn't do a thing for me," Jane reported. "I still carry them around with me, but I don't take them anymore."

As for Mrs. R., we had been trying for some time to get her to come into the office for a session or more with Jane in an effort to facilitate more forthright communication between the two of them. Mrs. R. resisted our requests as well as several from Bill. But given some encouragement, Jane asserted herself and convinced her mother to join us.

"I can't remember when I ever argued with her like that," Jane recalled. "But I told her that I had been ill and that in coming to the Program all these months I had begun to get well. I told her I don't think I'd ever felt better, but that I still wasn't completely well. I said I felt I would never be completely well until I could communicate openly with her, and to do that I really needed her to come with me to the Center. I let her know that it was very important that she help me with this."

Mrs. R. was quite apprehensive and fidgety when she sat down in my office. I told her that it had become clear to me in Jane's therapy that she and her daughter had many positive feelings about each other, but that the two of them seemed to be in conflict now. "My goal is to give both of you the opportunity to get off your chest whatever it is you've been storing for years, to get through your difficulties so that you can come back to the warmer feelings that are really there. I want to bring some real closeness into the relationship. Mrs. R., would that be important for you?"

"I've always been a good mother," Mrs. R. said. "I don't know what I've ever done to cause any problem for Jane. I don't know why I'm even here."

"We're not looking for guilt or blame," I reassured her. "We're looking to improve things between you, to make it possible for both of you to really open up about how you feel about each other. Because out of that comes a sense of closeness, mutual respect and caring. I'm sure you did the best you could all these years. I know it's not easy

to raise two children with your husband away so much.''
(I also pointed out emphatically that she did this while having considerable fears of her own, as Jane's disclosures had made clear that Mrs. R. was an undiagnosed agoraphobic.)

Mrs. R's face took on a pained expression as she said, ''I can't begin to tell you how *hard* it's been for me. I wanted to give Jane and her brother everything the other kids had, but I just couldn't. There just wasn't enough money. I couldn't go to work. It was hard making ends meet. So *hard*.'' Her eyes grew moist.

Seeing her mother's tears, Jane was touched and reached for a tissue to dab at her own eyes. I asked her how she felt about what her mother said.

Though moved by her mother's words, Jane said sharply, ''Well, I'm really angry at you, Mom, because you seemed to be so helpless all your life.'' Then, staring at her mother, Jane said quickly, ''But I don't really mean to upset you, Mom. I really don't.''

THE PERSON YOU TRY TO PROTECT IS STRONGER THAN YOU THINK

''Jane,'' I said, ''you were really feeling angry, but now you're feeling guilty about it. You're taking care of your mother again. I wonder if you could just repeat what you said about feeling angry, and see if your mother can handle it. I have a feeling that she's a lot stronger than you're ready to give her credit for.''

''I . . . I really don't want to make her feel bad,'' Jane said. ''But darn it all, whenever I say what I feel I *do* feel guilty because I'm afraid I'll hurt you, Mom.''

''I didn't know that, Jane,'' Mrs. R. said. ''I always wanted to know how you felt.''

Jane was silent and uncomfortable. I said, ''Why don't you tell your mother where you think the guilt comes from surrounding your fear of expressing your feelings. She's asking you and I think it's reasonable for you to let her know."

Her anger flashing again, Jane said, "All my life whenever I tried to express my feelings you always got sick! I don't know how many times you had me believing you were gonna faint or have a heart attack! And that really scared me. So I learned not to tell you what I felt. I was afraid to."

"*Please*, Jane, you know I've been sick all my life," Mrs. R. said. "Is it my fault you have a sickly mother? My mother was constantly sick, and I had to take care of her, too. I didn't make things that way. I tried my best for you, Lord knows I did. I don't understand why you blame me for all this."

Jane, looking down at her hands that were slowly rubbing together in her lap, said, "I really don't, Mom. I . . . I'm sorry."

I pointed out that the same thing that had happened five minutes ago had just happened again. "You expressed your feeling, but something going on between you and your mother has you feeling guilty and apologizing again," I said. "Mrs. R., is this making sense to you? Do you see how this happens?"

"I don't understand any of this. All I know is my husband leaves me all the time, my son left me, Jane left me. I'm all alone now."

"What is it like for you when Jane gets angry?"

Mrs. R. shrugged. "Everyone gets angry at times. It's natural."

"But when that happened just now," I said, "you began defending yourself as if Jane were making you a villain."

"Well, sure, she doesn't make me feel good. Saying I frightened her, saying she couldn't tell me how she felt."

"Mrs. R., when someone is angry with you, it doesn't necessarily mean it's your fault. Again, we're not trying to lay blame here. When people want to be close, they must have the opportunity to be angry with each other, and they must listen to each other. All of us try not to cause anger in someone we care about. My guess is that when Jane says she's angry with you about something, you start feeling guilty. Then you start to defend yourself, as you did just now. That's understandable. But I suspect you and Jane would get closer if you would just pay attention to how her remarks make you feel guilty."

"Of course I don't like to think I caused all Jane's problems," Mrs. R. said. "Look, I had this problem with fear all my life, and I was always afraid Jane would get it. To tell you the honest truth, I think my own mother had it, too. She was always afraid. And now look at all the problems Jane's having."

"Jane," I said, "did you know your mom was feeling guilty all this time about your problems?"

The young woman looked stunned, saying, "She never told me that before."

"How do you feel about it?" I asked. "Tell her."

"Well, I'm sorry you feel that way, Mom."

"Jane, you must know I really do love you. I've always wanted the best for you."

"I wish you'd told me that a long time ago," Jane said tearfully. "I really needed to know that you cared for me. I wasn't sure you ever loved me."

"I thought I did everything I could to let you know that," Mrs. R. said. "Didn't I walk to and from school every day for years? I was there every day at three o'clock waiting for you. What other mother cared that much for her daughter?"

"Yes, you met me after school long after the other girls were walking home together making friends," Jane said angrily. "You made me an outcast! You never wanted me to have friends, to go to parties, to have any social life. You wanted me home with you! You left me totally unprepared to go into the world after high school. I could hardly talk to anyone! I am angry at you for that! I am!"

Mrs. R. let out a sob and began crying.

"Mom, I'm . . . I know you did the best you could, please don't cry," Jane said.

BEING ABLE TO EXPRESS ANGER

In the next individual session with Jane, I emphasized that we had to break this pattern that blocked her from being able to express anger to her mother. Every time she did so, she felt guilty and apologized. I asked her what memory she might have of something terrible that happened after she expressed anger.

Jane started talking about a time when she had become very angry with her father. "I remember I was thirteen, it was just before he had a heart attack and went into the hospital," she said, sobbing softly. "There was a party, one of the few I was ever invited to. I asked my father to buy me a dress, told him I wanted to look nice." Tears were falling now, and her words came in bursts between gasping sobs. "Daddy refused to buy the dress, I don't know why. But I *screamed* at him. 'You don't care about me! You don't care how the other kids see me! You're just like Mom!' " She let out a long mournful sound. "The next thing . . . I knew . . . he was in the hospital." She cried uncontrollably for more than a minute.

When she regained control, Jane said, "I guess I'm afraid if I ever let myself feel that much anger again, that something will happen to my mother. I . . . I never thought of that before."

RELEASING SOME GUILT FEELINGS

This was a cathartic experience for Jane and helped her release some of her guilt. "From all of this perhaps you can see why it's been so difficult for you to express anger to your mother," I said, and Jane nodded. "Now it is crucial for you to let your mother know how you feel, because in the end it's for her benefit as well as yours. As long as you two are on poor terms, your mother will be just as unhappy as you are. There's no joy in the relationship for either of you."

Mrs. R. came into the next session saying she felt more comfortable. "I was scared to do this in the beginning. But I'm glad I came, because I feel much better when Jane and I talk on the phone."

Jane had already said she was willing to let her mother know of some changes she wanted to make in their relationship, and I asked Mrs. R. if she would be willing to listen to them.

"Of course I'll listen. I'll do whatever I can to help Jane."

At my suggestion Jane said, "I feel, Mom, that I'd really like you to call before you come over to see me. Sometimes it's just not convenient."

"I didn't know I wasn't welcome in your home," Mrs. R. said.

In a burst of anger, Jane said, "You always say things like that! Won't you ever listen to me? It's always the same! You never listened and you're doing it again!"

"Wait a minute," I said. "You told your mother about a change you want her to make, and she said she didn't know she wasn't welcome in your home. Stop and think about the feeling you got then."

"I felt really hurt," Jane said, "because it was like she didn't even hear what I said to her. No, actually I felt angry because she was criticizing me."

"Instead of saying your mother never listens," I said, "stay in the present and tell her what makes you feel angry."

"When I'm not being listened to, that makes me feel angry," Jane said.

In individual sessions with Jane she would tell me about her telephone conversations with her mother. They were a

good way to practice her small steps toward a new assertiveness, because she had the option of terminating the conversation whenever she got overwhelmed. When Mrs. R.
complained that she hadn't heard from Jane in several days,
Jane said she'd been busy applying for college. "Well, I feel
like you don't have time for me anymore," Mrs. R. said.
Jane, overwhelmed, said she was sorry and had to go, hang-
ing up.

"I guess I should have told her that what I felt was anger," Jane told me.

I then played the role of Jane's mother and said, "I feel
like you don't have time for me anymore."

"That makes me angry," Jane said. "You're always saying that and you know it's not true."

"All right, that was much better. You were angry and
you expressed it. Now you need to express your feelings
in a way that'll get through to her. Because essentially she
said, 'You don't care about me anymore'—a guilt-provoking
statement. And you came back with, 'You're always saying that'—another guilt-provoking statement. So for her to
hear what you say, stay with your feelings—not with her
behavior. Don't accuse her, just tell her what you *feel*. Try
something like, 'Mom, that makes me feel really angry, because I do care about you, but I have other things in my life
that are important, too, and I want you to understand that.' "

We role-played the exchanges until Jane was comfortable
with her new vocabulary. Then I emphasized how crucial
it was for Jane to make her points without being sidetracked
by her mother, without giving in to guilt, defensiveness and
apologies. "That's the way you've tried to placate her in
the past, and it hasn't worked for either of you."

Week after week in individual sessions Jane worked on
not allowing Mrs. R. to deflect her message: "Mom, the
main thing for me right now is that I'm making changes in
my life, and that's very, very important to me. I hope you
understand that. But if you don't, I'm gonna make those
changes anyway."

Jane did make those changes and became fully able to express her feelings—including anger—without guilt or apology. And Mrs. R. in time accepted Jane as an adult and stopped treating her as a child. Jane learned that you don't change another person by asking that person to change. You change another person by changing yourself. Then the other person is unable to respond to you in the same way, because you are simply not the same person. Of course, there are men and women who will not accept their child or partner's changed persona, and in these situations the goal is to put distance between them without feeling blame or guilt.

After starting college, Jane had two more sessions and then terminated her treatment. "Bill's taking me to New York for a three-day weekend to celebrate," Jane said, beaming. "When I first came here eighteen months ago I never thought I'd feel this good."

WE ALL NEED SOME ANXIETY, EVEN RECOVERED AGORAPHOBICS

Six months later Jane suffered a setback when her mother was diagnosed as having cancer. She came in and reported she'd had a lot of anxiety for a week and said she'd actually suffered a panic attack during her third visit to the hospital the previous evening. "I feel like I'm losing it all, as if I might totally relapse," Jane said, looking very upset.

I reminded her that she had every reason to be anxious about her mother, that anyone in similar circumstances would be. That's what stress does to people. Nonagoraphobic people can have panic attacks under stress, but she was fortunate in that she had the skills to cope with anxiety. "Use the tools you have," I said, "and anxiety will never get the best of you again. It's also important for you to remember that you did not create your mother's illness. You may have to repeat that fact to yourself for some time. When we've changed things we're anxious about doing out of fear that the changes will hurt somebody, it's not unusual to feel we've caused any subsequent hurt to that person."

Jane visited the hospital for the next three weeks without panicking. At that point corrective surgery had Mrs. R. on the way to recovery. As of this writing, almost five years after termination of her treatment, Jane was free of agoraphobia. A college graduate, she is now employed as a social scientist.

The Effects of Agoraphobia on the Family

LIVING WITH AN AGORAPHOBIC CHILD

For parents there is nothing more heartbreaking than to observe their child suffering from a lingering illness. When the illness turns the child's face into a mask of total fear and is seemingly incurable, parents are crushed. They believe they are failing their ultimate responsibility, which is to protect their child from frightening situations. Should these arise, the aim is to reassure and comfort the youngster. But parents of an agoraphobic child can do nothing when their daughter or son is suddenly seized by a panic attack. They stand there helplessly as their child trembles, in tears, often crying out for relief from the terror that's gripping her.

Parents don't know what they have done, but they feel responsible for their child's chronic anxiety, and they are torn by guilt. In spite of their desire to make everything right for the child, they are powerless. This often leads to a rift between father and mother on how to deal with the child. Parents often blame each other for the problem. Couples who have been communicating well will be brought closer together, their relationship strengthened. But agoraphobia in a child may drive a wedge between parents, bringing out long-standing animosities.

Usually parents turn to their medical doctor for help and

then to a psychotherapist, preferably one who has had success treating agoraphobics. Some parents feel bad about having a stranger take over the care of their child, and their guilt intensifies.

BE SUPPORTIVE, BUT NOT CONDESCENDING

In most cases one parent will adopt the attitude that their offspring is sick, whether he or she be fifteen or twenty-two, and will begin to treat the agoraphobic as a child. This leads to the kind of overprotection that may have fostered the problem in the first place, which is exactly what is not needed. In fact the person should be treated appropriately to his or her age, as an autonomous young adult. Parents should be supportive but not condescending. If an agoraphobic teenager is treated differently from her siblings, for example, her sense of self will be undermined, and she will feel that she cannot take care of herself. Whatever perception parents have of their children tends to be the perception their child will incorporate as her self-image. Parents should therefore encourage a teenaged child to be independent, to make decisions and act on them. This does not mean you should *force* your child to do something, but rather try to encourage with warmth and understanding. As agoraphobics gain self-sufficiency, both they and their parents benefit.

Parents tend to try to avoid saying or doing anything that could upset their agoraphobic child. Often they will sacrifice themselves and their own feelings for what they regard as the child's welfare. But the open expression of feelings helps everyone in the family. As you have seen, the inability to express feelings often leads to stress and anxiety.

Agoraphobia places a tremendous burden on parents. It

causes hurt, anger and resentment, feelings that anyone in similar circumstances would have. Those feelings should be accepted and expressed calmly and rationally. Communication should start with "I feel" phrases, such as "I feel annoyed about giving up my golf game to drive you around." Agoraphobics don't know much about open expression simply because they haven't experienced it, and such dialogue can be a new beginning for them. Open expression is sometimes difficult to achieve without the guidance of a therapist. But parents who learn that it is all right to express their pain, confusion, sadness and anger can feel their guilt begin to dissolve. And that's one *great* feeling.

SEPARATING FROM THE FAMILY HOME

Even before the onset of symptoms most agoraphobics have a difficult time moving out of their familial homes. They are fearful of stepping out on their own into the seemingly chaotic and unpredictable world at large. People in general need a strong sense of security to separate from their family home, and when the young person marching toward agoraphobia has not acquired that sense he or she constantly searches for it.

The way many of these people bring themselves to leave the "safety" of home is by marrying a spouse who seems to possess many of the characteristics of one of their parents. The more conflict there has been in the home environment, the more likely it is that the agoraphobic will choose a spouse with a manner and style similar to that of a parent. This is usually the father in the case of female agoraphobics. A familiar environment—even a bad one—is less scary than an unfamiliar one, which is why parents are sometimes exchanged for a surrogate parent in the guise of a mate.

THE HUSBAND AS PROTECTOR

Often the chosen husband appears to be a strong, totally-in-control individual. It's easy to see why a fearful young woman would join her life with someone so seemingly assured and protective. But while other young people leave their parental home in a move toward independence, the pre-agoraphobic woman simply transfers her dependency. She marries a man she sees as able to take care of *everything*. This kind of man offers many attributes, but open expression of feelings is rarely among them. Generally this husband needs to play the parent role, not the role of mate, and his wife's dependence reinforces this tendency. Even before the wedding ceremony he may have fancied himself as a kind of Pygmalion who would completely remake his wife and would guarantee that everything was all right. He may say to his wife: "Your parents were terrible to you, but that's over now—I'll save you."

THE PROTECTOR ROLE PERPETUATES HIS WIFE'S DEPENDENCY

Yet the husband of an agoraphobic soon discovers that his spouse is in no position to change. In addition, in assuming the protector role he perpetuates his wife's dependency, instead of helping her develop her own sufficiency. Thus, without meaning to, the husband maintains his wife's agoraphobia.

The couple's relationship may be fine initially, the husband-who-would-be-parent and the wife-who-would-be-child merging in a satisfactory way. But many pre-agoraphobic women suddenly find that being separated from their parents while also having to assume the considerable responsibilities of marriage is just too much for them to handle.

Their stress builds and panics begin. Onset may not occur for other pre-agoraphobic wives until after the birth of a child or two.

AGORAPHOBIA PUTS TREMENDOUS STRESS ON A MARRIAGE

But whenever the onset comes, agoraphobia puts tremendous stress on a marriage. Even among those couples who were interacting as equals there is often a breakdown in communication. The husband regards his wife as sick and in need of special care. He begins to swallow his complaints, to bury his feelings, in order to protect her.

We all tend to feel somewhat guilty about misfortunes that befall those we love, and that feeling is multiplied many times for a protector-parent husband. He thinks he should have been able to prevent the disorder from striking and he often begins to wonder how he may have contributed to his wife's panics.

Out of concern for the woman he loves and the desire to be available for her whenever possible, husbands may begin to give up most of the things they enjoy doing. Once he regularly stopped with colleagues for a drink after work; now he hurries home. He used to bowl Thursday nights; no more. On Saturdays in the fall he liked to take in a football game, in the winter to go hunting or skiing, and in the spring to fish in a nearby lake. Now on Saturdays he has to accompany his wife when she does the family shopping and other errands. Eventually she becomes too frightened to drive the car. The husband tries very hard to meet all of his wife's demands and requests. For some months he goes so far as to race home from work whenever she tearfully asks him to come, saying she feels as if she's going crazy.

THE HUSBAND TRIES HARD TO HELP, AND HIS WIFE GETS WORSE

He makes every effort for his wife, but instead of getting better she gets worse and the demands of her disorder keep increasing. He becomes frustrated as the symptoms of agoraphobia now dominate his every waking moment with his wife. Instead of sharing experiences that enhance a relationship, they are sharing anxiety. Instead of making plans for a relaxing weekend with neighbors, the couple conjures excuses about why they will be absent when friends gather. After a number of excuses, friends don't bother to offer them invitations anymore. And the family beset by agoraphobia may become totally isolated, enshrouded in a mystifying and terrorizing disorder.

And husbands who try to do everything, which of course is impossible, soon discover that none of the duties are performed satisfactorily. These men find themselves being pulled apart. Their wives' emergency summonses force them to be called out of meetings, they can no longer make evening sales calls or take out-of-town business trips. These are usually concerned, caring men who choose to respond to their wives' calls knowing full well they are jeopardizing their jobs. The husband employed by corporations that rotate executives around the country has to turn down such moves and the chance for advancement or pay the price of his wife's increased distress subsequent to a move. The thought of leaving home is extremely threatening to an agoraphobic, not unlike the frightening separation from the parental home. The husband may eventually become resentful, and some become fed up and begin to withdraw from the family.

Other husbands try to avoid the home scene. Virtually from the beginning of the wife's onset these men become workaholics rather than spend time at home. When the husband is home, he feels guilty about pulling away from the family in its time of need. Then he is often angry and rakes his wife verbally, and sometimes his children as well. The husband is now in need of help as much as his agoraphobic wife. Marriage and fatherhood were never meant to be like this and he just doesn't know what to do, except escape or sink into depression.

THE HUSBAND'S BURDEN WHEN AGORAPHOBIA CUTS HIS WIFE'S INCOME

Husbands whose wives were working at the time of onset sometimes feel terribly put upon by the abrupt reduction in the family income. One example of such a husband is a man we'll call Steve. He was a computer systems consultant married to a twenty-seven-year-old pediatrician, Carla, who was beginning to build a good practice. Six months after they had bought the house of their dreams, a house well within their means, Carla began having panic attacks. Increasing anxiety and panics soon caused her to have such difficulty functioning at work that she cut her schedule to part-time. Within months she had to stop working altogether. The large house mortgage and decreased income forced Steve to increase his work load to about seventy hours per week. He was always overtired and seldom available for Carla, who needed his support very much. Confused and disappointed, Steve began to resent the extra burdens her problems placed on him, including taking care of all the chores outside the house which they had previously shared.

By the time Carla came in for treatment at the Program three years later, her relationship with Steve was in a shambles and there was little communication between them. Steve, convinced that Carla would never again be the woman he married, had become totally wrapped up in his work. They both harbored unexpressed resentment, she feeling that he was withdrawn and unsupportive, he feeling that she had grown critical of him and no longer gave him understanding. Carla was unable to enjoy social events, though she pushed herself to attend a few. Steve knew she was miserable at parties and that she attended them only because he wanted to, so he felt profoundly guilty.

In some marriages conflicts are acted out in constant bickering. "You're abandoning me!" the wife cries. And the husband says, "You expect me to work, do the marketing, take care of you and the kids. You must be nuts! One person can't possibly do all that!" This causes the wife to panic. Any kind of ongoing stress can trigger an attack, although the agoraphobic is usually unaware of the connection between the two. Not knowing heightens anxiety and confusion.

THE WIFE'S SENSE OF DISCONNECTEDNESS

It is often a sense of isolation, of nonconnectedness with others that produces panics. People tend to meet their need for connections through their relationship with parents initially and then with a spouse and close friends. Yet agoraphobics usually have been raised in an environment that does not teach them how to connect with others. As children, they were not encouraged to express themselves freely. The general sense of disconnectedness is often the result of parents not having connected with the child through attention and acceptance of the child's feelings and thoughts. The agoraphobic's feelings of emptiness are filled only by the parent or relative they perceived as their "safe" person very early in life.

Whatever friends were made after marriage are usually soon

lost following the onset of agoraphobia. The wife's social anxiety is often present to some degree prior to her panics. She does not relax at large gatherings, particularly among strangers because she feels they are always observing and evaluating her. She is uncomfortable, anxious. Even those people who were gregarious and enjoyed a social life prior to onset may quickly become reclusive once they have experienced panics. They feel something will happen to them in the presence of friends that will cause them to lose control and look ridiculous. Fearing that they will be embarrassed, they start to worry about being around people. Scheduled events become terrifying, the anxiety building every day for a week as a bridge date or dinner engagement approaches. When it arrives the agoraphobic woman usually comes up with an excuse for not attending.

Most husbands go along with the growing isolation for a while. They give up most if not all of their recreational activities, the relaxing, leisure pursuits that refueled and replenished them. Eventually the husband of an agoraphobic may suspect that his wife is using her illness to avoid certain activities that she never much cared for. A wife who was uncomfortable at her husband's office picnics, but attended them without complaint, now refuses to go. That annoys him, for he feels that her absence will hurt his chances for advancement, that his boss will think he's married to a very strange person.

Agoraphobic people tend to be erratic in their behavior. They think they can do something, agree to do it, and then withdraw at the last minute. Even social events in their own homes become impossible. "We can't have them over, because what if I don't feel well that evening?" the agoraphobic wife will say. "How can I take care of those people if I have a panic?" When friends just dropped in unannounced while passing through the neighborhood, the wife felt trapped because there was no way she could escape. She was obliged to be cordial and serve drinks while feeling she might panic at any moment and make a fool of herself.

WHY SEXUAL DESIRE FLAGS

One of the most frequently heard complaints of agoraphobic women when they come in for treatment is, "My husband doesn't understand me. He never expresses any feelings. If he'd only *talk* to me!"

With some couples, sex is the lone aspect of the relationship that remains satisfying. But much more frequently when one partner is agoraphobic the couple's sex life is disrupted. To begin with, depression and constant anxiety have an adverse effect on all pleasurable activities. The resentment, frustration and anger that take over both husband and wife usually interfere with sexual desire, arousal and the ability to relax and concentrate. A good sex life is maintained and augmented by free and open communication, flexibility and frequent fantasies. But because an agoraphobic's time is spent obsessing about some upcoming event she can't bear to face, sexual considerations seldom surface. Initially the sex-life disruption tends to be sporadic, and husbands may feel used, as if their wives are offering sex only in exchange for something in return. As the agoraphobia continues, husbands tend to regard their wives' lack of interest in them sexually as a painful rejection.

It takes a tremendous amount of effort to keep a relationship viable among all this turbulence and anguish. The longer the disorder goes on, the more difficult it becomes to hold a marriage together. The husband may threaten to leave, which adds to the wife's anxiety. But most husbands feel so guilty that they seldom act on the threat.

THE AGORAPHOBIC MALE ALSO SEEKS A TAKE-CHARGE MATE

Not surprisingly, the male who becomes agoraphobic looks for some of the same characteristics in a wife that the female agoraphobic seeks in a husband: someone who is very responsible and well organized, a parental type who likes to take charge. Such a woman in turn tends to seek out a man who gives her the space to act independently. The wife's need is for a structured existence: this is when I clean, this is when I cook, this is when I shop, this is when I go to work. At the onset of agoraphobia the structure is invariably disrupted, which is stressful to the woman. Additional stress is brought on by the wife's feelings of guilt and helplessness in the face of her partner's panic attacks.

MANY MALE AGORAPHOBICS CONTINUE TO WORK

Some of the male agoraphobics we see are able to function fairly well, to work and to participate in social and recreational events. But they are limited in where and how far they will travel. Many are afraid of flying, driving through tunnels or over bridges, and riding on elevators, particularly in high-rise buildings. Thus they find the disorder to be very distressing.

In some cases the men are far more limited in their mobility and therefore can't hold a job. When her husband is suddenly out of work, the financial pressure on the wife can be extraordinary even if she is employed. Usually the man's salary was higher and now her income must cover the mortgage payments, the food bills and all the other costs of running a household. The woman tries to work harder, and if she has children she feels guilty about giving up time with them. Wives who have not been working, who do not have employment skills, have far more difficulty trying to support the family when agoraphobia incapacitates their husbands. Somehow given their strong characters, they endure and prevail, but not without paying a price. They become depressed and anxious themselves under the constant stress thrust upon them. They find it difficult to communicate with their husbands, who tend to withdraw into themselves and grow obsessive and hypochondriacal.

Of course, the man has never felt worse. Not only is he chronically anxious and regularly subjected to panics, but he feels abysmally guilty about his unemployment, his inability to support his family. The reversal of the sex roles is particularly destructive to men who subscribe to society's view that the husband who doesn't fill the larder is worthless.

FOR THE HOUSEBOUND HUSBAND, FAMILY LIFE ALMOST CEASES

Despite the fact that his wife is supporting the family while he is at home all day, he rarely takes any responsibility for running the household—cooking, cleaning, taking care of children. He becomes so wrapped up in his disorder that the family almost ceases to exist for him. In many ways the conventions of our society, which suggest that women should keep the home together and men should provide the financial support, makes it doubly difficult for male agoraphobics. Women are supposed to be domestic; they can hide their agoraphobia behind that domesticity, at least for a while. Men are expected to function in the world, and often, when they feel they have failed in that arena, they are incapable of making a contribution in what they consider the female arena. The male agoraphobic becomes another person for his wife to take care of and worry about.

Men and women alike tend to feel guilty when a spouse becomes agoraphobic, as if they caused the problem for their partner. They did not. People who become agoraphobic bring the preconditions into the marriage and onset appears to be inevitable. There is no question that spouses can *contribute* to the problem, if their own histories have led them to be irresponsible or alcoholic or otherwise not providing emotional support. Communication between spouses is a problem in many marriages, and it is a very serious problem with couples in which one partner is agoraphobic.

PARENTS HIDE THEIR AGORAPHOBIA FROM CHILDREN

Most agoraphobic parents go to extremes to hide their disorder from their children, and this is a mistake. Clients tell us they don't want their children to know about their anxieties for fear they will catch them. The hiding of fears is not only out of concern for the children but out of concern about what other people in the neighborhood might say about them once word of their disorder gets around. Agoraphobics are ashamed of their problem, and feelings of shame undermine their own sense of worth. Hiding their fears not only cuts them off from friends, but adds another anxiety: the fear of being discovered.

CHILDREN OF AGORAPHOBICS

We have interviewed scores of children of agoraphobic parents and few of them said they knew that a mother or father was so afflicted, even though they sensed something was wrong. Yet others in the family, such as uncles, aunts and cousins, said they were aware of the disorder. The children of an agoraphobic parent said, even into adulthood, they knew their father or mother never went anywhere, but they assumed that was by choice, that he or she was reclusive. Often this behavior is interpreted as the parent's not caring much about the child, and that is more hurtful than knowing the truth.

Hiding the disorder from children results in erratic behavior that the children can't explain, and that too is destructive. The child's interpretation is that life is unpredictable and dangerous, that one can't depend on anything. In the early years children tend to see themselves as the cause of all of their parents' behavior. When the agoraphobic parent does not show up for a PTA meeting, for a ballgame, for a child's appearance in a school play or for any event in which other parents are present in abundance, the child feels that is the treatment he or she deserves. The child feels that he or she is not worthy of love.

Daughters in particular are at risk of developing panic attacks and agoraphobia when they grow up in a home with a parent who has those symptoms. Thus there is a need for children to understand what's going on so they'll know how to cope if they should experience anxiety that spirals into panic.

In addition, as agoraphobic parents tend to be fearful about their children's well-being in general, the youngsters pick up the fearfulness. This is another reason why children should be told about a parent's fears, so they can work together on potential problems. What the parent basically needs to say is, "This is the way I behave when I'm afraid and it has nothing to do with you. I can't take you to the movies as we'd planned because I'm frightened, not because I don't want to take you. I love you, even though there are times when I'm too scared to show it. I do get frightened and there's nothing I can do about it, and nothing you can either. It passes, it always does."

Sometimes, out of desperation or the need for someone to count on, an agoraphobic parent will turn a child into his or her "safe person." The child will then be asked to accompany the parent whenever he or she leaves the house; the child will also be needed at home to allay any fears that arise. This role reversal, where the child takes care of and provides security for a parent, is very harmful to the child's development, even if the child seems to be coping well with it at the time, and can result in the young person's becoming agoraphobic later on in life.

ANXIETY VERY COMMON IN SOCIETY TODAY

An important fact that agoraphobics overlook is that anxiety is very common in today's society. Everyone has some fear, some trepidation, and everyone has relations or friends who have exhibited intense fears. The fact that you get frightened at times merely makes you a member of the human race. Admitting it helps reduce fears.

When agoraphobic mothers and fathers finally do decide to tell their children the truth about their disorder, the result is usually much greater understanding and closeness in the family. Not long ago one of our clients, who was recovering from agoraphobia, at long last told his now-grown sons why he could never bring himself to take them fishing or to ballgames. He was surprised to hear them say they knew something was wrong but didn't think they should ask him about it. Following the man's recovery he rented a house on a lake—the first time he'd been to the country in twenty years—and drove off on vacation. The day he got there so did his sons, their wives and his grandchildren. They threw a wonderful celebration in his honor. "I wish I'd told them years ago," he said later. "What was scary then seems silly now."

CHAPTER 5

The Two-Week Intensive Program

*T*he most successful innovation in our treatment of agoraphobics has been the Two-Week Intensive Program in which a group of six to eight clients works approximately eighty hours in ten days. In the early years of our program, treatment consisted of one hour of individual therapy plus a few hours of group travel work each week. But shortcomings emerged in this program, one being that it seemed to prolong treatment. People tended to progress rather slowly because all the time between sessions they were living under the same conditions that had the power, in a sense, to control the way they behaved. So it was much harder for people to make changes when they were in therapy for such a small portion of their week, four hours out of a total of 168.

In addition, after clients went through three or four weeks of individual therapy we found we were getting a fair number of dropouts. This seemed to occur when clients became aware of difficulties in their lives that they had not recognized before, particularly problems in their relationships. To some, that was sufficiently frightening that once they learned some coping skills they chose to withdraw rather than deal with the interpersonal issues. Often there was also some resistance to change from the significant figure in the client's life—spouse, lover or parent.

Thus there was a need for a way to support clients through the hard transition toward the beginnings of change and a need for a way to support the significant others so that they were not threatened by the changes their loved ones were making. The Two-Week Intensive has proved to be very helpful in overcoming these problems, clients working together with a therapist, a travel leader and one or more assistants from 9:30 A.M. to 4 P.M. for ten days, broken only by a weekend. And in those two weeks they accomplished what on a weekly basis would usually take six months' work.

It became immediately apparent that the intensive format made it much easier for people to let down their defenses and open themselves to change, because they were being supported by others with similar problems. The members of the group became like a family, caring for and helping one another at every turn. The intensity of the experience also caused issues to arise much more quickly than they do in extended therapy. And the radical change of patterns for two weeks allowed people to get a good strong hold on the new ways without falling back into old habits. In addition, motivation is higher for most clients because they see such rapid progress, and this encourages and builds confidence in everyone. The combination of all these things makes for a very powerful and effective experience.

Here we will take you through a Two-Week Intensive group so that you can get some feel for the experience. The group includes five women and one man. In the interest of space we will focus on only two of the women, each of whom had undergone three individual therapy sessions prior to the Intensive. Both of these women, it turned out, also had difficulties in their marriages that were connected to their anxiety, which is not uncommon among agoraphobics.

Norma was an attractive, charming, well-dressed thirty-eight-year-old who appeared far younger than her age. She reported in her initial visit to the Program offices that she was unhappy in her marriage and was thinking about a separation. She was constantly anxious, fearful of being alone in her house or of going out by herself to any place from which quick escape was difficult. When panic struck she said she often felt as if she couldn't breathe, and she had also experienced heart palpitations, dizziness and numbness in the extremities. These sensations increased her fear.

"Sometimes I think I'm going to have a heart attack and I get terrified," she said. "Other times I'm afraid I'm going to faint, or just totally lose control and do something foolish, you know, in public. It's awful."

Norma was the mother of a son, Jonathan (fourteen) and a daughter, Anne (ten), by her first husband, Lee. Both Norma and Lee had remarried other partners five years ago. "Jonathan decided he'd rather live with his father, and that's where he is," Norma said, and tears welled in her eyes. Anne and Norma were close, mutually supportive. An extremely conscientious mother, Norma spent much of her time caring for her daughter and wooing Jonathan during his visits. She missed him and hoped he would decide to return to her.

As a child herself, Norma said she was the overprotected oldest of six daughters in an upper-middle-class family. Her mother was somewhat agoraphobic and completely controlled by her very strict father, who would not even allow his wife to learn how to drive a car. Norma said she was the only person in her family who would talk back, though always politely, to her parents. She regarded herself as her mother's protector and advocate whenever her parents differed. Norma felt she was her father's favorite and she kept trying to reform him and to liberate her mother. On graduation from high school, Norma enrolled in college, studying to become a social worker. But her mother kept deriding her for attending college, saying she'd be better off taking a job as she would eventually marry and quit work anyway. After her sophomore year, Norma, feeling somehow guilty, did leave school and get a job. Within a year she married Lee.

Four months later she had her first panic attack. She described Lee as a man who was unsupportive, rigid and dictatorial. She wanted to leave him but was too fearful to do so. Lee was a successful businessman and she didn't know how she would fend for herself. In addition, she said she did not want to disappoint her parents by divorcing. As the children came she attempted to fill her life with them and to ignore her husband's coldness and criticism. But except during her pregnancies—when she was relatively symptom-free—she was essentially housebound for eight years. When she finally divorced Lee, her symptoms disappeared.

Within a year, though, she married again. Jack, a corporate lawyer, was also rigid and ungiving, and Norma felt that he constantly criticized and controlled her. Her symptoms soon returned and ran a fluctuating course through the five years of this marriage. She was no longer housebound, and in fact had returned to college and would soon earn her degree. She hoped to get a job in the fall and to leave Jack. But torn by guilt over thinking about a second divorce and what it might do to her children, Norma felt helpless. In recent weeks her anxiety had seemed to be almost without letup. She had taken a leave from college and had Jack do most of the shopping.

Norma had undergone psychotherapy for several years during her first marriage and for fourteen months prior to coming to the Center. She said the psychiatrists gave her some insights into the relationship between her marital unhappiness and her symptoms, but she saw no improvement in her condition. The antidepressant prescribed for her, imipramine, had provided no relief. She said small doses of Valium had helped her get through particularly stressful days.

In her individual sessions Norma had already learned some use of coping skills and was cutting back her use of Valium. "I'm not taking more than one a day," she said, "but I still carry a full supply. Just in case." She was again doing the family shopping, though at times she asked Jack to accompany her.

So that they could be guided and supported in their roles during the Intensive, the significant figures (husbands, parents, lovers) are expected to attend a two-hour orientation meeting and six two-hour group sessions during the two weeks. Jack was somewhat reluctant to participate in these sessions.

The second woman we'll focus on is Beth, a twenty-nine-year-old mother of two preschool children, who came in deeply depressed. She had difficulty relating to people, particularly to her husband, Ben. Six months earlier she had begun wondering whether she loved Ben, and whether she should leave him. Shortly thereafter she started having panic attacks while driving home from her part-time job. She gave up the job and also gave up driving, shopping only when Ben drove her. Though she spent most of her time in her house, her panic attacks persisted and became more frequent.

As with Norma's husband, we invited Ben in and explained his wife's symptoms, saying that Beth would be working to gain control of her fears and panics in group travel and group psychotherapy sessions during the Intensive Program. We explained that we would like him to work with Jack and the other spouses in group sessions. "Sounds good to me," Ben said, "anything to get Beth back together. If she's not having a panic attack she's withdrawn all the time, even from the kids. I tell you, I almost hate to come home sometimes."

All of the clients and spouses were present at the start of the Intensive on Monday morning, and they found it reassuring to see that their problems were not unique. First I introduced the other therapists who would run the group with me—Alex Tullis and Diane Coia—then the clients and spouses. Next we had a discussion about agoraphobia and its roots, the schedule for the Intensive and why we would be doing the things that were planned for them.

AS CLIENTS MAKE CHANGES, SPOUSES MUST ALSO CHANGE

I pointed out that clients would be making a lot of changes in their behavior, and that spouses should be prepared to change too. It's not uncommon for spouses to feel negatively about their partner's improving in spite of their best intentions. Many have told us that they worked hard for years trying to help their ill partner and made no progress, then they felt resentment when the spouse responded in treatment. Others have told us that they've felt somewhat threatened by the growing independence suddenly exhibited by the recovering person. So partners can expect to feel some stress, too, in this period and it's important that they have a chance to talk about those feelings in the group meetings.

Jack, Norma's husband, asked, "What can we expect at the end of this? Will Norma stop having panic attacks?"

I told Jack that we see much more mobility in people after two weeks. People are usually well on their way to no longer avoiding and in knowing how to cope with panic. They'll still have more anxiety than normal levels. But they can anticipate continuing decreases in anxiety over the months to come. We'll also have a good idea at the end of two weeks as to what stresses are present in each client's life. Most people complete the Intensive and continue in group or individual psychotherapy.

"What about depression?" asked Ben. "Beth, my wife, has been so depressed and I just wondered if this program will help her get rid of it."

I explained that agoraphobics tend to be depressed because they engage in so much negative thinking, and anyone who's constantly anxious inevitably becomes depressed. On the whole they grow much less depressed as they make gains during the Intensive.

At meeting's end the spouses left and therapist Alex Tullis said, "The rest of us will all have lunch together, which is a good chance for everyone to get to know one another. The restaurant's just two blocks away and we'll all walk over together."

Norma, who was seated next to Beth, saw how disturbed the younger woman looked, eyes lowered, lips set in a thin line. Striking up a conversation, Norma said, "I feel good about this, as if I'm finally going to get some help. I saw two psychotherapists for over a year and they couldn't do anything about my anxiety. For the first time I feel like someone understands what I have."

"I'm scared just thinking about going to lunch," Beth said.

"It'll be okay," Norma said. "We'll eat together."

As they headed for the restaurant, Norma revealed her desire to leave her husband, and for the first time life came into Beth's eyes. They fairly flashed as she said, "I've been thinking the same thing, and it's scaring me to death."

"It's scaring me, too," Norma said. "I've already been divorced once."

When they were crossing the parking lot in front of the restaurant, Beth said, "Oh, my God! I know that woman by the bakery! Don't let her see me. Walk in front of me, Norma."

Beth stepped behind Norma, but it was too late. "What are you doing here, Beth?" the woman said. "I haven't even seen you around the neighborhood in months."

"Oh, I . . . lunch, I'm just having lunch with a friend," Beth said, blushing and quickening her pace. "Nice, uh, nice to see you." She hurried into the restaurant, not even holding the door for Norma at her heels.

Beth was somewhat disoriented, and Norma cupped her elbow and guided her to a table. "I'm so embarrassed!" Beth said as therapist Diane Coia joined them. Diane said, "Agoraphobics are easily embarrassed. They think everyone is always looking at them and that's seldom true." Diane asked Beth to explain her embarrassment. When she did so Diane said, "It sounds like you made yourself anxious by catastrophizing, thinking something awful would happen.''

Back at the Center after lunch during the group psychotherapy session, therapist Alex Tullis asked about the medication clients were taking and pointed out that it was a good idea to reduce drug intake during therapy because while on them clients often did not ascribe to their own efforts the progress they were making. They tended to think the medication was responsible for their improvements. But he said all drug reductions would be done under the supervision of the psychiatric consultant at the Center.

"I'm on Tofranil, an antidepressant," Beth said. "I get these incredible panic attacks now, on Tofranil, and I'm afraid if I go off it the depression will get worse."

YOU GO OFF DRUGS SLOWLY—AT YOUR OWN PACE

"First of all you are weaned off all medication slowly," said Diane, herself a recovered agoraphobic. "You don't stop all at once because it's a shock to your system. I was on Tofranil myself for a couple of years, and I know that when I had a panic attack it tended to be the same with or without the drug. I think if you're gonna go off it, it would be a good idea for you and everyone else to do so with the guidance of the psychiatric consultant here. Check with him."

"I'm just about off Valium," Norma said. "I didn't take one today."

"That's great, Norma," Diane said. "There's evidence that tranquilizers can interfere with changing the fear attached to places. So it's far better not to use tranquilizers when we do our travel work. Beth, you look like you want to say something."

"I was just thinking that sometimes I feel like I'm not here," Beth said. "Like I'm floating, kinda looking down on myself, and I get smaller and smaller."

WHEN FEELINGS SHUT DOWN

"We call that depersonalization," Diane said. "When you are very anxious for a long time, you begin to feel that things around you are unreal. This is the body's way of protecting you against overwhelming feelings. Because when you are in this state it is like the feelings shut down, a kind of numbness and distance from things occurs. Of course, for agoraphobics this is just another sensation to be worried about. An important part of what we will be doing here is learning about the connection between unexpressed feelings and the development of anxiety, panic and agoraphobia.

"If we learn at a very early age that we are punished for expressing our feelings or if they are so strong that we feel overwhelmed by them, after a while we lose the ability to recognize those feelings. Then when something happens to stimulate those unwelcome feelings we experience them, instead, as anxiety. And for those of us who will become agoraphobic, the anxiety leads to panic.

"In order to get over that anxiety and its source we must learn to accept all of our feelings and how to allow them expression in direct and constructive ways."

"Basically feelings come down to 'mad, glad, sad and scared,' " Alex said. "Anything else is part of one of those four feelings. And we're gonna be talking a lot about them. Most of us don't allow ourselves to be mad or sad." Diane said, "A second very important part of our work will be the learning of anxiety and panic coping skills so that you can begin again to feel in control wherever you go."

Diane started teaching the various skills that serve to cope with panic. "These are the tools you'll be able to use to help you through an attack," she said. "The only skill you have now when panic hits is to run. It's also important to learn that panic will not lead to the things you may fear, such as heart attacks or going crazy. Panic hits and it peaks and it tapers off. But nobody stays in an attack long enough to find out that it tapers off and goes away. We're going to have people with you when the panic hits so that you can stay with it and see that nothing happens."

Alex, noting the fearful look on Beth's face, said to the group, "I don't want anyone sitting here catastrophizing about the next two weeks. Because all of this work will be done *gently*. No one's gonna be pushed out on a high bridge until you're ready to tackle a high bridge."

FIRST COPING TOOL: PROPER BREATHING

"Let me make it quite clear," Diane said. "*You do not have to participate in any travel assignment*. Okay, the first coping skill is proper breathing. Many agoraphobics breathe rapidly with the upper chest. This way of breathing goes along with being anxious, and we can reduce the anxiety by changing the breathing pattern to one associated with calmer states. Breathing in too much oxygen brings on symptoms such as dizziness and tingling in the fingers." The group was then instructed in diaphragmatic breathing described on pp. 42–43 and detailed in Chapter Ten. They spent the next twenty-five minutes practicing, getting feedback from the therapists. They were urged to practice at home for twenty minutes each morning and evening.

SECOND COPING TOOL: SNAPPING A RUBBER BAND

Next, each client was given a rubber band. "This is your next coping tool," Diane said. "Slip it on your wrist, and whenever you start to get catastrophic thoughts, snap that rubber band, just enough to feel it but not hard enough to hurt, and it'll bring you right back to reality. Agoraphobics are always saying 'Oh, my God!' and 'What if!' You set up yourselves for an attack.''

"Catastrophize," Alex said.

"So the minute you start to say 'Oh, my God!'—snap the rubber band and break that thought," Diane said.

Clients were asked to make a list of the catastrophic thoughts they frequently entertained and to notice how those thoughts caused anxiety. The therapists then helped them use the rubber band snapping to stop the thoughts.

THIRD COPING TOOL: STAYING IN THE HERE AND NOW

"The third coping skill is staying in the present," Diane said. "Your anxiety and panic take you away, you're often somewhere off in your history or future. Not here. Let's try to be in the *here and now*. Not the past and not the future—the present. Tonight when you worry about 'what they're going to do to us tomorrow,' stop and look around the room, see where you are, the color of the walls, the texture of the curtains—that's the reality. There's nothing to fear where you are.''

Alex had the group close their eyes and then asked questions "to see how present you've been the past forty-five minutes." He asked who could name the color of Beth's blouse, the kind of necklace Norma had on, the color of the rug in the room, how many people present were wearing glasses, etc. No hands were raised. "That gives you an idea of what it's like to be in the present," he said. "Many of us don't live very much in the present."

"Agoraphobics tend to walk down the street with their heads down, unaware, not there," Diane said. "Look around you, there are many wonderful things to see."

"Beth," Alex said, "you look like you're drifting off."

Beth snapped her rubber band and said, "I guess I was. Thinking about tomorrow, the travel. But I snapped back."

CHALLENGING THE SYMPTOM

Diane led them through another practice session of here and now focusing as covered in more detail in Chapter Ten. Then she said, "We need to be able to *challenge* the symptom; not avoid it, but work with it. When you experience symptoms coming on, stay with them and you will begin to trust that they pass and that nothing terrible happens." She said, "Let's do an exercise to demonstrate, and this exercise will also help you become less afraid of your normal body sensations. It also gives us an opportunity to practice some coping skills right now." Diane asked, "How many of you are frightened by a rapid heartbeat or by feeling out of breath?" Four of the members raised a hand. "Okay," she said, "everyone up on your feet. We are going to do some physical exercise to get the heart pounding and to create a sense of breathlessness. If you start to feel frightened, then remember to stop those catastrophic thoughts and focus on the here and now. And *keep going*. Jog in place now.———That's good.———A little faster.———Good."

Norma abruptly stopped and snapped her rubber band.

"Norma?" Alex said, as he signaled the group to stop jogging.

"My heart . . . I had a flutter," she said. "I got scared."

"Of what, that you'll have a heart attack?" Diane asked gently.

"Yes. Or maybe pass out." Norma looked anxious.

"This is a perfect time for you to challenge the symptom and learn that the catastrophe is not gonna happen," Diane said. "Try to bring it back. Let's all jog again, and if you get scared, stop the catastrophic thoughts and stay in the present. If you feel tension, try to focus on it as an observer, but try not to catastrophize about it." Two group members stopped on their own, saying that they were too frightened to go on. The therapists helped them use their coping skills to get calm again.

"I felt a little dizzy, scared," Beth said when she had stopped jogging. "But I tried to push it and not much happened."

"This is hard," Diane said, "but it'll come. You just have to remember when a symptom hits not to run—stay with it."

Norma was standing with her eyes closed, sweat beading her brow. Then she opened her eyes with an expression of disbelief on her face.

"Were you able to stay with it?" Diane asked.

"I . . . I got the flutter again and I didn't really push it," Norma said, "but I didn't stop jogging. I just . . . the fear went away." She smiled.

"Do you all hear that?" Diane asked. "Let the fear come, stay with it, and it goes away."

LET THE SYMPTOM COME

This exercise was to be repeated again and again for those who needed it until they were able to jog without fear. They were learning to increase their tolerance of body sensations, and it was a good opportunity to practice coping skills with the therapist there to give support.

Following a break, Alex asked participants to come up with three things they wanted the Intensive to do for them.

Beth said, "I want to be more assertive. I want the Intensive to make me care for other people. And"—for the first time today she smiled—"I want the Intensive to take away my symptoms."

Norma said, "Take away my symptoms, make me a happier person and help me make the right decision about my husband."

As the first day of the Intensive ended Beth walked out with Norma and said, "This stuff really scares me. I don't see how this is going to help me."

"I couldn't be more pleased," Norma said. "I actually stayed with that fear and it just—poof!—disappeared. I'd never done that!"

The next morning everyone met at the Program offices. Before setting out on their first day of travel work the group reviewed their coping skills and practiced switching from catastrophic thinking to focusing on the here and now. They practiced until everyone was able to gain some control over anxiety by being aware of *where they were at that moment.* When Norma had some trouble Diane said, "Stamp your feet, feel the floor."

Norma did so and said, "I'm okay."

As about 50 percent of the clients at Temple have problems with chronic hyperventilation—rapid deep breathing from the upper chest that produces such symptoms as dizziness, pounding heart, feelings of unreality, sweaty palms, rubbery legs and chest pains—everyone was asked to intentionally hyperventilate. Once they felt a symptom, they were to first clear the symptom and then use diaphragmatic breathing to calm themselves.

CLEARING THE SYMPTOM

Beth could not do so, because as soon as the slightest symptom appeared, she cried, "I'm starting to panic!"

To clear the symptoms quickly, I told Beth, "Take a deep breath, hold it as long as you can, then let the air out slowly to a count of six."

That cleared the symptom and Beth relaxed and said, "I'm feeling better. But I didn't like that. I felt dizzy, my heart was beating real fast, my legs felt weak and I felt like I might fade away. That's how panic usually hits me."

"They're all related to overbreathing," I said, "and everyone in this group has that problem at times." I then put the group through repeated trials of overbreathing and clearing of symptoms, then switching to diaphragmatic breathing. "This will help you build up a tolerance for your symptoms, help you see what causes them and help you learn how to control them. Proper breathing is very, very important, but it's the hardest skill to learn."

Beth was told she could go a long way toward eliminating panics if she changed her breathing pattern. Everyone was asked to monitor their pattern and to use diaphragmatic breathing whenever they found themselves breathing in an anxious fashion from the upper chest. Every Intensive day would begin with diaphragmatic breathing practice, and clients were told to practice at home mornings and evenings.

Next we moved out to the bus stop for a trip into downtown Philadelphia, and everyone was reminded to use their coping skills if symptoms arose. But as the bus came into view Beth, looking scared, said, "I can't get on that! I haven't been on a bus in months! What if—"

"Beth, you're catastrophizing!" I said. "Snap your rubber band, come back to the present. Check your breathing. Good!"

RIDING ON A BUS

She looked relieved as the bus, not ours, pulled away. "Remember it's not the place you're afraid of—it's the panic. Once you feel in control you'll be able to go anywhere. You're not on the bus yet, but you began to get anxious because of your *thoughts* about it. So don't welcome them into your mind. Stop them by snapping back to the present. If the thoughts come again, as they will, snap them away."

While we waited the staff helped everyone stay in the present and checked breathing patterns. As our bus approached I noticed that Beth seemed preoccupied and that she was taking fast, shallow breaths as if anxious. "What are you thinking?"

"I . . . I was worrying about being trapped on the bus," she said. "I won't be able to—"

"Stop! You're catastrophizing again! It really sneaks up on you, doesn't it? Now check your breathing and use your skills."

On the bus, staff members interspersed with the group to see how they were faring and to advise on the use of skills. Beth found herself going from moderately tense at first to feeling fairly calm at the end of the forty-five-minute ride. As we walked toward a department store I asked her how it had gone for her.

"I was scared when you told us what we were going to do, but I never really panicked," she said. "I think being with you helped a lot. You know, noticing when I was tensing up, telling me to use my skills. Now I realize how much catastrophizing I was doing, and how much I was over-breathing. I did have a few surges of fear, like when I suddenly realized I was actually on a bus!"

LEARNING TO RIDE AN ELEVATOR

At the department store clients were asked what they thought they needed to work on. Some said shop alone, others said ride the escalators. Beth and Norma both said elevators. "They're really hard for me," Beth said. "I don't think I'm ready for that yet."

"It may seem so when you think about it," I said, "but I think you are. Let's give it a try, what do you say?"

"I don't know. Can we just stand by the elevators and see how I feel?"

"Sure," I said, heading for the elevator bank. We stood there watching people getting on and off. Norma boarded a car with Diane and they went up.

"I don't know, Alan," Beth said. "All these people, I could get stuck in there."

"What are you doing now?"

"Oh, God, there I go again—catastrophizing!" she said. "Okay, give me a minute. Back in the here and now!"

"Okay, here's an empty car, let's take this one," I said, gently taking Beth's hand. "Just watch your thoughts and breathing. Good."

We stepped into the car and I pushed nine, the top floor. As the doors closed, Beth cried, "Oh, no! Oh, no!" She was alternately holding her breath and gulping air.

"It's okay, nothing bad is happening to you," I said. "Look around, feel the floor under your feet, get in the here and now. You're fine."

"But I am getting dizzy."

"You're over-breathing. So clear your system with a deep breath, hold it, let it out slowly. That's it."

Beth was very tense as the elevator ascended, watching the floor indicator. At floor three the car stopped and the doors opened. As a passenger boarded, Beth bolted for the opening. "Wait, stay with me," I said, but Beth was off and I followed.

"I just couldn't stay on there! The door opened and I lost it. Before I knew it I was out the door!"

"That's okay, you did really well," I said. "Just minutes ago you were saying you couldn't even get on an elevator."

"You're right," Beth said, calming herself and checking her breathing.

AVOIDING ALWAYS SETS YOU BACK

"Okay, now let's get back on and see if we can stay with it. Remember, every time you avoid by getting off you let the fear control you and that tends to set you back. But if you can just stay with it—and I'll be right there with you— it will get easier and easier, just like the bus ride. Keep in mind that if you stay on long enough, you'll be over the hump and elevator fears will be behind you in a few days. So here we go again."

The doors opened and we moved in hand in hand. Beth began to tighten up and she was told to use her rubber band if necessary and stay in the present.

"I'm still scared."

"I know, believe me I do. But this is the worst part, the first minutes. Breathe now, and stay in the present."

Again I pushed nine and as the car rose, Beth stared at the indicator, then snapped her rubber band. "Good," I said, "stay in the present."

But when the car slowed, approaching floor six, Beth visibly tensed and held her breath. "Snap back, Beth, and keep the breathing going," I said.

As the doors slowly opened at six, she took a step toward the opening, looking far away and lost in fear. "Wait, Beth," I said, stepping in front of her and placing a hand on her shoulder. "This is a choice point for you. Snap back and be in the present. Stay with me. It's okay. Look around, feel your feet on the floor. Let this peak pass without running!"

Beth calmed a bit and stood fast as a couple boarded the car talking. We went up to eight, where they got off, and I said, "Beth, that was sensational!"

"THAT'S THE FIRST TIME I LET THE PANIC COME!"

Tears welled in her eyes, and she said, "That's the first time I just let the panic come and I'm still here! I'm not crazy! I did it!"

"Great!" I said, giving her a little hug. "Now we just keep riding—the longer the better. It's just a matter of lots of riding on elevators now, repeatedly practicing."

We rode together for another twenty minutes and Beth did so with little anxiety. Then I suggested that she ride alone for twenty minutes while I waited on the main floor.

"Alan, I'm not ready for that!" she said, tensing.

"Where have I heard that before?" I said, smiling, and Beth relaxed and laughed. "Just give it a try, okay?"

"All right," she said, still smiling. "I've come this far, I might as well do the whole thing."

As the doors opened on the main floor and I stepped out, a whole flock of people started in—and Beth also got off. "What happened?" I asked.

"I wasn't ready for all those people getting on! I started to think I'd be crushed in there."

"Yes, we hadn't practiced with that many people," I said. "So how will you deal with the unexpected? We have to apply the same coping strategies, right? Watch the thoughts, get back to the present and be aware of your breathing. So let's try it again. I'll be right here. Check your watch and ride for twenty minutes, okay?"

RIDING AN ELEVATOR ALONE

Beth stepped into an elevator, and as the doors closed she gave a little smile. She rode for about ten minutes, and each time the car doors opened she smiled at me, obviously proud. Then the doors opened—and Beth wasn't there! But a few minutes later Beth waved from an elevator two cars away and continued riding. When her time was up she walked out of the car looking pleased.

"Why did you change elevators?" I asked.

"Well, this strange guy got on and I didn't want to be in there alone with him," she said. "So I got off and waited for the next car to come. I noticed that waiting was making me a little anxious so I thought I'd practice that too. I used my skills and it was fine."

"But you didn't get off because the elevator made you uncomfortable?"

"No. I was actually very comfortable. I felt like I could ride forever."

"Great, Beth. Very well done."

The clients and staff regrouped at a prearranged location and returned to the Program offices on the bus. Beth sat next to Norma and said, "I can't believe what I did! I feel terrific! I can handle elevators!"

"I can too," Norma said. "But did I panic at first! Thank God Diane was with me. I thought I was going to faint, or have a heart attack."

"You catastrophized and that caused you to hyperventilate," said Diane who was seated on the other side of Norma. "But you cleared your symptoms quickly. You know what to do now. Just take a deep breath and let it out *slowly* to a count of ten."

"That's true," said Norma. "I didn't have any other problems with travel after that."

Back at the Program offices, following a lunch break, everyone assembled in a large room for group therapy, seated in a circle on the carpeted floor. Beth excitedly told everyone about her breakthrough, and three others, including Norma, were equally enthusiastic about their improvements. But two clients had still been anxious returning on the bus and they were critical of themselves. Neither gave herself credit for having done as much as she did.

DO NOT UNDERMINE YOURSELF

"That's a problem we'll have to watch out for, undermining yourselves," Alex said. "Undermining statements can block progress so please watch them. In fact, along with your breathing practice homework I'd like you all to make a list tonight of the ways you might undermine yourselves and block progress through these two weeks."

Then Diane placed a record on the stereo phonograph and said, "We'll start the session with music and I want you to concentrate on the words. It's an exercise in the present, in being in the here and now. Many times I know you've started hearing a song or gone to a movie and you weren't with it because your mind wandered. So as you listen to this song if you find yourself drifting off, snap your rubber band and bring yourself back to the music. I'd also like you to look around at each other during the song. Make eye contact, reach out and touch someone next to you. But be with each other and don't feel like you're *all alone in a room.* Which is often what you feel like when, as you say, you're not there."

John Denver's "I Want to Live" filled the room and Alex asked everyone to sing along and several people joined in the chorus, which was repeated five times: "I want to live, I want to grow/I want to see, I want to know/I want to share what I can give/I want to be, I want to live."

"If there are no objections, we'd like to make this the group theme song," Alex Tullis said afterward. "Isn't that what this is all about, living, growing?"

RECOGNIZING AND CONFRONTING YOUR FEELINGS

During the group work Norma brought up the issue of divorce, and Beth said, "That's something I've been thinking about, too. Whether I still love my husband and want the marriage."

"That's been going on with you for some time," said Diane, who had seen Beth in several individual sessions prior to the Intensive. "But the point now is you're *saying* it. It's out and that's good."

"It's scary," Beth said. "My kids are small . . . and it just scares the hell out of me that I even have thoughts like that."

"It's a thought many people have, but it doesn't mean that marital difficulties cannot be resolved. That has happened to many people while in this program. But it's also true that you can still be a terrific parent and not be married."

Norma grew tearful and Diane asked her what was making her feel sad.

"When I got divorced I lost my son," Norma said, reaching for a tissue in the box on the floor. "He lives with his father."

Diane moved over and sat next to her, asking quietly, "What's his name?"

"Jonathan."

"Tell Jonathan you miss him," Diane said, sensing that losing him was an issue behind Norma's anxiety. Norma was choked up and Diane said gently, "Get a picture of Jonathan in your mind and talk to him."

"He resents the divorce and he resents me when he comes to visit weekends," Norma said tearfully.

"Talk to Jonathan," Alex said softly, trying to help her release her feelings of sadness.

"I miss you, Jonathan," Norma said.

"Tell him you love him and that someday he'll understand the divorce," Diane said.

"I love you, Jonathan, and some day you'll understand why I had to leave your father," Norma said. "Some day you'll forgive me." Then she burst into uncontrollable tears and could not continue.

"That's all right," Diane said gently, patting Norma's arm. "When you're ready you'll get it out. You need to let out that sadness."

In a few minutes Norma was again composed and actually felt better over having released a bit of her sorrow.

PRACTICING DIAPHRAGMATIC BREATHING AT HOME

The following morning, and every day of the Intensive, clients were asked if they were able to practice diaphragmatic breathing at home.

"It was hard for me because I have so many things to do," Beth said.

"Yes, I know how it is," I said. "But it becomes a matter of priorities. It's really important to realize that you have the right to take time to practice and that we are talking about something that can literally change your life."

"Alan, during this Intensive I just have to crowd in so many things," she said. "Every day I wake up with all these things on my mind that I have to do, including the work here. This is like when I was working."

"Diaphragmatic breathing helps keep you calm, and if you do your self-maintenance work you can be free of panics and therefore more efficient and less preoccupied," I said to the group. "So I would suggest twenty minutes of focused breathing each morning, at lunchtime and in the evening. I know that's a lot and that no one's going to be able to do this *every* day, but make an effort and it will become a habit."

"I still have some trouble breathing from the diaphragm when I'm standing up," Norma said. "And when I get real anxious I just completely lose it."

"That's typical early on," I said. "We'll begin each practice here on the floor, then go to sitting, then standing until you get the feel of it. Do this at home as well. If you lose it, start over. For now the breathing will be difficult to use when you most need it—when you're frightened—but with steady practice it'll gradually become part of you and more available when you need it.

"Remember when you're frightened, please start by using your rubber band to stop the catastrophic thoughts, then focus on the here and now, and *then* go to diaphragmatic breathing. It'll be easier than if you try right off to change your breathing. Any questions? Okay, let's begin by lying on the floor."

ENLARGING THE TRAVEL WORK

After practice the clients agreed to follow up on the work done yesterday: bus rides, elevators, walking about in the crowded city. And the entire group would also visit the outside observation deck of a tall building in the center of the city. The elevator there would also be a big step because it was twenty stories high.

While waiting for the bus, Beth said to Norma, "I'm not nearly as scared as I was yesterday. Just thinking about it made me anxious. Now I want to see how I do today."

"That observation deck doesn't sound too appealing to me," Norma said. "I don't know."

The two women who had been anxious on the return trip the day before again experienced symptoms on the bus ride in. One was able to use her coping skills to stop her catastrophic thoughts and then regulated her breathing and calmed. The other suffered a full panic attack before Alex got her to employ her skills to bring herself back. "That was very good," Alex told her. "Now the next time you get anxious snap yourself back and use your other skills right away and you won't go into panic."

"I'm still having trouble with breathing, I just get so tense," the woman said.

"That's all right for now," Alex said, "just use your other skills. Snap back and focus on your present surroundings. You haven't really had enough practice on diaphragmatic breathing to use it effectively yet. That's why you need to do lots of practice on your own. It'll come naturally in time."

The elevator we used today was quite different from those

in the department store. It was small, with padded walls and low-level indirect lighting. Beth said she was a little apprehensive and asked if I would accompany her on the first ride. I told her she had all the skills to manage herself and it would be better if she tackled it alone. She rode it for about thirty minutes with short periods of increased anxiety but without a hint of panic.

THE NEW YOU BEGINS TO EMERGE

As we walked to the building with the observation deck, Beth said she was very confident about her ability to ride elevators now. "But you know something, Alan, I'm kind of confused. Part of who I am is someone who can't ride elevators. I feel strange, kinda like it's not me doing this, like it's someone else."

"Well, you are a different person, Beth, one who now *can* ride elevators. It's understandable that at first you feel strange. You are going through lots of important changes and it will take some time for you to get comfortable with the new you."

This point was made to the entire group when we reached our destination. We rode up to the large observation deck and stepped onto it through swinging glass doors. Then we walked around the large space, stopping at various places by the parapet to gaze out over the city. At first Beth was apprehensive about moving close to the parapet. But when she grew anxious she called on her coping skills and was fine, stepping up and leaning on the parapet. "You can really see a lot," she said.

BEHIND THE TRAPPED FEELINGS

Meanwhile Norma walked around a corner on the deck that was out of view of the doors leading back inside the building. Suddenly her eyes widened and her hands began to tremble. "I'm getting really anxious!" she cried.

"What are you feeling?" Alex asked.

"Scared, like how am I gonna get off here quickly?" Norma said. "I don't even know where the door is. I feel trapped."

"Is it similar to the feelings you have about your present life?" Alex asked.

"Yes, that's the way I feel—trapped," Norma said with a certain surprise in her voice.

"What's keeping you trapped?" Alex asked.

Norma's eyes welled with tears. "If I leave my marriage, I'm afraid I'll lose my daughter, too. I'm afraid Lee will get her to join Jonathan." She burst into tears and cried for a few minutes, then calmly wiped her eyes.

"What are you feeling now?" Alex asked.

"Relieved," Norma said. "I feel as if a big burden has been lifted off my shoulders."

Norma not only stayed out on the observation deck without having any further anxiety, she walked over to where Beth was standing by the parapet and said, "You know, the view is really beautiful from up here."

This exchange occurs frequently during travel work. When anxiety is triggered and panic then threatens because of a reminder of highly charged memories of a serious interpersonal conflict, there may not be conscious awareness of the content but the body reacts anyway. Norma, seeing herself on the observation deck, assumes that she is responding only to the physical confinement, but when helped is able to make the connection which leads to understanding of a more subtle cause of some of her panics. This experience, repeated many times, helps her learn to seek out for herself these subtle connections as well as contributing to her ability to gain a sense of control in the situation.

During the next two days of group psychotherapy Norma came to realize that she had chosen both of her husbands largely because of their similarity to her father. All three had rigid, controlling styles and she had been attracted to her mates "by their strength, the feeling they could take care of things," Norma said. "But I wanted some independence, too, and I thought they understood that, particularly Jack, my current husband. I thought I could change them. But neither of them would give me an inch."

SET YOUR OWN PACE AND DON'T BE PRESSURED BY A SPOUSE

Meanwhile in the spouses' group meeting, Norma's husband, Jack, said, "It was great that she's doing so many things she was afraid to. In fact, I told her she really ought to go out on her own at night or that I'd go with her any place she wanted to speed up the process." I said it was fine for Jack to share Norma's enthusiasms for her progress, but suggested that she would do better in the long run if she set her own pace. "I was trying to help," Jack said, and it was clear that he was acting out of genuine concern. He was told that was understandable, but that a spouse cannot play therapist with a loved one as it only leads to resentment. "Norma may have some trouble making decisions," Jack said. "I've always been the one in the family to decide things."

"Maybe she didn't feel she had that option," I told Jack. "But now Norma is changing, and in the interest of the growth of your relationship you will need to make some changes too. I know that these changes can be very hard for you, too, Jack, so let us know what you need to help you through them."

Ben, Beth's husband, seemed very comfortable with his wife's changes. "I can't wait to pick her up every night," he told the group. "She's so excited about what she's doing. I haven't seen her like this in years. I mean, she tells me about the coping skills she's learning and how they work. She wanted to try driving last night. We went out for an hour and she was great! Just great!

"The only problem was, and I want to bring this up because it confuses me," Ben went on, "we got home and I was so excited I called my brother to tell him the good news about Beth. He invited us over for coffee, he's only two blocks away. I said great. Beth was feeling so good I figured she'd love it. But she said she didn't want to go. She was tired. Then she withdrew again, back to her old stuff. She does it with the kids as well. It really confuses me. One minute she's up, excited. Next minute she's down, withdrawn, silent. I really wanted to pop over to my brother's, and maybe I should have even though Beth wouldn't go. But I stayed home. Sometimes I don't know what the hell to do."

DON'T GIVE UP SOMETHING YOU RESENT LOSING

"A good rule of thumb," I said, "is not to give up something that you *resent* losing. If you can stay home without feeling angry and resentful, that's fine. But if you stay because you feel guilty about going and resent it, it's important for you to go. Do take the time, though, to explain how you feel, because it's important for both of you not to give up activities if it breeds anger and resentment. Those feelings will only lead to more distance between the two of you. Keep in mind that setting an example for Beth will let her know she's entitled to not sacrifice her interests for you when that would make for resentment. All of this may help you toward warmer feelings for each other."

Ben said he would try to discuss his feelings with Beth. "But when she withdraws—forget it. She doesn't want to hear anything or do anything. I'll have to pick my spots, but I'll try."

Beth continued to do well in travel. She even took the elevator to the office where she had worked and was delighted to learn that she would be welcomed back any time she was ready. She used her tools to cope with her anxiety and felt good about her accomplishment. But while practicing driving with Ben the previous evening she'd had a panic attack and pulled over. Ben had driven home and she'd gone right to their room. She hadn't been able to stay with the panic and the only feeling she had was "scared."

The next afternoon, after again doing fine with the group travel work, Beth showed up for the psychotherapy session looking depressed, her face pinched, her eyes cloudy, her lips compressed into a thin line. When Diane asked her how she was, Beth said in a low, pained voice, "I feel really bad."

"What are your feelings?" Alex asked. "Mad, sad, glad, scared?"

"Mad," Beth said.

"Okay, tell me about 'mad,' " Diane said, moving over to her on the floor.

"I NEED TO ACCEPT MY FEELINGS"

"I'm still mad that—I guess I'm mad at myself. That I feel I won't get what I want. I need to accept that I have feelings to not let them scare me so."

"You're right," Diane said. "And you're starting to do that. It won't happen all at once, but now you're aware of your feelings, you're starting to identify them and expressing them here helps that important process. Any other feelings now?"

"Scared," Beth said. "I'm also really scared to deal with what's going on with me at home."

"Tell Norma about it," said Diane, knowing they'd become close and that they faced a similar conflict.

"Like Norma I'm feeling trapped in my marriage," Beth said. "You know that, Norma."

Norma nodded. "Do I *know* the feeling," she said.

"And I'm not sure that'll straighten out," Beth continued.

"On the one hand I feel I love Ben, and on the other hand I feel I don't . . . after nine years. And I'm not sure why. I'm not sure if it's just the agoraphobia that's put me down with everybody and cut off my feelings with everybody."

"With *everybody*?" Diane asked in surprise. "Is that the truth?"

"With just about everybody," Beth said. "With some people it's worse. With Ben I shut down more."

"Who are the exceptions?" Diane asked.

"I think people I'm not real close to."

"With them you can maintain a certain openness, and with people you're close to you shut down?" Diane asked.

"Yes, I think so," Beth said. "I'm just not sure of what I want. I don't know. I have a thought of leaving my marriage . . . and," she choked, "it's scaring the hell out of me."

"Who's most difficult to shut down with in this group?" Diane asked.

"Norma. I'm most open with her."

"And who do you most shut down with?"

"David," she said, referring to the lone male in the group, a sensitive, caring twenty-four-year-old.

GETTING IN TOUCH WITH YOUR FEELINGS

Alex had Beth try a dialogue with David. She moved close to him, as directed, but could barely look at the young man. "Get in touch with what it is about him that makes you shut down," Diane said. "Look at him."

Beth looked up and said, "I'm starting to feel close to him." She said to David, "I like you and I'm afraid if I get close, I'll lose you."

"What's the danger if you like him, the threat to you?" Diane said. "Afraid he won't like you?" Beth struggled for a long moment. "What's liking, loving mean to you? What happens?"

"Well, for me right now, I'm married," Beth said.

"That's not the bottom line here, that's secondary to the issue," Diane said, probing for the truth that Beth needed to understand. "What happens when there's a possibility of a love ending?"

Beth struggled silently, and Alex asked, "What's happening inside now?"

"A lot," Beth said. "Maybe I'll lose what I have now."

"Would you get close to David if you weren't married?" Diane asked.

"No. I'd be too scared."

"Don't think about the answer—*feel* the answer," Diane said, knowing from Beth's demeanor that she was not scared but sorrowful. "What happens when you love somebody you get close to?"

"I get hurt."

"Say, 'I don't want to get hurt.' "

"I don't want to get hurt," Beth said.

Then Diane had Beth say, "I don't want to get close to you."

"Take it all together," Alex said.

"I don't want to get close to you because I don't want to get hurt," Beth said. Then she lowered her head and began crying quietly. She wiped her tears and blew her nose, looking up.

"What are you sad about, from your heart?" Diane said. "What are you feeling now? Who did you get close to and then get hurt?" Diane reached over and touched Beth's arm gently. "From the heart."

FEELING THE LOSS OF A LOVED ONE

Beth sobbed and started talking about her first love. The boy was eighteen, she was seventeen when she bore his child.

It was a daughter she put up for adoption. The child was named Caitlin. She was nearly fourteen and beautiful. Beth had seen her recently.

Diane put an arm around Beth as she wept and spoke, comforting her, wiping the tears from her cheek with a tissue, then dabbing at her own cheeks, a mother sharing a daughter's sorrow over a loss she had never mourned.

"Feel the loss of Caitlin," Alex said softly.

"Say, 'I hurt,' " Diane said.

Beth said, "I hurt. I *hurt!*" She said it again and again and again, acknowledging her pain, her sorrow, really experiencing it. She repeated Diane's words, "I was only seventeen when I had you, Caitlin, a child myself. I had to give you up. I didn't want to but I had no choice. I did what I had to do, for you, for your benefit, your future."

"Tell each of the women here it was the hardest thing you ever had to do," Alex said.

"It was the hardest thing I ever had to do, Norma," Beth began, then went around the room and told each woman present by name, and there were many tears.

After a pause, Alex asked, "If Caitlin was here, what do you think she'd say about all this?"

"I think she would say," Beth said firmly, " 'Mom, I know that you really love me. I know you did what you had to do.' "

"Tell her," Alex said, " 'I really need you to know that you understand I did what I had to do in order for me to have some peace.' "

Beth said that with deep emotion, then repeated, "I was just too young when it happened, not much older than you are now, Caitlin."

"All I wanted was love," Diane said.

"All I wanted was love," Beth said. "I'd do anything for attention back then."

"Your marriage is troubled right now, and you're not going to open your heart in or out of your marriage until you resolve this loss," Diane said. "Move to David and tell him about that."

Beth slid over by David again, but lowered her eyes and said nothing.

"Are you shutting down getting close to him?" Diane asked.

"I want to just get rid of it," Beth said. "All the pain."

"You shut down with your husband, even with your children in your way, and you shut down with anybody who comes along," Diane said. "Then you go into depression because you're lonely, Beth. You won't be lonely when you share your feelings with others."

MAKING PEACE WITH YOURSELF

"It's time to say good-bye to Caitlin," Alex said. "Are you ready to say good-bye to her, Beth?"

She nodded, and Alex handed her a pillow and told her to picture it as the infant Caitlin. "Cradle her in your arms and tell her you loved her, that's why you had to give her up."

Beth hugged the pillow to her breast and her eyes filled with the infant as she rocked it. "I loved you so much— that's why I did what I did," she said, choking out the words. Then she collapsed on the pillow and wept as Diane at her side rubbed her back, comforting, her own tears raining down on the young mother.

When the spasm passed, Beth sat upright again, and Alex said, "Pass Caitlin to me." He reached out his arms.

"You've got to say good-bye," Diane said tearfully.

Beth, her eyes never leaving the infant, passed the pillow to Alex and murmured, "Good-bye."

"Say it again," Alex said, nuzzling the pillow against his cheek. " 'Good-bye.' "

"Good-bye," Beth said, staring at Alex's arms through moist eyes. "Good-bye, Caitlin."

"Feel the loss," Alex said. "It's all right to let the pain in."

"Good-bye!" she said in an anguished cry. "Good-bye, Caitlin!" Then she broke down and wept for several minutes, while the others dabbed tissues at their cheeks.

When Beth regained her composure, Alex said, "What's the final thing you want to say to Caitlin?"

"Caitlin, I love you," Beth said firmly, "and that's why I did what I did. I'm making peace with myself now. Good-bye." She turned to Norma and nodded, looking relieved, her face no longer pinched or her lips bloodless. Her eyes were red from weeping, but they were bright, alive.

In subsequent sessions the therapists worked with Beth on slowly letting go of her guilt and on coming to accept her loss completely. As she moved through these stages it also became easier for her to begin sharing her feelings with her husband.

INTENTIONALLY HYPERVENTILATE, THEN PRACTICE CLEARING SYMPTOMS

Beth said she still occasionally had fears of dizziness and feelings of unreality. So we decided to get her into a difficult situation, with her permission, and have her intentionally hyperventilate, then practice clearing her symptoms. On day eight of the Intensive we went to the Franklin Institute, a science and natural history museum that is always mobbed. There we walked into a huge mockup of a human heart in which one feels quite enclosed because the passageway is narrow and the line of people in front and behind does not allow for a quick exit. We were about halfway through the heart when Beth said, "This is hard for me. I'm feeling really trapped in here."

"What are you thinking about?" I asked.

"I'm thinking that if I lose control I'm gonna have to push

past everyone ahead to get out," Beth said. "And I'm getting dizzy and that scares me."

"Okay, there's enough room here for people to pass so let's stop and see what we can do about that."

"Okay, but wait, let me take a minute to get control," she said, snapping her band and looking around to be present, then checking her breathing. Very soon she was feeling better.

"That was great, Beth!" I said. "Really great. You didn't need any help."

"Yeah," she said, chuckling. "I just do it now."

"Good, now see if you can create your symptoms by hyperventilating. Then in order to clear away the symptoms take a deep breath, hold it as long as you can and then exhale very, very slowly."

Beth started breathing very rapidly until she began to feel lightheaded. Then she stopped and gasped, "Oh, Alan! This really scares me. With all the people."

"That's good. Now just take a minute to clear the symptoms."

Beth did so and in a minute or so said, "Yeah, I'm better now."

YOU CAN DRIVE AGAIN

Beth repeated the exercise several times until she could calm herself with ease. In fact, she began using this coping skill more than the others and she found it particularly helpful while driving. She and Norma had pushed themselves hard and found that they could do far more than either ever expected. They both wanted very much to be able to drive again without anxiety, as Beth wanted to return to work and Norma to college next semester. Ben had gone out in the car almost every night with Beth, and she was feeling comfortable behind the wheel except on crowded expressways.

"The two times I've driven on one I've had to keep clearing symptoms," she said.

"You're able to clear them though and keep going, aren't you?" I asked.

"Yeah, and I'm not getting those trapped feelings as much now," Beth said. "The first night on the expressway I went right to the middle lane because that's where I used to drive. But I was going a little slow and all of a sudden a car came right up on my tail and others whizzed by on either side. I felt real closed in and said, 'Damn, Ben, how'm I gonna get off here?' Then as I was clearing my symptoms, he said, 'Flick on your directional signal and I'll tell you when it's okay. But you're doing fine and we're headed downtown, so why get over?' Of course I was thinking about getting *off* the expressway, but after he said that I decided, yeah, I am doing fine. Later I told him about what I was thinking, and he laughed."

Norma had tried driving practice with her husband only once because Jack, she said, made her uncomfortable. What he regarded as helpful suggestions came to her as instructions. So Norma practiced with a travel therapist. She began with local streets and slowly advanced to the expressway, each move up to more congested thoroughfares sending her anxiety shooting up. She used her coping skills, but still didn't feel comfortable on expressways. On them she often felt trapped.

DEALING WITH YOUR SPOUSE'S NEW INDEPENDENCE

Meanwhile, when the family members met in their last group session, Ben told everyone that he was happy Beth was beginning to share her feelings with him. "It's nice to talk to her and not have her suddenly withdraw not only from the conversation but from the room," Ben said. "I'm not saying she doesn't still withdraw some, but she's generally much more open. And more sure of herself. You know, funny, just last night she shocked me. My brother was over. As he was leaving, he said something like, it'd be nice for us to shoot some pool again. Then he saw Beth had overheard him and apologized. Beth said, 'I think it would be good for you to go shoot some pool.' I almost fell over. I mean, she never wanted me to go out at night. I went out for an hour, then came back a little fearful. I was worried she might have changed her mind or got upset. No problem."

"The next thing you know, Beth may be going out at night with friends," I said. "As she becomes more assertive and independent and expressive of her feelings and needs, it could be scary. In the past you could predict how she would respond to you, but her responses will be less predictable as Beth makes progress. That may make you uncomfortable. And where you've rejoiced that she's feeling better and sincerely want her best interests served, you may also be scared by the change in her and find yourself saying things that could undermine her progress.

"It's not uncommon for spouses to fear that they may lose their loved one when he or she is no longer dependent but autonomous. That fear is fueled by the strains and resentments from living with an agoraphobic. Once made secure by your partner's inability to get around much, you may now feel insecure. Now that won't lead to conflict if you can talk about your concerns calmly and openly while supporting your partner's new style. That will strengthen the relationship."

Jack said that he was already in conflict with Norma. "I don't object to her making some decisions, but she wants to chip in on *everything* now," he said. "I've always been the decision maker and problem solver in the family. She liked that when we got married. It's a bitch now, because I don't know if I can change. I really don't. That's a major step, a lot to give up."

In further discussion, it became apparent to everyone that

Jack's insecurities left him unable to give up control. He concluded that he should try to deal with this issue in psychotherapy himself.

BLOCKED FEELINGS HURT

On the next-to-last day of the Intensive, Beth decided she would drive Norma and me into the city for the travel work, while the rest of the staff and group rode in other cars. Beth was unusually quiet all morning, particularly on the drive back to the Program offices. I noticed she had a burst of anxiety as we pulled into the parking lot because she cleared symptoms.

"I don't understand it!" Beth said. "I haven't had any problem for days, and now this happens."

"You've been rather quiet all day, Beth," I said when everyone met for group psychotherapy. "Is something bothering you?"

"I don't think so."

"What have you been thinking about?"

"Well, tomorrow's the last day and I guess I've been getting kinda prepared for that," she said.

"How?"

"I don't know, just pulling back, I guess," she said, lowering her eyes briefly. "When I see these people—" Beth glanced at Norma seated on the floor beside her and looked away.

"Well, pulling back is cutting off feeling, isn't it? If you were to not pull back, how would you feel?"

"Real sad."

"And it scares you to go through feeling really sad," I said. "But as you know now, when the feeling is blocked it has consequences. Let's try it a different way, okay?"

"I'll try."

"Okay, would you go around the circle and tell each person here how sad you are that this group's ending?" I said.

Beth told each of us, tears filling her eyes, just how sad she felt. When she got to Norma she burst into sobs and Norma threw her arms around Beth and joined her in crying, accepting their mutual sadness. In minutes they wiped their tears and rejoined the group, looking relaxed and open again.

At the end of the Intensive, Beth was quite mobile and Norma needed only to work on her driving in heavy traffic, so she signed on to work with a travel therapist. She and Jack also agreed to join Beth and Ben in couples therapy with Alex. But after the initial session Jack quit therapy entirely, saying, "I was fine until Norma came here, and I'm still fine as far as I'm concerned." Norma moved into individual psychotherapy while Beth and Ben continued to work together with Alex.

LEARNING TO SHARE WITH YOUR SPOUSE

Gradually Beth came to know that she could get close to her husband and she began sharing with him, giving to him—and to her children—secure in her belief that she would not lose them. Beth had a brief setback while working with the fear that she was not worthy of being loved, but Ben was very supportive and giving in helping her see the truth.

Ben also had a problem during the seven months of couples sessions, shortly after Beth resumed her part-time job midway through the period. She went out with girlfriends after work a couple of times and Ben was not only surprised to find that he was jealous but angry even though he'd given his okay for her to spend the evenings with colleagues. Once the couple expressed their feelings openly in several sessions, Ben began to relax. When Beth went out once a week, Ben did the same with his brother. After the couple got home they would discuss their evening over coffee, an occasion they both came to look forward to.

Beth remained in therapy fifteen months, terminating some four years ago. Ben recently said, "I never imagined this marriage could be this good. I mean, sometimes I have to pinch myself and wonder, 'Is this a dream? Is this the same woman I married? Who, virtually the day after the ceremony, began withdrawing from me? And who now is everything I always wanted in a wife?' Well, it is a dream—a dream come true."

Says Beth: "I am very happy too. We talk over everything. The only thing is, Ben never shuts up. Sometimes I have to tell him, 'Enough!' " She laughed.

FACING DIFFICULT DECISIONS

Norma continued in individual therapy and said of Jack's dropout, "That's exactly what I expected from him. He's the typical 'I'm-all-right-Jack.' " She was determined to move toward a separation, and those plans were virtually the only items she discussed in her sessions. Clearly, she was told, it was the initial thoughts of separation that had produced the overwhelming stress that brought her to us.

For weeks she discussed the pros and cons of staying married and of separating.

Two months later Norma said in her individual session: "I'm finally ready for a separation." When she came in the next week she was depressed, saying she had been suffering panic attacks and was very anxious. Suspecting the prospect of separation was triggering her panic attacks, the therapist asked her to stay with her feelings while saying goodbye to Jack. Norma panicked, but connected her panic to the fear of losing her children to her first husband.

Norma's feelings about losing Jonathan were explored and it turned out that she had never grieved his loss. She had kept his room just as the boy had left it and, though she knew better, fantasized that he would return. She had avoided accepting his loss as it was too painful. And thoughts of leaving Jack took Norma back to the apparent consequences of her earlier divorce from Lee.

MOURNING A PAINFUL LOSS

It was agreed that before Norma could move toward separation, she had to say good-bye to Jonathan, to mourn the loss. In eight sessions through the next four weeks Norma went over all of the painful memories in chronological order related to Jonathan's departure, repeatedly retracing the same sad ground. The stronger her feelings, the more she was asked to accept them in therapy and to herself at home.

She was also encouraged to spend considerable time in Jonathan's room, with the caution not to engage in her old rationalization that "It isn't so bad after all." She faced the truth. In this period Norma went through anger at her husbands, the hurt of being rejected by Jonathan and guilt over feeling she was an inadequate mother. Finally the past was causing only mild pain. She began attending Jonathan's sporting events, cheering him on, and taking pleasure in his smiling acknowledgment of her backing. She was able to enter his room and sit there without more than a tinge of sadness. On her own she decided to turn the room into a study and to give away the belongings that Jonathan had left behind.

By this time Norma had completed college and begun working part-time. It was a bit stressful at first, but soon she was working full-time as a hospital social worker. She proceeded with the divorce and Jack moved out, leaving Norma and her daughter Anne in the house.

At this writing Norma has been out of therapy for nineteen months without any recurrence of symptoms. "When Jonathan visits now," she said recently, "he no longer resents me and I have to say Lee is doing a good job. And Anne and I have been having some wonderful times together. But I guess I've got to start preparing myself for the end of that." She laughed.

"Anne's almost thirteen now and she had her first date last week. The boy was cute, red curly hair and freckles all over his face. I asked Anne how he was; she said, 'Nice, Mom, but he's so shy. And he couldn't decide what we should do. First he wanted to go to a movie, then he said he heard there was a good show at the museum, next he talked about the rock concert at the park.' Finally she told him, 'I like fresh air and music—how about going to the concert?' and off they went. When I heard *she* made the decision I gave her a big hug and said, 'You're all right, sweetheart!' "

CHAPTER 6

The Importance of Communication

Communication is a major problem for both agoraphobics and the significant figure(s) in their lives. Often this fact becomes dramatically clear to all on the second week of a Two-Week Intensive when clients, their spouses, parents or lovers meet in a combined group for two hours of work. The abridged meeting presented here is typical in its revelation of how very important it is for both clients and their loved ones to express their feelings to one another. It often takes great effort to develop the ability to express feelings, though most agoraphobics don't realize the need for it.

We will focus primarily on the three married couples in attendance and the dialogues between agoraphobic and spouse as guided by therapist Julie Weiss, who had been counseling the "significant others" in their group sessions during the Intensive, and therapist Alex Tullis, who was co-leading the clients group. The couples:

CLIENT	SPOUSE
Mike	Bonnie
Leonard	Sally
Ellen	Thad

Other clients were twenty-year-old Dante, accompanied by his father, Vito; twenty-one-year-old Talia, whose boyfriend was taking college exams and could not attend; and another married man, Don, whose wife had been sent out of town by her job. Their remarks will be brief but telling.

The meeting was held in a large room at the Center and everyone sat on pillows on the carpeted floor, a posture designed to encourage openness and a relaxed atmosphere. Julie asked everyone to get comfortable and introduce themselves. Then Alex asked first the clients and then the "significant others" to describe their experiences in the Intensive. The clients all agreed with Ellen that "It's been scary but well worth it, very satisfying." Her husband Thad spoke for the loved ones when he said, "It's been very helpful and comforting in many ways."

Julie asked if the agoraphobics realized their loved ones also needed comfort, and Mike said, "I feel that way. It seems as though Bonnie is giving 95 percent of the time and I'm only giving five. I should give more."

" 'Should,' " Alex coached, " 'or want to'? "

"I will give you more," Mike said to his wife. "I will change, talk to you more openly."

Bonnie, smiling faintly, said, "That would be a nice change."

WHEN NOT GOING PLACES IS A MATTER OF CHOICE OR AVOIDANCE

Vito raised a question about whether or not he should push his son to go places, such as visit relatives, and Dante said the choice should be left up to him. "When I say 'No,' it means I don't want to go."

"Do you know when you're saying 'No' because you're afraid and avoiding that place?" Alex asked the clients as a group.

"I think from an agoraphobic's view you may go just to prove you can do it," said Leonard. "I mean when you really don't want to go. Sometimes an extra push is good, sometimes not. But I don't know if there's a signal you could learn that tells you."

"You have to be agoraphobic to learn that signal," said Don. "Whether you just don't want to go—"

"Or because you're afraid to go," Leonard said, nodding his head.

"As soon as I say 'No' it pops into my head, 'Am I avoiding this?' " Don said. "There's some confusion here."

"I've had that confusion myself," Leonard said. "Lots of times I would go someplace just to prove I could—and ended up with a good day out of it."

"I cop out a lot," Mike said. "If Bonnie and I are going to a high school football game, say, even before I go I'm there in my mind, panicking. So I stop myself from going."

"When you decide not to go, what do you do?" Julie asked.

"I just lie around," Mike said.

"How do you feel?"

"Guilty," Mike said.

"Are you disappointed in yourself maybe?" Julie asked.

"Yeah," Mike said. "But then sometimes I'll say, 'The hell with it, I'm going.' No matter how I feel."

THE STRAIN OF LIVING WITH AN AGORAPHOBIC

"Anyone find it a strain to live with an agoraphobic?" Julie asked.

"At times, yes," said Bonnie, Mike's wife. "Before Mike came here, um, he would just lie in bed. When he came downstairs in the morning he'd have his breakfast in the kitchen or take it back upstairs with him. And when he'd come down later he'd lie on the sofa. Constantly, day after day. I'd say to him, 'Do you want to go out?' 'No, I don't want to go.' I couldn't say, 'Come on, it'll do you good to get out.' I just became aggravated. It seems if I put more pressure on him he just withdraws."

"You can't win either way," Julie said.

"Yeah," Bonnie said. "And, well, we don't argue. If there was something we disagreed about, he would go upstairs and I would stay downstairs. Nothing would be resolved. But he and I talked the other day at the meeting with you. It seemed to help. We've been talking."

"Maybe that's where some of the comfort you mentioned came in," Julie said. "Having someone to talk to about your frustration."

"I think living with an agoraphobic is a big strain," said Thad, Ellen's husband. "I never know what she is thinking, or what she wants, or if she really cares for me and the kids. She seems to have a lot of preoccupations, to be consumed by her agoraphobia. And sometimes I try to be a therapist. I really shouldn't be. But it's frustrating watching her go through what she goes through without being able to do anything about it."

"Most people go home from work and have a personal life," Julie said. "But when you live with an agoraphobic, you never get to have a personal life. I mean, when is it *your* turn? Anything you'd like to ask for yourself?"

"Like, 'How about me for a change?' " Alex said. "Let's look at *my* wants."

"Thad, I don't feel you're giving me a lot," Ellen said. "But I realize I've really shut you out. Shut the kids out."

"Is there anything you want, Thad?" Julie asked.

"A lot of what I want is really for Ellen," Thad said. "I want her to be not as dependent on me as she is. She knows that. We've talked about it. Financially I have to work two jobs. I don't like doing that. My second job drives me *nuts*. I get all *wound up* about it. It seems like I'm always tired, but I don't tell her that."

EXPRESSING WHAT YOU WANT

"It's hard for you to tell her what you want," Julie said. "Go ahead, talk to Ellen."

"I want a balance in my life, Ellen," Thad said. "So much time at work, so much time with the kids, so much time with you. And it's not there. It's all work. It frustrates me when the kids say, 'Hey, Dad, you have to go to work again.'" He paused, then added, "Maybe I don't have to work that other job."

"What can Ellen do to help?" Julie asked.

"I see her really frustrated at home, with the kids, with the house. She always wants to go out, but she can't because of her agoraphobia."

Julie said to the group, "Do you notice how difficult it is for Thad to *ask* for something?"

"I imagine it happens a lot that 'Since so-and-so's ill I'd better not make any extra demands on him,'" Alex said. "Does anyone else feel that?"

"Yes, I do," Bonnie said. "Mike often thinks that I don't understand. But I do. So when something comes up I feel I shouldn't burden him. And I keep everything inside. As I said, we don't argue. I don't throw things. I just cry. And it's all right for a while, then it just builds up again."

"How about you, Sally?" Julie asked.

"It hurts to be shut out, it really does," said Sally, Leonard's wife.

"I'M LONELY, DON'T SHUT ME OUT"

"It's lonely sometimes for spouses," Alex said. "But it's really okay for all of you to ask, 'Hey, don't shut me out, I'm feeling lonely.'"

"Sometimes I just can't give it emotionally," said Mike, "I'm so tied up in myself. It's very hard."

"I just want you to be aware of the other important person in your life," Alex said, "aware of the frustration and loneliness in his or her life."

"Leonard, you look as if you want to say something," Julie said.

"You mean that's my problem?"

"What's it like for Sally?" Alex prompted.

Sally, seated next to her husband, leaned over to Leonard and said, "Shutting me out, not sharing. Loneliness."

"I know about those things," Leonard said, speaking of himself, "because I let you go off with our daughter and travel."

"It's lonely without you," Sally said softly.

"She'd tell me that, that she'd like to have me go along," Leonard said to the group. "But I used to think it was better not to let them know—"

"Talk to *her*," Alex said.

"I thought it was better not to let you know my feelings, Sally," Leonard said.

"That hurt," Sally said with emotion and patted her husband on the arm.

"Well, that hurt me too, but I didn't want you to know. I felt that not saying anything would be better for you."

"How about asking Sally if keeping your feelings from her was best for her?" Alex said.

"Was that best for—" Leonard started, then turned from Sally smiling. "I know what she's gonna say."

"I want you to tell me," Sally said to him. "I *want* to know what you're feeling so I can help you."

"I can't understand how that's gonna help."

"*I* feel lonely when you don't tell me. You know that."

"Oh, yes, because you told me."

"But you still think it's best not to tell me?" Sally asked.

Leonard didn't answer, and Alex asked him, "Have you ever told her about your loneliness?"

"No, you didn't," Sally said.

ASK FOR SOMETHING THAT WILL MAKE YOU LESS LONELY

"Sally, maybe you could ask him for something that would make you less lonely," Julie said.

"Well, when you won't go somewhere I need to know if it's because you don't really want to go, or if it's because you're afraid to go. If you'd just tell me, then I could deal with it."

"Whenever I didn't want to go anywhere it was because I was afraid," Leonard said.

"But when you don't tell me it hurts," Sally said. "I love you, you know that."

"I do know that. I just wasn't able to do things. We used to go to movies and then go out to eat almost once a week. Restaurants. We started going dancing, driving into the Poconos. It's just that everything had to be done in a radius of thirty miles."

"How big's your radius now?" Alex asked.

"Home's over a hundred miles away and now that's no problem," Leonard said, proud of the progress he'd made in travel work. "I drove to Atlantic City the other day. And we plan on coming back to Philadelphia for a weekend next month. We've enjoyed it these two weeks."

"Sally, is there anything else you'd like from Leonard?" Julie asked.

"Well," Sally said, looking into her husband's eyes, "I still need to know how you are feeling."

"Now I tell you," Leonard said, and over the friendly laughter of his co-clients, he shouted, "I started yesterday! I *did*. It was hard for me, what the hell."

"Having held in feelings all your life, it isn't easy to let them out," Alex said.

"That's what I'm doing," he said and turned to Sally. "I'm working on communicating my feelings to you. I am."

Sally smiled, very pleased, and touched her husband's arm lovingly.

"He's got a lot of feelings," Alex said.

"I'm sure, but why does he keep them in here?" Sally said, tapping her chest.

"I didn't think anybody'd want to know when somebody wasn't happy," Leonard said.

"*I* want to know! Your feelings are very important to me."

"You know, it's crazy but that's the reason I didn't tell her!"

"And," Alex said, " 'if I told you my feelings I was afraid that'—what?"

"Aw, I was afraid that I would be sad myself," Leonard said.

"So what—we can be sad together!" Sally said.

"I hope you learned in our group work yesterday that *you can't have all the joy without some of the sadness*," Alex said. "When you keep all the sadness in, some of the joy's going to be kept in too. Would it be all right with you two if I used you as an example for a few seconds?" He nodded at Leonard and Sally.

"I'd like to hear it," Leonard said.

THE THINGS WE WANT MOST ARE HARDEST TO ASK FOR

"What I want to point out is how difficult it is to actually communicate our feelings, our wants," Alex said. "And the things we want most are the things we have the most difficulty asking for. We want our loved ones to express their feelings, and somehow we can't seem to find the way to express our own. And sometimes when the wants are expressed the other party has difficulty responding to them. Now the last ten minutes or so were awkward for Leonard. But I imagine everyone around the room has had some trouble expressing feelings at times. Communicating is difficult."

"I was wondering if anyone would like to do some practicing here?" Julie asked.

"I would," Ellen said.

"Want to try a dialogue with Thad?"

"I do, but I just feel so held back," Ellen said. But she

took a deep breath and twisted her body to face her husband. "I get a little afraid sometimes."

"Why?" Thad asked.

"Because of your reactions. When I get panicky in the morning. Like the other morning, you said, 'Why are you panicky? You just woke up.' I just shut down after you said that. There's always a reason for panic. But you got angry."

"If it seemed that way," Thad said, "I . . . I was just confused. How anybody can wake up and be that panicky, when it appeared that nothing had happened—I was just confused. I'm not ever angry when you panic. Maybe I get to a point where I'm frustrated and confused."

"Well a lot of times I don't tell you when I'm panicking. I think you're tired of hearing it. And you are."

"Yeah." Thad laughed. "Sometimes I am. But I'm . . . I'm really not sure."

"You get a look on your face," Ellen said. "A lot of times your reaction to the things I say, the things I do . . . maybe I get scared, because suddenly I won't go any further."

"I'll see that you're panicking whether you tell me or not," Thad said.

"Sometimes when he says, 'What the hell are you panicking for now' it seems like he's angry at you?" Julie asked.

"Yes, and I can't deal with his anger," Ellen said.

"Then a lot of times you won't tell her you're tired from working two jobs," Julie said to Thad. "What keeps you from telling her when you're really tired?"

Thad thought a long moment and said, "I don't know."

YOU DON'T PROTECT A SPOUSE BY NOT SHARING FEELINGS

"I do," Ellen said. "Because we always protected each other. Always."

"From what?" Alex asked. "Can you be specific?"

"I'll come from the Intensive and the dishwasher's broken, the car—"

"You handle those things better than I do," Thad interrupted. "I wish I could handle those things as well as you do."

"I get upset when I have to tell you all these things fell apart," Ellen said, looking at her husband. "And I get upset because of what your reaction will be. We know what that reaction'll be. So I'll wait—"

"Leave me notes or something," Thad said, smiling. "Leave me a note."

"You're afraid of his anger?" Julie asked.

"Yes."

"You hear that, Thad?" Julie asked.

"I hear it."

"And what are *you* afraid of with her?" Julie asked Thad. "She says you always protect each other.

"I don't know if I'm *afraid* to tell her," Thad mused. "Or, 'She doesn't need to know.' "

"Check it out with her," Julie said.

Ellen smiled.

"You'll be in a really good mood and I think that if I tell you, you'll get angry," Thad said.

"That's the protection," Ellen explained, then turned to Thad. "I know you want me to be independent. But there are certain restrictions. For example, when I used to go out with my girlfriends, you'd say, 'I don't want you going out without me. Why can't you stay home?' Know what I mean?"

"I talked about that with my therapist," Thad said. "But I can't change overnight. It didn't hit me until I was thirty years old, 'Hey, I'm jealous.' I'm *trying* to change it. It's hard to change something immediately. It will take time."

"Ellen, how do you protect him?" Julie asked.

"I guess by not going out and doing the things I want to do, because I think he'll get angry. Things like going out with girlfriends. I wouldn't do that, even though I wanted to. I guess to avoid what would happen if I did."

"So you protect yourself from his anger," Julie said.

"Yes," Ellen said.

"Do you ever get angry, Ellen?" Julie asked.

"Oh, yes!" Thad cried. "She gets angry like Bette Davis does! It takes a lot for her to scream. But then she *explodes*!"

"Ellen, I might suggest that one of the things you protect Thad from are *your feelings,*" Alex said.

"Yes."

"And that's her way of protecting you and herself," Alex said. "There are a roomful of people here who're trying to make everything safe for those they love."

Seeing Bonnie nod, Julie asked her if there was anything she wanted from Mike. "He's made you an offer to share with you, but he's going to need a lot of help. Tell him something you'd like from him or he's going to miss the mark."

"It's going to take time, too, to feel comfortable about saying what I feel," Bonnie said. "Because I'm basically a shy person."

PRACTICE ASKING FOR WHAT YOU WANT

Julie had Bonnie tell Mike that directly, then said, "Can you come up with anything now that you'd like from Mike? Even the smallest thing, just for practice."

"Okay, I'd like you to go pick raspberries with me when we go home."

"All right, I'll do that," Mike said.

"How did that feel, Bonnie?" Julie asked.

"Strange. Very . . . strange."

"When we spend a lot of time *not* asking for what we want," Alex said, "it is strange when we begin to do it.

But it takes practice, lots of practice, and then it becomes easier."

Julie addressed the two clients whose "significant others" could not make this meeting and asked Don what was going on with him.

"During the last six weeks that I've been in individual therapy here and then this Intensive, I've been talking with my wife much more," Don said. "And Debbie told me that she has been holding back on asking for things, and telling me how she's feeling. That bothers me. And I said to her that I'd held back, too. As Leonard said, I didn't want to tell her I was feeling nervous, a little panicky. I had a real hard time telling her when I'm not feeling well. I didn't want to bring her down. But she told me, 'I really want to know how you're feeling, it's important to me.' So I understand what Sally's saying. And our communication has changed in the last couple of weeks. I've changed. Both of us have. Debbie's more willing to tell me what she needs no matter what I'm feeling, and I'm more willing to tell her what I'm feeling. It's much better. It's been *great*, really."

"I think it's the same for everyone," Sally said, "thinking you are saving someone by not sharing your feelings."

"Exactly," Don said. "If all of us could just express our feelings . . . agoraphobic or not."

AGAIN: "PANIC APPEARS WHEN FEELINGS ARE NOT BEING EXPRESSED"

"Agoraphobics have a little more difficulty identifying their feelings and then expressing them," Alex said, "because that's usually what is behind the symptoms. Often panic appears when very intense feelings aren't being recognized for what they are, sadness or anger perhaps. That's why part of the Intensive has been given to *learning to identify feelings* and learning to tolerate them."

"That's a good point," Julie said, "the difference between agoraphobics and nonagoraphobics. We other folks can also have a very difficult time expressing our feelings. But agoraphobics have more trouble *identifying* what the feeling is. We all feel anxiety, we feel scared, sad, lonely, angry. And for agoraphobics it is usually very difficult to even recognize what the feeling is. Talking about it when we are upset is the way to sort the feelings out."

"As an agoraphobic I think I lost the idea that all these other people are feeling these emotions, too," Don said. "And when you get limited in your mobility and are feeling panicky, then any kind of disagreeable feeling becomes part of the sickness. And it scares me even to get that depressed feeling. Yet everybody has depressed feelings at times. They're all part of life. Some of us just blow them up a bit." He laughed.

Julie next called on Talia, at twenty-one the youngest woman, and asked how she was faring.

"Well, my boyfriend Jim didn't understand at all," Talia said, smiling shyly. "He'd make me feel that I was crazy when I got anxious or panicked. Then I'd get even more shut down because I was embarrassed to tell him how I felt. But since he went to the 'significant others' meeting last week, he really understands a good deal more often. Now if I get a panic attack or get anxious, we can actually sit down and talk. We are really communicating, and it makes me feel really, really happy. Now any time I'm feeling sad or lonely, Jim's always there for me. He'll say, 'We'll get through this.' He's very helpful. We didn't have a really good relationship for a long time. Now I feel like I did when I just met him, and it's really nice now."

Julie asked Vito, Dante's father, if he had anything to offer.

"My situation's different with my son," Vito said. "These people are husband and wife, so I don't quite relate to what they're going through."

"The line's the same—communication," Alex said.

"That's true, and I must say I'm very happy about these

sessions Dante's been having. They really seem to have helped him. He's been opening up and I've been opening up in the evenings. I can see that what you have to do is really tell each other exactly how you feel. Whether it makes somebody mad or not. So I think these sessions have been a big benefit for me as well as Dante."

Julie and Alex thanked everyone for coming as the session concluded. Then Alex said, "I'd like to leave you with one statement: Communication is healing—withholding is destructive."

Two Recovered Agoraphobics Relate Their Experiences

ALICE

Alice was in her twenties and had been free of agoraphobia for two years when we talked to her recently.

Alice: I was sixteen when the symptoms started, in high school. I felt anxiety in class before a test, after a test, whenever I had to speak in front of the class. When a teacher would ask me a question, I wouldn't answer. It just terrified me. I had heart palpitations, hyperventilation, sweating, constant blushing. I was terrified that I would do something wrong and make a fool of myself.

The first year, when I was a junior, I had only two or three full panic attacks in school. But my senior year they were *so* intense! The last attack the teachers were really afraid something was seriously wrong with me and they sent me home. They took my blood pressure and it was pretty high.

I was so embarrassed. I didn't tell anyone, not even my parents. But on the way home from school I went to my family doctor and she gave me a prescription for Valium. I took it for two weeks and stopped. I didn't have another panic attack for about six months. Then they started coming real often, in specific places. Like going to the dentist. I knocked four bottom teeth loose in a car accident. I had three unsuccessful root canal treatments over the next couple of years before they pulled them out. It was awful. I had panics all through this period.

Then I had allergies and I was getting allergy shots, and I had real bad reactions. Every time I got shots I broke out in hives all over my body and my throat closed up. Once they almost took me to the hospital, my throat closed so tight. And I couldn't make a decision to stop taking shots because my parents were pushing me to take them. I kept having this fear that eventually my throat would close up and I would choke to death. When the fear came it turned to panic.

All through this time I was also having problems with friends, relationships with guys. I really couldn't communicate well with people. I was a real hysterical person. The littlest thing devastated me, as far as relationships went. I felt I wasn't good enough. My high school was full of upper-class kids. They had lots of money and there was lots of competition, lots of cliques. I didn't feel like I fit in anywhere. Then I got into the drug scene. I found I couldn't do grass because I was allergic to THC. I hallucinated badly. But I used cocaine, speed, Quaaludes, anything to get me to a point where I was comfortable around people. Drugs seemed to help me relax, escape from fear. Speed made me feel like I was keeping up with everybody.

Meanwhile I had a few long-term relationships with guys in high school, and the endings were devastating. The guy I went with the last two years, we moved in together after graduation. I went into this with *great* excitement about getting out on my own. I was going to be independent. But I was seventeen and I had no idea what it would be like to live with somebody. We were supposed to share everything. Well, that wasn't the way it went. I ended up having to do everything, and I couldn't deal with *anything* going wrong.

Finally I moved back home, and that was a bad experience because it was like I had failed. I had been accepted at college, but I decided I couldn't handle school anymore. I really *hated* high school. I felt I wasn't up to everybody else. I just barely passed. So in September, I just stayed on in the job I'd taken at a library, a clerk's job that a five-year-old could do. And I started having panic attacks going to work. Then I started having attacks on the way home. I didn't have attacks at home, where I felt safe. But going and coming I had them all the time. I was dizzy twenty-four hours a day, it seemed. I think I hyperventilated in my sleep. I was nauseous all the time. That's how bad it was.

I went to so many doctors it was incredible. I had so many drugs—for nausea, dizziness and I don't know what else. My family doctor told me I had an anxiety neurosis and I began seeing a psychologist. I was so disoriented during the sessions that I'd leave and not remember what we talked about. The psychologist told me about the program here. But when she told me about the travel work, I was too scared to come here. By this time I was so scared that I would only go places I was used to.

I started getting worse, though. I was having disassociations, where you feel like you're outside your body and you can't really function. And you look really weird because you don't have any control over yourself. You actually feel like you're going crazy, like you're going over the edge. And once you go over—you're never gonna be able to come back. It's terrifying. Some of these disassociations would last for three minutes, and that seemed like three hours.

I had to quit my job. A month later I joined the program here. My father drove me at first, but by the second week I was driving myself.

I got better really fast, compared to others. Everyone's different. I was completely mobile in two months, doing everything on my own. Perhaps because I was so young. Also, I didn't have the burdens of those who were married and had families, kids to take care of. I had a lot of motivation. People have said to me, "I don't have that much to look forward to, I've lived with agoraphobia for so long."

It almost becomes a part of them. I don't mean that anyone ever gets used to it, but they kind of come to expect it.

My treatment started with a Two-Week Intensive. One day the therapists said they were gonna take us on the bus into center city. I hadn't been anywhere in so long, I said, "I'm not getting on that bus!" But I'd learned my coping skills that morning. I had my rubber band to snap back. I knew the breathing techniques. I knew how to ground myself by focusing on the present. They encouraged me to use those tools on the bus ride. I did and I was fine. The fear was all this stuff I'd built up in my head, and I handled it.

My biggest problem proved to be recognizing that I was feeling something other than anxiety. The therapists basically explained to us that often, when we are anxious, there is another feeling going unnoticed. The situation was really not what we were afraid of but what the situation *represented* to us, like being in stores and feeling trapped. That situation was a reminder that I was feeling trapped in a relationship. Or trapped by the fact that I had to be home and taken care of by my parents when I wanted to be independent. So I learned all that.

But I still had trouble expressing my feelings and I kept working on that in individual therapy. I had to learn to get angry, learn to assert myself, learn how to have a better self-image. I had to learn how to get sad and not be ashamed to cry when I was sad. It took nine more months for me to learn how to express what I was feeling directly. That's when I really started feeling better.

It's not easy learning how to express your feelings when you've spent most of your life not expressing them. I'm still working on that two years later. Like I can say to somebody, "I'm really angry." But I don't *sound* angry. Still, I am getting better.

I'm also in my second year of college, majoring in psychology, and I'm amazing myself. I'm getting A's in everything.

* * *

*A*lice's story shows us the power of motivation. She was always more than willing to take the sometimes frightening steps involved in recovery. She was just as frightened as anyone else but *trusted* the staff enough to really give her all while accepting their guidance.

DANA

Dana was in her late thirties and had been free of agoraphobia some three years. She recently received her degree in social work.

Dana: I had agoraphobia for eleven years. Initially there were just a few things I couldn't do, but the symptoms grew progressively worse. I had seen five different therapists in the early years, then I saw a psychiatrist for seven years. But if I hadn't gotten the right kind of help I think I would have become housebound. Just to go two blocks from my house to the market was awful. I had terrible panic attacks.

I'd become depersonalized and felt as if I was fading away. Everything around me became unreal. The sidewalk would start to come up at me. My vision became unfocused and it would get darker and darker as if I was going blind. And I'd hyperventilate, become so dizzy I felt like I would faint. Black spots would appear in front of my eyes in this very narrow dimly-lit tunnel-like vision I had. I'd have to hold onto something, grasp it and hang on to keep from collapsing.

I was always by myself, too. I was embarrassed and never told any of my family or my friends that I had this problem. Only my husband knew, but he worked so much he wasn't home a lot. It was up to me to go to the stores, to the bank. I would go quickly and come back as fast as I could. I'd just *force* myself to go. I took a lot of Valium. A lot.

I thought it helped. But that's basically what my psychiatrist did for me—prescribe Valium or Stelazine, a stronger tranquilizer.

I'd always been a passive kind of patient. But I finally got so bad that my husband drove me to my psychiatrist and I told him, "I've been with you for seven years and I'm getting worse! What can you do?" At this point I was in *constant* panic and just going outside was a problem. My husband confronted him and demanded to know why something couldn't be done for me.

He told us about the program at Temple and wrote down Alan's phone number. Then he said, "You can call him if you want to, but I don't think his program will work for you. I think you want to be the way you are."

I had been just completely shut down in all those years of therapy, which was all analytical. I never got angry, I never cried, but I was physically sick. Very hypochondriacal, fearful of cancer. I was always running to my family doctor for blood tests. But I had no feelings. I felt sick, fearful, that was it.

It took me two years to really identify my feelings and begin to let them out. I had been an abused, battered child. My mother did this. She was schizophrenic, in and out of hospitals. I took care of my brother, who was two years younger than me, kind of raised him until I got married at seventeen. And I could tell my analyst about this perfectly calmly, with no emotion. No rage, no sadness. As I said, I couldn't even cry. But with Alan's therapy, I finally started to tear a little, then cry a little, then the crescendo came when I felt sad.

My husband was great when I was ill. But trouble began when I started to get better. He became very threatened as I became more mobile and developed new interests. For seventeen years I had been home every night; my social life had always been him. But as soon as I got better I went back to college two nights a week and that upset him. I made friends in the Program and we went out to dinner. I took tennis lessons, because I love sports. All this independent socializing without him was upsetting to him. He began acting out, staying out all night. This was something he'd never done before. He felt threatened and tried to scare me. It was horrendous.

Then he took off and I didn't know where he was for a year. It was total abandonment. The old injury again. I became depressed, as anyone would in those circumstances, and I had a high anxiety level again. I started getting symptoms, but thankfully no panic. Alan and my new friends kept getting me out, supporting me. I was even gonna drop out of college, but Alan kept talking to me and I stayed in. I also had a teenage son I had to take care of. But it was the experience of being alone without some attachment to hold you up that brought the terror. Abandonment is the agoraphobic person's worst fear. So I had to work through that and learn to become independent. It wasn't easy, but I was forced to do it and it was good for me.

The marriage ended when my husband appeared again. I was very hurt that he was nonsupportive of me when I was getting better. He went into therapy, too, and his therapist told him to come and talk to me and to his son, to explain the pain that he was going through. He did that, and it made me see what I did. I wasn't just this innocent little sick person. It takes two. But I closed down and just because I didn't argue I thought I was victimized. I realized you can be lethal silently, too, and I could understand his feeling of rejection. That meeting kind of bridged the gap between us and we're friends now. We understand each other's pain and what happened.

Since then I've been working on my relationship with my mother, and I have some peace with that now. I have some good feelings about her. She's seventy-seven, and I wanted to do that before she's gone. No one wants to go all through life having bad feelings about their parents. I even tracked down my father and made peace with that relationship after all these years. I hadn't seen him since I was five. I'd known that he was in the area, but I just pretended that he wasn't within reach. Then I made some phone calls, reached him and went to see him. That worked out real nicely.

*D*ana's story tells us of the devastating effect of a persistently traumatic childhood. It illustrated how the resulting emotional scars and defensive habit patterns interact with the agoraphobia and necessitate more prolonged therapy for a successful conclusion. It should also provide hope for the most severe of agoraphobics, as Dana was as badly traumatized and severely anxious as anyone I have ever seen. Yet she is now a respected and competent professional who has truly fully recovered.

This story also points up the necessity of including the close family members in the therapy. Perhaps, if her husband had been able to be part of the process, the marriage would have survived the crisis and actually been strengthened.

CHAPTER 8

The Male Agoraphobic

*F*or many years agoraphobia has been called "the housewife's disease." Those who would not agree with the accuracy of that phrase include John N., a salesman; Al R., a plant foreman; and Joe Z., a state civil service official. These men are just a few of the scores of male agoraphobics we have treated over the years, even though our clientele has been composed of 85 percent females. Most men who seek treatment are men whose lives are very seriously disrupted by panic attacks, often to the point where they are threatened by the loss of their family or employment. Unlike women, for whom staying at home is still acceptable, men are expected to go into the work world; there is no way for them to hide.

Male agoraphobics find it extremely difficult to seek help because of the social-role training of our culture, which teaches men to always be self-sufficient and to not admit to having fear. Certainly, no one wants to admit that he is afraid of something as prosaic as riding an elevator in a tall building. But this happened quite suddenly to John N., a six-foot-five-inch former all-city basketball player, who was in the process of setting a first-year sales record for his company. As the elevator climbed higher and higher, out of nowhere John's heart started thumping so loudly he could hear it in the otherwise empty car. His legs and stomach were quivering, sweat flowed down his face, and he felt so dizzy that he grabbed the handrail behind him with both hands and hung on for his life.

John did not die. He had suffered his first panic attack. Three weeks later he suffered another one while driving to work on a heavily congested freeway. He was moving rapidly in the middle lane until the traffic abruptly slowed to a crawl and finally stopped dead. With no way to get to an exit, he felt trapped, and the terror squeezed him as if he was in the bowels of a sinking ship.

MALES OFTEN USE ALCOHOL TO CUT ANXIETY

In subsequent months similar attacks occurred when John was driving through the Lincoln Tunnel into Manhattan; when he was headed across the Tappan Zee Bridge in New York and again when he was strapped into an airplane as it lifted off the runway. He was still shaken when the stewardess came by selling drinks, and he ordered three. Before he had finished the second he felt better, as if the glow from the alcohol numbed his anxiety.

From then on, whenever he could, John used alcohol to fend off or reduce his anxiety. When he had to fly on business, he downed several drinks before boarding the aircraft. Tunnels, bridges and bumper-to-bumper highways were avoided whenever possible. Instead he would take circuitous routes to his destination, no matter how much time it cost him. He always had a bottle of Jack Daniel's stashed in the console of his car for emergencies. When there was no way he could avoid traversing a bridge or driving through a seemingly endless tunnel or negotiating a fear-producing highway, John sipped from the bottle of whisky and managed to get through the ordeal. He was often high when he pitched to his customers, but he was a good salesman, quick with a joke or a sports anecdote, and he was a nice guy to deal with.

At one juncture in his career John N. was offered a much better job. It included a five-thousand-dollar raise plus the opportunity for swift advancement. The company was situated on the thirtieth floor of a Manhattan office building. John stopped for three drinks before going for his interview. But the elevator rushed upward at what seemed to him rocket speed, thrusting his stomach into his mouth. He panicked, jabbed his finger at button number four and exited the elevator, gasping for breath. He took the next car down and did not change jobs. "Going down in an elevator or an airplane never bothered me much," he said years later in therapy, "because I always felt like I was headed for safety."

John functioned well enough to earn a good living for fifteen years, until he became so dependent on drink that he lost his job and ended up in an alcoholic rehabilitation facility at age thirty-six. When he stopped drinking, he learned that he was agoraphobic. A therapist at the rehab center made the diagnosis after John had multiple panic attacks daily and suggested that he might want to try our program. He was taught the skills to cope with panic, then went through a Two-Week Intensive where he overcame his avoidance and cut his panic episodes by half. During the Intensive he discovered that when he panicked he often cried, which suggested that it was not fear but sadness he was feeling. His mother had died shortly before his first panic attack, and behind his sadness lay the fact that he had never grieved her loss. He spent five months working through his mourning reactions, shedding many tears and at last saying a final good-bye to his mother. Fears had been masking his real feelings of sadness, and when he was able to grieve the fears gradually disappeared.

Males suffering from agoraphobia are so ashamed of and embarrassed by their fears that they usually reveal them to no one. That was John N.'s situation, until the depths of his feelings were experienced in the presence of a therapist.

"I think I'm going nuts!" he shouted. "They're gonna lock me up and throw away the key!" John N. had many lovers over the years, including a woman with whom he lived for almost a decade, yet he hid the symptoms from them. It is not unusual for a male agoraphobic to be fearful and avoidant for twenty years in a marriage without his wife ever being taken into his confidence concerning his symptoms. John N.'s partner, whom he married while he was recovering, reported, "As time went on there were more and more places John wouldn't go, things he refused to do at the last second. We'd have dinner dates, sometimes with one of his customers, and I'd have to call with an excuse. John always came up with some excuse. But I never had any inkling that he was scared all the time."

In our society men are taught to be aggressive, confrontational, responsible and independent. They are obliged to go out and earn a living for themselves and their family should they choose to have one. Thus male agoraphobics push themselves to work, striving as long as they possibly can in the face of anxieties to remain employed, often relying on alcohol to mute their fears and to keep them mobile. The three-martini lunch and the evening cocktail hour(s) are still acceptable ways for men to relax. One study of alcoholic rehabilitation facilities revealed that 45 percent of the men in them were agoraphobic.

On the other hand it is acceptable in our society for women to be more helpless and dependent than men, to avoid situations that seem to make them fearful, to spend most of their time at home caring for their children. Women will readily take their fears to the family physician, who usually prescribes a mild tranquilizer for them. Valium, Tranzine and Xanax are the female equivalents of the alcohol used by the majority of men in an attempt to defuse anxiety.

WHEN MEN BECOME SEVERELY AVOIDANT, THEY SEEK HELP

Men tend to be less avoidant but no less distressed than women by the symptoms of agoraphobia. But when the man begins avoiding going to many places he once enjoyed, then he usually seeks help. Listen briefly to Al R., a fifty-one-year-old plant foreman, whose first panic attack occurred in a restaurant: "Suddenly my heart started beating wildly and I thought I'd either have a heart attack or go crazy on the spot. After that, before I'd sit down in a restaurant I'd walk around and locate all the exits. I'd figure that I would run out this door or that one if I had to get out to a safe place. Then I'd look around the restaurant and see there was no danger, even though I was feeling it. That's when I started to think I was crazy.

"It's not what I did but what I didn't do that became important after a while. Because I stopped going to restaurants, theaters, ballparks—and, hey, I loved football—supermarkets. . . . Any place I'd had a panic attack, I wouldn't go there again. My whole life became geared to *not* doing things. So I wouldn't have a panic attack, so my heart wouldn't beat so rapidly that it would wear out and stop, so people wouldn't think I was crazy."

Al R. saw a psychiatrist for seven years. "I'd leave a session with him feeling pumped up and thinking I had the answer to what was wrong with me," Al said. "But that feeling wouldn't last until the next session. It was like filling up my gas tank for fifty dollars and then running out of gas two days later. As time wore on my feelings of hopelessness were reinforced. I was convinced that I'd never be like everybody else."

Traditional psychotherapists too often do not deal with the conditioned fears that beset all agoraphobics, and those fears *must* be brought under control before the underlying issues that trigger the panic can be resolved. When Al came to us, it took several months for him to master the techniques for managing panic. Then, in psychotherapy, it was found that frequently when Al panicked it was not fear he was feeling but guilt, a normal reaction to what had transpired in his life nine years earlier.

"My cousin lived for a long time on a kidney machine," Al said. "He needed a transplant, and I was the one picked to give him a kidney. I went along with it because that's what the family told me to do. But when time came for the transplant, I wasn't able to do it. My sister gave her kidney instead. Three years later my cousin rejected the kidney and died."

During several months of therapy, Al made peace with his guilt, learned coping skills and pushed himself to go places again, and his panic attacks ceased.

IDENTIFYING FEELINGS, A MAJOR PROBLEM WITH MALE AGORAPHOBICS

Most male agoraphobics have a great deal of trouble identifying what they're really feeling. And in addition to the conditioned reactions brought on by panics it is a feeling— usually anger, sadness, grief and occasionally joy—being cut off, somehow too scary to face, that results in panic. Helping clients to identify the feelings that ignite anxieties in them is a difficult task for therapists. But persistent effort pays off, as in the case of Joe Z., thirty-eight, who came into a Two-Week Intensive after panic attacks while driving to his job caused him to miss six days of work.

Surprisingly, after only two days of practicing coping skills while traveling around Philadelphia with the group and on individual assignments, Joe was driving again without incident. "When I came here I thought I'd do it, because I was determined," he said, smiling. "But not this fast."

Joe looked comfortable during his travel work, but he looked tense during the afternoon group-therapy sessions.

They were led by therapist Alex Tullis and Diane Coia. They asked Joe to tell them about the onset of his symptoms.

"It started with a racing heart, then went to numbness in the hands," he said. "I was approaching a bridge that I'd driven over many times. I stopped and asked a kid to drive me across. He must've thought I was a nut, but he did it."

"Did you have any problems in your life at that time?" Diane asked.

"No, I'd gotten married and my son was born that year," Joe said.

But he looked rather sad and Diane, wondering if Joe was plagued by unresolved grief, asked if his parents were alive.

"They're both deceased," Joe said. "I had a bad time when my mother died. I was close to my mother, closer than my three brothers."

"Did you feel the loss more than them?"

"I probably felt it more because I had a lot of problems in those days. When she died I had all kinds of problems. Am I supposed to say all this?"

The therapists assured him and everyone else that they should feel free to be open about everything in their lives. "Trust is a hard issue for agoraphobics," said Diane, herself a recovered agoraphobic. "And this is a good place to learn to trust and to share with one another. This is also where you'll relearn the process of handling anger, sadness, grief and all of the feelings you may have buried. Many of your parents did not encourage expression of feelings."

"You'll also learn to *identify* your feelings," Alex said.

"I know for myself as a child, I never got mad, never cried," Diane said. "I was taught that was wrong, to show emotion, feelings. I became a quiet, perfect little lady. I had to relearn not to be a perfect lady all the time. I was angry and I was sad, and I had to express those feelings, finally."

The other male in the group said, "It's hard for guys to

show feelings, particularly to cry in front of others."

Joe nodded in agreement. "I don't care who cries," he said, "but I don't want to cry."

"How long has it been since you cried?" Alex asked.

"Long time."

"Where did all the sadness go?"

"I've cried, but only by myself," Joe said. "Even when my mother died I went off by myself."

"Joe, I'd like you to share some of your sadness during these two weeks," Alex said. "I'd like you to see what your other side feels like. The side that is lonely."

"In my house if you cried, they said, 'What's he crying for?' " Joe said.

Diane, still sensing that Joe had some feelings of sadness about his mother's death, returned to that subject.

"I felt guilty about it because I put her in the hospital where she died," Joe said. "And my brothers all thought she should have gone to a bigger and better hospital. I always felt guilty about that. I said to them, 'If you don't like the hospital, move her.' My oldest brother Bill, her favorite, said 'Leave her there now.' "

Joe paused, seated among the group in a circle, and lowered his eyes. "That was a bad time," he said, "a bad time. Because I had a lot of other troubles too. They all piled up. And then she died. I almost felt at one time during my troubles like I could've cried."

The therapist pursued a dialogue around Joe's missing his mother, including some Gestalt work in which Joe talked first to his mom, then assumed her voice and had her talk to him. But Joe revealed no profound sadness.

He continued to excel in his travel exercises, both during the mornings with the group and in the evenings on his own. One night he drove his wife all the way to Atlantic City—where he'd once had a panic attack—and back, traversing the very high Walt Whitman Bridge both ways without incident. He was thrilled by his accomplishments.

"I DON'T LIKE TO BE SAD IN FRONT OF MY WIFE"

But Joe remained reticent in the group psychotherapy sessions. At times it appeared as if he were going to let go, that there were things he wanted to say, yet couldn't quite get them out. On Friday, though, day five of the Intensive, dialogue with another client around sadness caused Joe to say, "I don't like to be sad in front of my wife."

"You have memories about being sad with your wife?" Diane asked.

Joe was silent, eyes lowered, and Alex said, "You look sad right now. What's going on, Joe? What are you remembering?"

"I don't want to say it."

"Is this what you do, Joe, kind of shut yourself out from people, instead of sharing?" Diane asked. "I'm feeling you closing up. Anybody else feel that?"

Several other clients said, "Yes." They were all rooting for Joe, their travel star, a big, gangly guy who had tried to encourage and help them in their work in the city.

Joe looked up at the clock on the wall and said, "It's after the hour, isn't the time up?" The other clients smiled, but *with* Joe, telling him it was okay, to keep working with Diane, as several had begun to get in touch with their feelings and felt better for it. It had been hard, but worth it, for there seemed to be light ahead.

"That kind of behavior means you're really lonely," Diane said softly, her compassionate expression reaching out to touch Joe. "If you don't share your inner self, what do you do with your hurt, sadness?"

"I cry sometimes."

"That's good. But sometimes you can get through that a lot faster if you can sit down with someone and share it. Maybe that's why the sadness has lasted so long in your life."

Alex said, "Will you try and make a statement to the group

around, 'If I let you people see me cry I imagine that—' what?"

"I don't think you should cry," Joe said.

"So tell us," Alex said, "those of us who have cried the last five days—"

"That's okay for them," Joe said.

"What would happen if somebody saw you cry?" Diane asked.

"Probably laugh at me."

"Laugh at you? And what would they call you?" Diane asked.

Joe paused. "Oh, maybe 'stupid.' "

"Of the group members," Alex said, "is there one person who would be easier to share your sadness with?"

"With Diane," Joe said.

WHAT IS THE SADNESS ABOUT?

Diane Coia slid over on the carpeted floor in front of Joe. "Can you give us some clues as to what your sadness is about?"

"Yeah, my mother dying."

"Think about your mom," Diane said. "You talked to her at the hospital?"

"Yeah, we talked."

"You tell her you love her?"

"When I was a little kid I did," Joe said. "I guess everyone in the family did then."

"How about in the hospital?"

"I told her then," Joe said with emotion.

"Does that bother you?"

"No, it doesn't bother me."

"Well, tell her, 'Mom, I really wanted you to love me as much as Bill.' "

"Mom, I really wanted you to love me as much as Bill," Joe said.

"That's what I really wanted," Diane coached.

"That's what I really wanted," Joe said strongly.

"I tried to make that happen," Diane coached.

"I really did try to make that happen," Joe said.

"Tell her how you tried."

"Aw, I used to do a lot of work around the house," Joe said. "I tried to make something of myself . . . because I never made you happy. I tried to make you happy by working hard. I thought making something out of myself would make you proud."

"I wanted you to like me," Diane coached.

"I wanted her to like me," Joe said. "But I knew when she died she liked me. She liked all of us."

"Tell her what you felt when she was in the hospital," Diane said.

"When you got sick I did all I could for you, Mom."

"Tell her what your brothers thought," Diane said.

"They didn't like the hospital, thought it was the wrong place."

"Where was your older brother Bill?"

"He was working down in Maryland," Joe said. "It was up to me. I did the best I could've done." He paused a long moment. "But I had troubles—and it was me who put her in the hospital!"

"Did your mom blame you?"

"She didn't, but I felt the family kinda felt that way," Joe said. "That my problems put her in the hospital."

"You feel responsible for her death?" Diane asked.

"No, because I checked. I didn't think I did kill her. She had a gall bladder operation and an infection set in. Then she died," Joe said with emotion.

"Tell her, 'It's not my fault, Mom,' " Diane said.

"It's not my fault! I didn't put her in the hospital the first time. I think Bill did, or somebody. See, the first time she went in the hospital, I was getting a divorce," Joe said, his eyes growing moist.

"You were married before?" Diane said in surprise.

"I was only married a short time. Two weeks. That I know made her feel bad."

"Are you Catholic?" Diane asked.

Joe nodded. "First in the family to get divorced." He lowered his head, grabbed a tissue from the box near his knee and quickly rubbed his eyes dry. "I was the fourth kid."

"Tell your mom there was nothing wrong with divorce," Diane said.

"It wasn't the divorce that bugged me," Joe said. "It was the stuff that came out. She went into the hospital right when that all happened. I felt like I put her in there."

"Was the divorce your choice, Joe?"

"Oh, yeah. It had to be done."

"She was aware of that?" Diane asked.

Joe looked at her, his eyes wide, as if to say: Are you kidding! And the rest of the group burst out laughing.

"It's great that we finally got some laughter in here," Alex said, and Joe, relieved somewhat, smiled.

"What was your wife's name and what was her trip?" Diane asked.

"Denise. She thought she was too beautiful and all the guys were after her. And a lotta guys *were* after her. But she thought she had to go with every guy that went after her. She was beautiful, but no brains. I decided I didn't want that anymore."

"Had you dated her for a while?" Alex asked.

"Not too long. About a month."

"Infatuation," Diane said. "How old were you, twenty-one?"

"Twenty-two."

"Many people do that," Diane said emphatically.

"Marry and divorce in two weeks!" Joe said incredulously, letting out an embarrassed laugh. "That's why I didn't get married in the Catholic Church again—I thought I couldn't."

"Is that a mortal or a venial sin?" Alex said.

"A big-time sin," Joe said. "Everything was bad. It all happened in April, you know—during Lent."

"You got divorced and moved back home at the end of Denise?" Diane said, and when Joe nodded she asked, "Were you hurt, did you feel bad?"

"I was angry," Joe said. "And dumb and mad. You know, she was a waitress, and I'd go in the restaurant where she worked"—his laugh was embarrassed but ingratiating— "and I'd see all these guys around her. I knew what the hell was going on!"

The room broke up, and Joe joined in the laughter, feeling acceptance, camaraderie, enjoying the story he was relating as much as his fellow clients.

"Twenty-two-year-olds are very hopeful and romantic," Diane said emphatically.

HIS TEARS NOW WERE FROM LAUGHTER

"You're that way at all ages!" Joe cried. "But you're a little stupider then!" His tears were from laughter.

"A lot of guys married young and divorced," Diane said, getting back to work. "Tell your mother, 'I didn't do anything wrong.' "

"Mom, I DIDN'T DO ANYTHING WRONG!" Joe fairly shouted.

Alex, smiling, said, "Was it a good two weeks?"

"Yeah," Joe said. "And the month before was okay, too!" He laughed so hard he almost fell over on his side, and everyone was hysterical, totally relaxed and enjoying the story.

"It was a great two weeks, Mom," Alex said, laughing.

"I should have never brought this up!" Joe shouted over the laughter, backhanding the tears of merriment from his checks.

"How long has it been since you talked about this?" Diane asked.

"I *never* talked about it!" Joe said.

"Thank God you did!" Diane said, smiling at Alex. "He's been talking about his 'troubles' all week."

Alex laughed. "I was scared you'd done something horrible."

"Well, they were troubles," Joe said. "That was a bad time. That was crazy, the family reaction. They tied it in with her being in the hospital. Somebody said, 'She's got enough trouble—and look what you do.' "

"So tell all the family to get off your back," Alex said.

"I think only one person said that about me," Joe said. "Bill probably."

"Sibling rivalries are tough," Diane said.

"Oh, I don't rival him," Joe said. "I still visit him, and my other brothers. We have picnics. It's a close family. But don't do anything wrong to your mother or father."

"Typical Italian Catholic background, just like mine," Diane said. "Okay, finish with your mom. Look at her and say, 'I'm not done talking to you, Mom. I'm going to settle all this with you.' "

Joe repeated those words to his mother and added, "I did the best I could."

"With no help," Diane said.

"With no help," Joe said.

"And with my own trouble," Diane said.

Joe repeated and, on mention of the word 'trouble,' laughed, and everyone joined him.

JOE HELD IN HIS SADNESS AND SYMPTOMS RETURNED

On the eighth day of the Intensive, Joe, who'd had no problems with travel work, had an anxiety attack in the Penn

Mutual Tower elevator, which had a window looking out on the city. Diane noticed him looking sad and asked him what he was thinking.

"I'm . . . I'm a lonely bastard," he said tearfully.

When the group got off at the top floor, Joe was dry-eyed and Diane said, "As soon as the tears came the symptoms stopped, right?"

"Yeah," Joe said.

"What do you feel your symptoms were covering up?"

"That it's going to be hard for me to leave in two days," Joe said emotionally.

Diane addressed the other clients. "What happened to Joe is important for everyone to understand. He's done this elevator many times in the last week, but when he did it today symptoms came out. That's because now a lot of feelings are stirred up, and the end of this group is in sight. So rather than feel that, which is to feel sad and maybe cry, the symptoms came on. Then his feelings broke through and he had some tears. Over separation and leaving—loneliness. So that shows you when you choose *not to feel* something, symptoms result."

Following the Intensive, Joe joined a group that met weekly and worked hard on identifying and sharing his feelings. He had considerable and understandable sadness surrounding the breakup of his first marriage and the death of his parents, which had to be aired and dispelled. He has been free of symptoms for more than two years since terminating treatment.

CHAPTER 9

Drugs and Agoraphobia—
Be Wary

*V*irtually all who join our program arrive with what they call a "survival kit" that they feel will help them gain control if they start to become panicky. A survival kit contains things like a list of phone numbers of "safe" people to call for help, such as a therapist, physician or friend; some reading material to distract the mind; and occasionally a container of alcohol. Many also include a soft drink or thermos of ice water with which to wash down medication. The vast majority of clients we've treated also come to us carrying some drug, usually Valium, Xanax, some other tranquilizer or one of the antidepressants.

Everyone wants a medication that calms her quickly, and she believes that without the drug the panic will grow beyond control. In the minds of agoraphobics the drug becomes a kind of savior.

Claire is typical of those who use drugs in order to do things they would otherwise avoid. During her evaluation she said that she took a dose of Xanax any time she left her house and always carried a supply with her. Whenever she gets upset she takes a Xanax fearing that if she doesn't she'll have a panic attack. Even with the Xanax she often has panics, but not always when anxiety first strikes. So Claire relies on it.

Al also always has tranquilizers with him, though he hasn't taken any for several months because he has not had any intense panics. He carries a shoulder bag and makes sure there is Valium in it, along with a can of soda, before leaving his home. Just in case.

Barbara relies on vodka to cut her anxiety. "I keep a pint in the door pocket of my car and a flask of vodka in my purse," she says. "I never get really drunk because I don't like to lose control. But when I'm a little high I'm not as anxious. I admit I've had panic attacks while a little high— but I've had a helluva lot more of them when I wasn't."

Many people with agoraphobia have tried drugs, including alcohol, and become so fearful of losing control that they refuse to try them again. Drugs often have side effects—dizziness, light-headedness, feelings described as "zombie-like," and a mouth so dry it feels as if it's full of cotton—that are very scary, in part because they are so similar to the effects of a panic attack. "I'm fearful enough without taking a prescription that scares me," is a common complaint.

Most clients have said that medication proved to be at best of minimum help in "taking the edge off anxiety," at worst of no use whatsoever. In some instances, certain medications—the tricyclics and MAO inhibitors—have alleviated panics, reduced anxiety and led to marked changes in the ability of agoraphobics to function.

MINOR TRANQUILIZERS

The medications most often prescribed for people suffering from panics and phobic avoidance are the minor tranquilizers. Among these are Valium, Xanax, Ativan, Tranxene, Serax and Librium. These drugs have been used in various forms for a long while, and results with them have been consistent over the years. They have been popular with agoraphobics because the tranquilizers give very quick relief from anxious feelings, though not from panic or from the fear that arises in particular places. But the relief is also very short-term. And what is not widely known is that for some people who take these drugs regularly, doses must be increased because users develop a tolerance to them. Also, with Valium, for example, it is generally accepted that doses of thirty milligrams or more per day for two months or more leads to physiological addiction. Even minimum doses of tranquilizers can be psychologically addictive.

The addictive nature of Valium was not discovered until long after the drug was in widespread use and widespread abuse, often with the encouragement of prescribing physicians. Xanax, which is clinically close to Valium, is now touted as the miracle drug and is very heavily prescribed. Some people claim that Xanax may have antipanic properties, but this has not been conclusively demonstrated. And it appears that this drug may be more addictive than Valium. There is more evidence that this is also true of Ativan.

With Xanax withdrawal effects often begin at a point when the original dosage has been cut in half and continue until the person has been off the drug for two weeks. The primary withdrawal effect is intense anxiety, and people report they feel as bad or worse than they did before going on Xanax. The result is that many people resume taking the drug to avoid the withdrawal effects.

On the plus side is the fact that for some people minor tranquilizers are useful in helping them cope with short-term stressful situations. But because agoraphobia tends to be chronic, these drugs produce no long-term benefit. The fact is that in eighteen years of treating agoraphobics, I have never encountered anyone who showed marked lasting improvement while on these drugs.

After taking tranquilizers for a time people will notice that as soon as they put a tablet in their mouth they feel better— well before any chemical effect could have taken place. This is clear evidence of a psychological dependency on the drug, and that the anxiety relief comes from the thought rather than from any chemical effect. Meanwhile, users of tranquilizers are loading their systems with these extremely powerful drugs that can have various detrimental effects. For example, it has been proven that chronic use of Valium leads to depression in some people. It has also been found that traces of Valium are still in the body even a month after quitting it.

Even for those who take tranquilizers only now and then when they feel they might panic there are problems. The drug continues to have its short-term effect, but the agoraphobic's dependency upon it is most destructive to the process of regaining a sense of control over one's own responses to things—and to recovery from the problem.

MAJOR TRANQUILIZERS (ANTIPSYCHOTIC DRUGS)

The most common names for these drugs are Thorazine, Mellaril, Stelazine and Haldol. These drugs were never meant for treatment of panic or agoraphobia. But occasionally physicians, usually nonpsychiatrists, will prescribe them erroneously. These drugs don't help in any way; rather, they often make the user feel more anxious. Most agoraphobics will not take the drugs beyond a trial period because they tend to produce unpleasant side effects, such as dry mouth, agitation, tremors, constipation, inhibition of ejaculation and amenorrhea. Any physician who prescribes a major tranquilizer for agoraphobia is not up to date on proper treatment, and help should be sought elsewhere. (Note: These drugs in large doses are appropriately used for psychosis. Sometimes phobic-like fears will accompany psychosis, but when this is the case symptoms other than phobic ones will be present and lead to a nonphobic diagnosis.)

BETA BLOCKERS

These drugs principally affect peripheral autonomic functions by decreasing such responses as heart rate, hand trembling and blood pressure. Beta blockers are often prescribed for mitral-valve prolapse, a benign condition that sometimes causes slight disquieting sensations. But beta blockers are also prescribed occasionally for agoraphobics, particularly when a patient reports to his physician that he is afraid of such body sensations as increased heart rate, twinges, or pains in the chest and trembling hands. The drug does not change the phobia in any way. For a few patients whose major fear is increased heart rate or trembling hands, the drug may provide noticeable temporary relief. But it will not provide even temporary relief for the vast majority because heart-rate fears are just one of the multitude of distressing symptoms of agoraphobia.

Even where beta blockers seem to help, the basic fear of increased heart rate is usually not actually changed. Using a drug to decrease heart rate on those who fear rapid heartbeat is like treating those who fear heights by having them avoid tall buildings. When the drug is no longer used and the heart is allowed to function properly, agoraphobics are usually right back where they started. They still fear rapid heart rate and they have uselessly subjected their bodies to a very strong medication.

ANTIDEPRESSANTS

There is considerable data on the effects of two antidepressants on agoraphobia and panics. These are (1) the tricyclics, marketed under such brand names as Elavil, Tofranil and Norpramin; and (2) the MAO inhibitors, marketed most commonly as Nardil. Both of these drugs were originally used in treating depression, but now some psychiatrists believe they are helpful in treating panics.

A comprehensive review of the outcome of research that tested the usefulness of antidepressant medication was published in 1983. The study was conducted by Michael Telch and his colleagues at the Department of Psychiatry, Stanford University School of Medicine, and it confirms a number of observations that clinicians have noted for years.

First, up to 25 percent of those suffering from agoraphobia refuse to take these drugs. Most often this is a result of an overall fear of medicine. Many agoraphobics also know that to make progress while in therapy it is necessary that they not take medication. Until they feel in control of themselves without medication, they will not think of themselves as well.

In addition, among those who begin medication, many stop very quickly. One reason is that with the tricyclics the side effects—which include dry mouth, constipation, dizziness and general feelings of agitation—are unpleasant and sometimes frightening. Some people grow hypersensitive to the drug and suffer from insomnia, jitteriness and irritability, all of which tend to increase the kinds of fear that led to taking the drug in the first place. Those who use an MAO inhibitor must not eat certain foods, including cheeses, beer and nuts.

Published studies of those who are treated with antidepressant medication show that up to 40 percent drop out of the drug treatment program, compared to a dropout rate of only 10 percent among those in nondrug behavioral treatment programs. In studies of agoraphobics who had stopped taking antidepressants two years earlier, the relapse rate ranged from 31 percent (Zitrin, Klein, Woerner and Ross) to 100 percent (Solyom, Hesaltine, McClure, Solyom, Leduidge and Steinberg). This compares to relapse rates of 0 to 10 percent among those in behavioral exposure treatment programs.

The Stanford review found that there were just as many studies showing tricyclics and MAO inhibitors to be of no help in the treatment of agoraphobia as there are those that show the drugs to be helpful, which indicates that there is no reliable evidence of the effectiveness of drug treatment alone. In most of the studies showing the medication effective, the subjects were also receiving other treatments, usually exposure therapy, and thus it was not possible to say accurately what caused improvement. These studies indicate that there is no reliable evidence of the effectiveness of drug treatment alone. In summary, the Telch review says: "Recent research seriously questions the efficacy of antidepressant pharmacotherapy by itself as a treatment for agoraphobia. Moreover it is argued that the disadvantages of drug treatment—namely agoraphobics' reluctance to take medication, physical side effects and relapse upon withdrawal of the medication—caution against their routine use in clinical practice."

Although research findings are far from conclusive on the effectiveness of antidepressants on agoraphobics, proponents of the drugs have had a tremendous influence on psychiatrists and physicians in general. The result is that most doctors who cannot provide appropriate psychological treatment will prescribe the drugs. Unfortunately, some insufficiently informed physicians believe that panics and agoraphobia are biochemical in origin, and they erroneously maintain that people with the problem *must* take drugs.

Where do these flawed assumptions come from? In a study by Pitts and McClure, people who suffered panics and a control group who didn't suffer panics were given sodium lactate. Both groups experienced symptoms such as numbness in the extremities and muscle tremors, but the former group suffered panic reactions more frequently while on the sodium lactate. In a later study, when these people were given an antidepressant prior to taking the sodium lactate, they were less likely to report a panic response.

From these findings it has been reasoned that people with panic disorders are biochemically different from others and it is a chemical imbalance that causes panic and agoraphobia.

Because antidepressants sometimes lessen panic reactions, it is assumed that the drug is correcting the chemical imbalance. Proponents of this view argue that because the condition is biochemical in origin, recovery can *only* occur through drug treatments.

This seemingly compelling argument is flawed at many levels. Start with the fact that anything that we experience must be registered in our bodies biochemically or we simply would not experience it. Everything that we respond to in the environment causes biochemical changes in us. For example, a startling loud noise produces swift body sensations—rapid heartbeat, sudden alertness, faster breathing and a surge of fear—that announces profound biochemical changes occurring inside us. Even the slightest movements, the raising of a finger or closing of an eyelid, are mediated by biochemical changes.

It is clear that chronic states of stress not only change one's biochemistry at the moment, but lead the body to change its biochemistry further by attempting to adapt to that persisting state. The result is a relatively long-term change in our biochemistry that returns to normal only some while after the stresses are removed. Consequently, the chemistry of people suffering panic attacks is quite different from that of people who don't.

What the Pitts–McClure study actually shows is that panic-prone people have different reactions from others to sodium lactate, not that the biochemistry underlying that difference causes panic.

To better understand this, consider an example from research on depression, which is more advanced than research on panic. We have long known that biochemical differences are present with depression. But what is cause and what is effect? Take the case of a sixty-year-old man whose wife of thirty-five years dies suddenly from a heart attack. Not surprisingly, he becomes extremely depressed, has trouble sleeping, loses his appetite and when tested he shows profound biochemical signs that are linked with depression.

Do we consider that his biochemical state caused his depression? No. The death of his wife led to the depression that is expressed not only in his feelings and overt behavior but also in his biochemistry.

Of course, most of life's stressors are less striking than this example. They are the product of ongoing conflict, such as feeling trapped in an unhappy marriage, discontent with one's role in life or work situation, or conflict over separation from parents or other loved ones. In a study we did at Temple (Goldstein and Chambless) 95 percent of the subjects reported that panic and agoraphobia began at a time of severe conflict in their lives.

Subsequent studies of lactate infusion have concluded that differences between panic-disordered and control groups, reported in Pitts and McClure and other earlier studies, were due to the panic-disordered subjects' fear of the experimental situation. In the experiment the subjects were confined and a needle was inserted into a vein so that the lactate could be infused over a period of time. Panic-disordered people were likely to attribute the unpleasant effects of the lactate to rising anxiety; the anxiety would make them panic and they would report their panic. Subjects who had no history of panic attacks correctly attributed the sensations to the physiological effects of the lactate; they were not frightened. These more recent studies seriously undermine the very foundation upon which the whole tenuous notion of biochemical causation is built.

Those who believe that agoraphobia is a biological disorder point out that panic attacks run in families. It is true that if a parent, sibling or close relative has such attacks, there is a much greater chance that others in the family will eventually also suffer a panic attack. But everyone responds to excessive stress with some kind of physical and/or psychological reactions. Some people will get ulcers, others will get high blood pressure or headaches or low-back pain. Whatever the stress reaction, it will very likely run in families. Does that mean that everyone in society is suffering from a biological disorder? Certainly not, but it is likely that the propensity to respond to excess stress in a particular fashion is either genetic in origin or learned in families or, most probably, a combination of both.

Do we ignore the signals from our bodies that something is wrong in our lives and look only for external medical solutions to our problems, or do we listen to the body's wisdom and begin to pinpoint the inner problems we need to work on? I suggest that more meaningful and more lasting solutions will follow from the latter. In a study at our program at Temple, in which no drugs were used, 67 percent of our clients were free of panic six months after beginning treatment. Whether agoraphobia is basically a biological disease, a psychological one, or a combination of both it is clear that it can be treated effectively without medications.

In closing, there are some additional points to keep in mind if you are deciding about taking medication. The documented facts are that women are more likely to be put on medication than are men who present the same complaints. Most agoraphobics are women of childbearing age. None of the drugs discussed here should be taken during pregnancy, and pregnancy often is not detected for many weeks. Also, many of these drugs are in the body long after the last dose is taken, so drugs ought to be used with great caution and for as brief a period as possible. When there is no appropriate psychological treatment available to you or when psychological approaches have failed, then drug treatment might very well be the most appropriate treatment of choice. Occasionally we find a client who is so profoundly depressed or so anxious that she is unable to participate in treatment; antidepressant medication or tranquilizers along with supportive therapy may ameliorate the depression and anxiety symptoms enough to allow the application of the preferred treatment for agoraphobia. At our Center, once some coping skills have been learned to allow clients to control fear, they are slowly weaned of drugs.

Remember, too, that even if there seems to be no appropriate psychological treatment in your immediate area, there are now intensive treatment programs around the country well worth seeking out. There are also several excellent mail programs on the treatment of agoraphobia, so please check out the listing at the end of this book.

A Program to Help You Get Out

No doubt many readers who have come this far in the book have seen yourselves, or some familiar aspects of yourselves, in earlier chapters. You are now well aware that you are not unique, you are not alone. Millions of people suffer from agoraphobia, and many of them are in treatment with therapists. But for those of you who have been unable to find relief from this disorder, particularly those who have become bound to their homes by agoraphobia—you *can* help yourselves. You have unknowingly gotten into some destructive habits that have turned you into a prisoner of your feelings. Once you start changing those habits, you'll be on your way to freedom.

You are now ready for a program designed to let you get out of your residence. Or if you've been able to go out, yet avoided certain places, you will learn how to go any place you wish, without anxiety, without fear. You have suffered enough.

You did not acquire those destructive habits overnight, and unlearning them will not be easy. Progress may seem very slow at times, and there will surely be setbacks along the way. But there are no time limits on progress and no rigid goals; some people will respond more quickly than others. It is important to be reasonable about what you can expect to accomplish with a self-help program. Even with a lot of professional help, those who have avoided uncomfortable situations for a long while or are having frequent panics find it very difficult to trust themselves enough to face their fear squarely. Understandably they need a lot of encouragement, and going through the steps to recovery with someone they trust makes it easier. So it is best to enlist help if you can do so from someone who will be there to cheer you on when your courage fails and to let you know how great you are doing when you have a hard time seeing it for yourself. Even so, progress may seem excruciatingly slow at times. You must expect setbacks too. After having a few good days or weeks you can wake up to a day that is as bad as it ever was. At times like this it is only natural to become discouraged. But it is important to remember that progress cannot be measured by any one day. With continued effort the weeks will have a greater percentage of good days, though you are likely to have bad periods when you are under added stress.

Premenstrual hormonal changes, strife with a family member or at work, circumstances triggering unresolved feelings from the past, and unrecognized feelings of anger or sadness are all examples of events that often cause temporary worsening of symptoms for people with agoraphobia. When your symptoms suddenly reappear, try to turn these setbacks into opportunities by stopping to go back over in your mind the last few hours or days; see if any of these situations apply to you at that time. There will be repetition of particular themes for each person. Recognition of the connection of these events with a worsening of symptoms will in itself reduce anxiety and in addition suggest what changes you may need to make in your life.

With the aid of a self-help program and a very large amount of motivation and self-discipline, it is reasonable to expect that you can become able to go most places. Your anxiety in these places will be greatly reduced and your episodes of panic will be less frequent, perhaps even completely disappear. It is not likely that your day-to-day anxiety level will be reduced as much as you would like. This will require resolution of the conflicts that set you up for development of agoraphobia in the first place, and that resolution will probably require professional help. Keep in mind that self-help may simply not be for you. Often the extreme anxiety and/or depression accompanying agoraphobia can leave you so depleted that you can't do all that is suggested here on your own. Nevertheless, the gains to be had from self-help can make a very big difference in your life.

You also need to know that these techniques tried casually will not work for you. They require *disciplined* and *repeated practice* and are not easy to learn, particularly in the face of great fear.

If you try them and they do not work, do not become discouraged about being helped. You probably need the more powerful presence of someone capable and knowledgeable working with you.

If you end up seeking help at a program other than that at Temple, you will probably not find exactly the same skills training. That's okay. Give their way a fair chance. These are not the only possible techniques or necessarily the best ones for you. There are a lot of very competent professionals who have worked out their own skills-training approaches which may be as good or better for you.

What you have to do is in *no way dangerous*. All you need is desire and determination. If you can truthfully say to yourself, "I want to stop avoiding, I want to stop being anxious and fearful, I want to live life!" here's how to start.

While you are probably focusing on control—on stopping the panics and trying to function without feeling anxious—you have learned that attempting to do so directly does not work. The fact is that in order to stop something you need to do something else! Always checking to see how anxious you are, trying to be calm, will likely make you more anxious, not less, and indeed can actually cause you to have panics. In addition, the constant watching of your anxiety level is accompanied by a lot of scary self-talk that often begins, "My God, what if—" and ends in a full-blown cat-astrophic thought that something awful will happen. Add to this the fact that you are burdened by lots of physical sensations such as rapid heartbeat, dizziness and throbbing temples, among others, and you can see why you have dif-ficulty staying in control.

To actually gain control we must break the process down into manageable steps, acquiring some mastery over each one in turn and then combining them into a workable over-all strategy. There are several stages, and at each stage sev-eral steps are to be learned.

Phase I: Anxiety coping skills
    Stopping catastrophic thoughts
    Staying in "the here and now"
    Breath control
Phase II: Getting out and using your coping skills
    Cardinal rules: never avoid, use your coping skills, and
        never let your feelings dictate your behavior
    The importance of making a schedule
    Take credit for what you do
Phase III: Reducing anxiety triggered by body sensations
    Controlling hyperventilation symptoms; racing heart,
        dizziness, tingling in the extremities
    Reducing fear of rapid heartbeat and the feeling of not
        being able to get your breath

ANXIETY COPING SKILLS

I know you need to acquire the sense that you can accept whatever happens, a sense that your feelings are friends and not dangerous enemies. Well, this *can* be accomplished if approached systematically and persistently.

To begin with, you need to learn specific coping skills to manage panic and to reverse the upward spiraling fear that leads to panic. We will practice each skill separately and then combine them to maximize their effectiveness.

PHASE I: LEARNING ANXIETY COPING SKILLS

In earlier chapters we have discussed the destructive aspects of *catastrophic thinking*. Now you can begin to give it up. All you need is a rubber band, a pad and pencil, and time to practice the skill. To begin, I suggest you schedule four fifteen-minute practice sessions daily, and try to work during the same times each day in the interest of sticking with the program.

Day One

During your first fifteen-minute session make a list of your typical catastrophic thoughts. To help you identify those thoughts that are catastrophic, here are some guidelines: They are almost always future-oriented and concern frightening things that *are going to happen*. Examples are, "If I go to the grocery store I may get hit by a runaway panic and faint!" "What if I can't get to the department store exit quickly and people see me lose control?" "I can't go to the bank! How can I possibly wait in line without being overwhelmed?" "If I don't get help for this problem soon I'm going to go crazy!"

Catastrophic thoughts increase your anxiety. Often they occur when you notice that you are unexpectedly someplace that you regard as dangerous, or when you learn that someone expects you to do something that frightens you, or when a memory of something scary suddenly pops up. Catastrophic thoughts are likely to follow any time you get a quick little jolt of fear.

For example, a close friend calls to say he is getting married and he wants you to be in the wedding party. Instantly there is a charge of fear and the thought, "Oh, my

God, what am I going to do! I can't go to that wedding and stand up in front of all those people! What if I start to shake—I may HAVE TO RUN OUT OF THERE!" All the while you are feeling the initial fear response (which would be short-lived without the acceleration caused by your fearful thoughts), and your anxiety keeps going up. As the wedding day approaches you may find yourself having panics more frequently!

What is causing all this anxiety when you are not yet at the wedding, not yet standing in front of all the guests? It is your habitual thinking pattern that is doing you in.

The increased anxiety caused by catastrophic thoughts leads you to avoidance. Once your anxiety level begins to peak you will do whatever you can to decrease it—which is perfectly natural. The problem is that what you have learned to do is to avoid. You decide not to attend the wedding, and in the end that is very destructive to you, because avoidance simply sustains your fears.

Some people know a number of their catastrophic thoughts; others have trouble summoning them. So begin your list. If nothing occurs to you, or if you want to extend your list, think about some upcoming event that will be difficult for you. Two examples: Perhaps you are planning to pick up your child at school some afternoon soon, or there is a big party that you feel obligated to attend. Think about either of these events and your catastrophic thought will be immediately present. Make a list of all such thoughts. For example, "Oh God, how can I pick up John today when I'm already feeling so bad?" or "I said I'd go to that party, but what will everyone think if I have an attack there?"

If there is nothing potentially upsetting on your horizon, then create something. Pick a task that is possible to do and that you have thought about doing, such as saying to yourself, "Later today I am going to get in the car and drive to the department store, go in and pick out a dress that I will try on." Then pay attention to your thoughts, for again you are likely to be besieged by catastrophic thoughts, with relief coming only when you say, "I'm not going to that store!"

Once you complete your first fifteen-minute session (if it takes longer, that's fine), your assignment is to continue to be aware of whatever scary thoughts pop up. You will be surprised as you write them down that so much of your waking time is spent entertaining such thoughts. There is no need to try to change them yet. Just work on noticing them, being aware when they are present and watching how they work. Again, set yourself in a task like going to the bank, for example, then think of yourself standing in line. The catastrophic thought will be something like: "What if I lose control and have to run out of there in panic?"

At the next scheduled fifteen-minute practice go over your list again and remind yourself that *these thoughts are your enemies*. Again stimulate them by thinking about an upcoming event that frightens you, or by creating such an event. Notice how automatically catastrophic thoughts slip into your mind. Be aware of how they affect your feelings—and how those thoughts have been controlling you. The thought comes, followed by avoidance.

The third and fourth fifteen-minute practice sessions are to be spent in the same way. Understand that you are building self-awareness, and that is the first step to change.

Day Two

In today's four sessions we are going to begin practicing a skill that will be used to reduce anxiety whether catastrophic thoughts are related or not. In the meantime, continue to be aware of and list your catastrophic thoughts throughout the day.

Staying in "the here and now." We call this process here-and-now focusing. The point is to bring yourself totally into the present moment through the use of one or more of your five senses—seeing, touching, hearing, smelling or tasting. Most of the time we are not in the immediate present in our thoughts but somewhere else—in the past, re-membering; or in the future, anticipating, planning or catastrophizing. We may be thinking about a conversation with someone or we may be fantasizing. Rarely are we aware of what is actually around us, even in the most familiar surroundings. We are lost in our thoughts and this creates tension, the degree depending upon our habits of thought. To focus on the immediate is instantly calming. All relaxation and meditation systems rely on this fact. And consistently focusing on the immediate present over several months will unquestionably leave you feeling much less anxious. However, at this point we are most interested in taking advantage of the phenomenon to help you get beyond your fears.

Begin by trying out your senses, starting with *sight*. Look around you at the colors, textures, shapes and play of light in your surroundings. Try to do so quietly without commenting on what you see and without categorizing things. For instance, if you find yourself saying, "That's blue" or "That's a chair," you are limiting what you see. Instead pay attention to the qualities that you have called blue, to the contours, textures and shades of light that make up the form you call a chair.

Associations will occur from the things you see, so watch out for wanderings that have you thinking things like, "That's blue . . . oh, George has blue eyes . . . I remember when—" Any time this happens just come right back to the present visible experience. Stop and check out your present setting for a couple of minutes.

Okay, let's try the same thing using the sense of *touch*. Allow your fingers to run across different kinds of surfaces, such as glass, cloth, wood or the skin of your arm. Notice the different sensations at your fingertips. Now stay with each surface long enough for it to become familiar. Again do so without speaking or categorizing. Practice this exercise for a couple of minutes. Good.

Now let's try the same with *hearing*. Sit quietly and be aware of the sounds around you. Some sounds that have been there all along will become apparent for the first time— evidence of how we are unaware of present experiences most of the time. Sit with a quiet mind for a couple of minutes and listen to the clock ticking, the refrigerator humming, a bird outside peeping, a car pulling out of a driveway. Don't forget: When your mind wanders bring it back gently to the sounds.

Touch, sight and hearing can be used anywhere, any time, and are therefore the most useful for your practices. But the same principle can be employed with *smell* and *taste* where appropriate.

These exercises using the senses to stay in the present will also help you to develop concentration. For anyone who is anxious, concentration is likely to be hard, even for a few seconds, so do the best you can and give yourself credit for making the effort. With practice your concentration will increase slowly at first; as you advance it will increase dramatically. Remember that all the while you will be building the coping skills that will help free you from fear.

Repeat these exercises during the three additional practice periods scheduled for Day Two.

Day Three

Again schedule four fifteen-minute practice sessions.

We are now ready to begin to stop catastrophic thinking by using the rubber-band method. We will combine this tool with here-and-now focusing in a way that will allow you to begin using both skills when you actually get out into situations where rising anxiety threatens to overwhelm you. Do not expect to completely trust this strategy immediately, and try not to worry about it. It will take lots of practice in situations that are difficult for you before you master the technique. But with practice there will be at least small rewards quite soon, and they will encourage you to press on.

To begin, get out your list of catastrophic thoughts, look it over and add any new discoveries. As you study the list remember that these thoughts are unwelcome, destructive guests in your mind, and make a firm decision to stop entertaining them. Slip the rubber band around your wrist. It will help you stop those thoughts. Any time you become aware of one of those destructive thoughts forming, snap the rubber band and simultaneously say under your breath: "Stop!" You need not snap the rubber band hard enough to hurt, but hard enough to scatter the destructive thought and bring you back to the present. Sometimes it may take more than one snap. Remember, this technique is to be used against *thoughts only*. It will not reduce anxiety that is unrelated to thoughts; for that you use your here-and-now focusing.

Summon a catastrophic thought, snap your rubber band to bring yourself back to the present, and immediately use your here-and-now focusing until you are calmer. You may find the catastrophic thought returns quickly, and that's okay. As soon as you are aware of it sneaking up on you, stop it again by snapping your rubber band and go right into your here-and-now focusing by concentrating on your surroundings. In the beginning you may have to repeat this process numerous times to achieve calm, or you may use it successfully almost immediately. In any case, continue to practice. When you are calm again, start the whole process over by thinking about some unsettling upcoming event, snap the rubber band to stop the thought and swiftly focus on the here and now.

Once you have completed the fifteen-minute practice session, remember to use this strategy whenever catastrophic thoughts arise. As you go through the day, each time you notice the rubber band, notice the content of your thoughts and snap away the catastrophic ones. Be sure to use your three other practice sessions this day in the same way, as each will help add to your growing skills.

Remember that learning this strategy is at least as difficult as learning to ride a bicycle. So whenever you get discouraged just recall how many times you fell off a bike and how long it took before you really felt in charge of the machine. Those of you who have learned to play a musical instrument will remember how much practice was required before you could really play smoothly. So keep practicing this strategy. Your ability to use it effectively *will* come.

Day Four

Breath Control. When we are relaxed we tend to breathe in slowly, deep breaths using the diaphragm. The breath seems to be drawn into the stomach, causing it to expand as we inhale and contract as we exhale. Movement of the upper chest is minimal as the diaphragm does the work.

But when we are frightened we tend to breathe in quick, shallow breaths using our chest muscles more than our diaphragm. On the inhale there is expansion in the upper chest and on the exhale the chest contracts, with little movement of the diaphragm and stomach. We frequently hold our breath when we are scared. This breathing pattern is adaptive for really dangerous situations, as it increases the oxygen supply and reduces the carbon dioxide level in the bloodstream and prepares one for the "fight or flight" response. In other words, when you are suddenly in a situation in which you must either fight or take flight, then the body provides additional oxygen to aid you. But when you feel fear in a situation in which you neither fight nor literally run to burn up the extra oxygen, you are left with an imbalance of oxygen and carbon dioxide that leads to hyperventilation symptoms. You get light-headed, feel dizzy, and experience tingling sensations in the extremities.

The total body response that occurs here includes increased heart rate and blood pressure, with the rerouting of blood from the internal organs and skin to the muscles. All of this would help you deal with a life-threatening danger, but you face no such circumstances, no animal or person that you must fight or run away from. But since all of these physical reactions are part of a total interconnected body response, we can reverse them all by gaining control of any one of them.

The systems involved are all part of the autonomic nervous system that is not usually under conscious control, but breathing *can* easily be brought under conscious control. You can consciously increase or decrease the speed of your breathing even though breathing is otherwise unconscious. So the control of breath is a way to reverse the fight-or-flight response and return to a state of calm.

It has probably been a long while since you experienced the deep diaphragmatic breathing that accompanies contentment, so the first task will be for you to come to recognize it.

On Day Four again schedule four fifteen-minute practice sessions, and remember as we expand your skills that you must keep applying those learned earlier *every day*.

We begin this practice period by taking a position that will automatically produce diaphragmatic breathing. Lie on your stomach, then spend five minutes becoming aware of what it feels like to breathe in a calming fashion through your nose. Notice the expansion of your abdomen as you breathe in and how that feeling is made more obvious as your abdomen presses against the floor with each inhale, and how it contracts away from the floor as you breathe out. Be aware of the pace of your breath: breathe slowly and deeply. Pay attention to the movement of air *in through your nostrils* and all the way down to your stomach as if you are blowing up a balloon inside your stomach on the inhale and emptying it on the exhale.

Now, lie facedown on the floor, placing one hand with palms down atop the other where your head will come to rest. Rest your forehead on the back of your top hand and focus on your breathing for five minutes. Then check how you are feeling; you should be calmer than you were when you started. If you are not calmer, you probably allowed your mind to wander rather than concentrating on your breathing. Should you find yourself physically uncomfortable, try lying on a softer surface. Then go through the process again for another five minutes and get a good clear feeling of what this calming breathing pattern is like.

In your second practice session on day four, resume the prone position, on your stomach, head resting on the back of your hand, and spend a few minutes getting more familiar with this breathing pattern. Then slowly assume a sitting position, all the while being aware of your breath. See if you can continue to breathe using the diaphragm. Remember the image of filling and emptying a balloon in your stomach. If you lose the breathing pattern, return to the prone position for a minute or so and again move slowly, without interrupting your even breathing, into a sitting position. Spend the rest of the period getting familiar with the feeling of diaphragmatic breathing while seated. Any time you lose the feeling, start on the floor again and move to a sitting position.

During your third practice session, once again start in the prone position until you feel the diaphragmatic breathing, then slowly move to the sitting position and remain there for several minutes focusing on your breathing. Next, slowly rise to a standing position while being aware of your breath. Stand and focus on your breathing pattern for the rest of your practice period. Any time you lose the pattern, return to the prone or seated position, keeping your back as straight as possible so your diaphragm is free. Then stand again. This is difficult. Repeat the third practice exercise in your fourth session of the day.

As you will see as you progress, diaphragmatic breathing can be used in conjunction with the other coping skills you've practiced, or it can be used by itself. Be aware of your breathing pattern from time to time throughout the day. If you fall back to using upper-chest breathing, recall the image of filling and emptying a balloon and focus on that until you return to diaphragmatic breathing. Practice this both in calmer moments and whenever you feel anxious. Be assured of one all-important thing—practice will bring about a change in your ongoing breathing pattern that will result in a *lowering of anxiety.*

Day Five

Today you will need to schedule not four short practices but two longer sessions. Ideally you will find time for one thirty-minute-session and one forty-five-minute session. Today you will begin to combine the coping skills you have been learning into an overall system for maximum effectiveness.

For the first session we want to start by generating some discomfort for you to deal with. So let's plan an outing that would ordinarily be difficult for you, one that you will actually carry out on day one of Phase II. Right now think about what that outing will be. Perhaps it's just walking out to the mailbox by your curb, or to the corner, or even taking a walk around the block. Whatever you decide, it should be just a small step farther than you can go comfortably right now.

As you think about what you will do tomorrow, you will develop some anxiety. Already you may be saying, "Oh, no, I can't do that!" Now is the perfect time to practice using your skills.

First be aware of your catastrophic thoughts; then snap your rubber band and say "Stop!" Next focus on the here and now by using your sense of sight, touch or hearing in your present surroundings. Stay with the here and now until you are calm again.

Then start from the beginning once more. Repeat the thoughts about going out tomorrow; strengthen your resolve to do so. If catastrophic thoughts pop up, stop them with the rubber band and turn to the here and how until you are calm once more. Continue this practice over and over again throughout this session.

Later in the day, during the forty-five-minute session, start by repeating what you did in the first. Throughout the process see if you can be aware of your breath pattern. Are you using your diaphragm? Just let the breath pattern stay in the background of your awareness as you go through the coping process. Try using diaphragmatic breathing instead of here-and-now focusing and see how that works in calming you. Stop the catastrophic thoughts with the rubber band and immediately turn to breath awareness.

Play with these coping skills and work out the combination that seems to be most effective for you. Every individual is different. You can be creative in taking advantage of what you have learned about controlling anxiety. Whatever works best for you is what you should develop.

PHASE II: GETTING OUT AND USING YOUR COPING SKILLS

There are several important rules to remember as you begin to get out.

RULE ONE: Never retreat in the face of anxiety or panic. Recall from your own experience that panic arrives, rises, peaks and fades away. This sequence occurs whether you run or not. It's important to recognize that panics will pass rather quickly unless you try to fight them or you feed them with catastrophic thoughts. There may be times, in spite of your best efforts in using your coping skills, when panic will break through. But do not be discouraged and do not retreat.

Staying with panic and not trying to avoid it is an important emotional learning experience, because it tells you that the terrible fate you conjured up did not occur. You did not have a heart attack, did not faint, did not go crazy, did not make a fool of yourself. You had a panic attack, stood fast, and it went away leaving you intact. Once you have gone through several panics without running—just standing firm and using your coping skills—the anticipation of panic will rapidly lose its capacity to frighten you. Since it is the *anticipation* that leads to panic—the fear of fear—once you have conquered that anticipatory fear, panic will no longer be part of your life.

RULE TWO: Always use your coping skills. Remember your rubber band, your here-and-now focusing skills, and your diaphragmatic breathing.

RULE THREE: Carry out your assignment no matter how you are feeling. You may awake one morning feeling that if you go out you are sure to panic. This is the *time when most progress can be made*. Don't let your feelings dictate your behavior; don't fall back into the habit of avoidance by not going out.

Phase Two—Day One

All right, you now have the rules and you've practiced your coping skills. You're ready to go out. Let's say the goal you decided on yesterday was to visit a grocery store six blocks from home that you haven't been near in months or years. On the first day aim to go one-third of the distance to the store. When you reach that point, stand there for three minutes and employ your coping skills. Do not head for home until you are feeling calm.

On the second day go two-thirds of the way to the store and stand there for five minutes while using your coping skills to maintain, or regain, calm.

On the third day go all the way to the store and stand outside for five minutes, employing coping skills as needed.

On day four walk just inside the store and stand fast for five minutes while using your coping skills. Any time you feel the anxiety begin to rise, be sure to stay where you are. Use your coping skills: stop the catastrophic thoughts by snapping your rubber band; bring yourself into the present by focusing on something in the immediate environment; breathe slowly from the diaphragm. If the panic gets out of hand, use the opportunity to learn that you can stay where you are and the panic will pass so long as you don't feed it with catastrophic thoughts.

On the fifth day you will actually do some shopping in the store, employing your coping skills to carry you along.

The above are your goals and you *must* write them down in advance. It's also a good idea to share them with a relative or friend, and say, "This is what I'm going to do this week." Make it clear that you don't want them to push you. Support and encouragement are fine, but you don't need an overseer.

Every Anxious Experience Is a Healing One If You Don't Run from It

Be realistic yet gentle with yourself in setting up assignments, but be tough with yourself in carrying them out. You are going to have catastrophic thoughts on your excursions. Snap your rubber band to stop them and instantly switch to the here and now. Seize every opportunity in which you are frightened to use the tools you've learned to get through the fears and become calm again. Every anxious experience is a healing one if you don't avoid it by running. Never head for home until the specified time is up and you are once more calm.

It is also vital that you not cut back your plan once you are under way. Be persistent and finish it up. Some days you will be feeling so positive and determined that, having reached your preset goal and completed your assignment, you'll want to go further. Fine, decide on an additional distance to go and do so. If you become scared during the extra steps, use your coping skills and finish what you planned.

Some people when frightened unknowingly gulp in too much oxygen and feel dizzy, as if they might faint. Again, this is a state we call hyperventilation, and it also happens to those who are not burdened by agoraphobia. If it happens to you, simply take a deep slow breath and let it out slowly over a period of ten seconds; then focus on the diaphragmatic breathing you've been practicing and your light-headedness will swiftly disappear.

Take Credit for What You Do

Please remember as you work through this program that any progress that leads toward the end of agoraphobia should be celebrated. Congratulate yourself on small victories, because they will be followed by large triumphs as you move along. Keep in mind that the key is repetition: Going out and practicing your coping skills over and over again will advance you to ultimate success. Practice, practice, practice.

Anticipatory Fear Will Pass

You may be disappointed with your progress because the anticipatory dread of going out seems to remain. That is to be expected. You will continue to have some anticipatory fear of doing something or going someplace long after you have done it once or twice fairly comfortably. This nagging fear may occur even after you have achieved considerable mobility. You may say to yourself after a carefree visit to the store: "Well, I made it without a hitch. I guess I was lucky. But the next time could be disastrous."

Once you've comfortably made numerous trips without incident, though, the anticipatory fear will diminish and ultimately become a thing of the past. You will steadily be building confidence. In subsequent weeks, cross off your list any formerly feared place that you have now visited at least twice without thinking about it. For example, by week six you may be doing your own shopping at the nearby supermarket without giving it a second thought. Cross the supermarket off your list. Each time you strike an item from your list, you will become more confident and you will feel better.

Whenever you discover you are avoiding something that

was not on your original list, add it. Keep adding items until you have eliminated all of those places you were afraid to visit and all those things you were afraid to do. Be determined and have faith, because this kind of program has worked for hundreds of people who could not leave the house before they engaged in the program; now they can go almost anywhere without fear of panicking.

PHASE III: REDUCING ANXIETY TRIGGERED BY BODY SENSATIONS

Agoraphobics tend to be fearful of such body sensations as headaches, heart pounding, rapid pulse, dizziness and tightness in the chest. Because fear of these sensations can often spiral into panic, you avoid situations which cause those sensations. Now that you have begun to get out, have consolidated your coping skills and are less overwhelmed by your fear of panics, you can begin to stop avoiding discomforting body sensations. To build up a tolerance for these sensations, you will practice staying with them until they are no longer sensations you fear, and you will come to accept them as normal twinges that everybody experiences.

Our goal for the five days given to Phase III are designed to help you begin to change your habit of avoiding body sensations that tend to make you anxious. For it is only by facing those body sensations, by letting them come and acknowledging them, that you render them unable to cause you anxiety.

LEARNING TO FACE YOUR BODY SENSATIONS

Day One

Find a quiet comfortable place to sit or lie down. Set a cooking timer for three minutes. For those three minutes concentrate on your body. Focus on any sensations you feel, such as your pulse rate, heartbeat or throbbing temples. At first this may be frightening, because you've gotten into the habit of associating those body sensations with panic. You want to avoid them, but instead concentrate on them. You may think I'm asking you to lie on a railroad track in the path of an oncoming train. But no train is coming; *these sensations cannot harm you*.

Concentrate on those sensations. One may become more prominent than another—say an increased pulse rate surpasses the feeling of throbbing temples. Focus on the more prominent sensation. Concentrate and do not try to change it. The idea is to be aware of it as if you were an outsider looking in.

Do not try to make it go away, even though the feeling is making you uncomfortable. Try to stay with it until the timer goes off. Try this several times a day until you can stay with the body sensations for three minutes. The more you can stay with and not avoid these body sensations, the faster the anxiety they occasioned will lessen. Gradually the full anxiety will be reduced to a slight anxiety, and that will later become discomfort, then slight discomfort . . . and finally those body sensations will be no more than the twinges everyone feels. Of course, all of this will take time and persistence, and remember: Any time you feel anxious, *use your coping skills*.

Some people have trouble summoning a body sensation. If you do, create one. Breathe deeply and rapidly for thirty seconds, and you will feel dizzy. Then focus on that feeling. Stay with it. If a pounding heart frightens you, then push up your heart rate by walking up stairs or jogging in place.

For the Next Four Days

Repeat this exercise *at least twice each day*, more often if you can manage it. Remember, the more you do the exercise, the faster you will improve to the point where your body sensations no longer make you anxious. The more you stay with these sensations, the sooner you learn that nothing happens if you simply let them play themselves out. They don't get worse; on the contrary, they become easier to accept and acknowledge. You'll say, "I have a headache. Big deal. It'll go away."

When you've been able to stay with a sensation for three minutes, increase it to five. Repeat the exercise for five minutes twice the following day.

Once you've mastered the exercise for five-minute stretches at least twice a day, you will have accomplished two things. First you will have built up a tolerance for your own body sensations. Second, you will have reinforced your new habit of *facing* your fears.

By the end of your first week of Phase III perhaps you'll be able to practice sitting for five minutes focusing on and trying to increase a body sensation. Some days are bound to be better than others. You may have handled the exercise for three minutes one day, then only for one minute at a sitting the following day. Again, don't be discouraged. We all have cycles of energy that at times make concentrating difficult. Push hard on day three and you may be surprised that you can hold your focus for three minutes. Congratulate yourself and make a determination to aim for five minutes on day four. Once more, maintain your resolve and don't worry about setbacks. Your desire will overcome them.

Remember there is no such thing as failing. Realize that ninety-nine out of one hundred people will complete the first three phases of the program feeling frustrated, as if they did poorly. But people suffering from agoraphobia tend to see themselves negatively, and that attitude will likely prevail here. Just keep in mind that while you strive for success, you cannot accomplish everything in a few weeks. Each person's progress is different, and the key is to be patient—but persistent. Keep trying, and you will make progress at your own individual pace, week after week.

Some of you will overcome your anxiety on your own; others will reach a plateau beyond which progress seems impossible; others will not be able to make progress independently. Understand that this chapter deals with overcoming only the conditioned-fear aspect of agoraphobia. The problems that caused you to develop agoraphobia in the first place (see Chapter Two) are not likely to be changed by this at-home program. If you feel the need of further help from a therapist who understands agoraphobia and its treatment at all levels, see the listings at the end of this book of agoraphobia treatment available throughout the world.

If you think your disorder is not underpinned by the fear of fear but developed because of unexpressed feelings of anger, resentment, guilt or overwhelming sadness, you will also want to consult an experienced therapist. An example of one such case is a woman I treated recently who was afraid to drive her car into center-city Philadelphia. When I asked if she thought she could ride along while I drove, she said she would try it. And she was fine until we arrived downtown. Then she started crying and said she was having a panic attack. As she looked more sad than scared, I asked her what was going through her mind. She said she was thinking about her father, who had died three years ago in his office in downtown Philadelphia.

We returned to the program office and reviewed the history of her father's death. And through the next several weeks we went over and over that segment of time, again facing the thoughts that led her to feeling out of control.

If you pay attention to what you are feeling when you're frightened and those feelings involve some loss, such as that of a beloved father, the fact is that you may be afraid of the feeling of sadness, not the feeling of fear.

If you discover as you do your travel work that when you get frightened you are actually feeling anger, resentment or guilt, do seek help. Turn to the last chapter of this book and check the treatment program listing in your area.

CHAPTER 11

Ways You Can Find the Strength Within Yourself to Overcome Agoraphobia

◇   ◇   ◇

Through the years of development of our center, we have been extremely fortunate to have attracted highly talented staff members who have made unique and important contributions. Each has brought a richness of background with which we have been able to strengthen our program.

Diane Coia and Alex Tullis come from a Gestalt therapy background, which places heavy emphasis upon the value of recognizing and expressing feelings. Diane and Alex have been a valuable source of learning for the rest of our staff and have agreed to share with you, in this chapter, some of the therapeutic exercises and the philosophy that they have brought to our program. You shall see in reading through the remainder of this chapter, which they have written, their understanding of human inner processes and how the imparting of skills for developing these inner resources has contributed immensely to the improvement of many of our clients.

◇   ◇   ◇

"In each life there are moments that leave an imprint in the mind and heart and heart and spirit, moments that transcend lesser times and enable a person to stretch beyond what he has known into a new realm of discovery. In such moments the person feels his feelings, he hears his own inner dialogue; he feels his footsteps and knows them to be his own."

—*Clark Moustakas,* THE CHILD'S DISCOVERY OF HIMSELF

In the preceding chapter you were presented with exercises to help you acquire the skills to cope with anxiety and with frightening situations. This chapter will provide you with additional exercises and techniques to use in your struggle to overcome agoraphobia. Overcoming fears takes great courage and perseverance, and the following exercises are designed to help you find those strengths within yourself.

The exercises are based on two simple but significant concepts. The first is that human beings are responsible for themselves, for their own lives: We are not victims of circumstance! The second concept is that the important question about human behavior and living is not Why? but How? Human beings are free and most certainly have the capacity for radical change.

All of the exercises and suggestions in this chapter evolved out of our many years of working with agoraphobics. Hundreds of clients have reported that one or more of these exercises proved helpful in their path toward recovery. There is no right way or wrong way in which to do these exercises. Some you will like and find very helpful, while others may not have as much impact on or meaning for you. That's okay! But we encourage you to try each of the exercises at least once, and preferably twice. Find those that are most helpful to you, and USE them.

If you have already begun practicing the techniques for controlling anxieties and symptoms that are offered in the previous chapter, you probably realize they do work. But for them to become almost second nature takes time, patience and much repetition. The same is true with the following exercises. It took a long time for your agoraphobic behavior and for your thoughts and feelings about it to develop, and it will take a fairly long time to erase those thoughts and feelings and then to replace them with new, more positive, nurturing ones.

To begin, we are going to ask you to write two letters, and we urge you to do this even if it feels silly or awkward. The first letter is from you to the agoraphobia that's troubling you, and the second is the agoraphobia's reply to you. There is no right or wrong way to write these letters, and you need never share them with anyone unless you wish to. You are unique and your letters will be, too.

EXAMPLES OF LETTERS TO AND FROM THE AGORAPHOBIA

These excerpts are from first letters composed by previous clients who decided to share them in the hope that this exercise would help others as much as it helped them. Let them be a guideline for the letters you will write.

Letters to the Agoraphobia:

"I feel very awkward writing to you. I've never thought of you as something real that could be addressed in this fashion. I don't really know quite what to say to you. That is, I don't know quite where to start. Right now, even as I write, I feel like crying. You cause so much pain in my life. For example, just yesterday my little girl asked me to go on a school outing with her, and I can't! That hurts me! And it makes me so angry at you!"

* * *

"I don't know why writing to you never occurred to me before. I have a feeling this is going to take *a lot* of letters from me. I AM FURIOUS AT YOU! You are causing so much damage in my life. I have been unable to work for years. I am still unable to finish college, and I have lost many friends. I just wish I could get rid of you once and for all!!"

* * *

"Why are you doing this to me? I've done nothing to deserve this. Won't you *please* leave me alone? You scare me. I'm so afraid of you I don't know what to do. I pray to God every night that He rid me of this terrible problem. I don't know what else to do. . . ."

Replies from the Agoraphobia's Point of View:

"I was not pleased to receive your letter. Up until now you've never given me any trouble. I've had a free rein with you. I've been in control. Are you trying to change that, change the balance? If you are, I want you to know you have a fight on your hands. I've been around a long time and I don't intend to give up all that easily."

* * *

"I received your letter and have read it several times and given it much thought. I had no idea how much distress I've been causing you. I am certainly open to discussion with you and perhaps something can be worked out."

* * *

"I have no idea what you are talking about! How dare you say that I, the agoraphobia, am your enemy. Don't you realize that I keep you safe? The world is a scary place and I protect you from venturing out in it . . ."

These excerpts make clear the fact that there are many different kinds of letters that can be written. In some the agoraphobic feels a certain defiance and some fight, while in others there is a sense of helplessness and defeat. In the letters from the agoraphobia, all sorts of different personalities are attributed to the disorder.

Take time now to write your two letters, then reread them and see if you can determine your position. Do you evidence some defiance or have you given up? Which of your two letters is the stronger? Does the agoraphobia have the upper hand, is it a stalemate or are you on top?

Hold onto these letters and try to think of beginning a regular correspondence with the agoraphobia. The tone and theme of your letters will change the more you get to know each other, and we can assure you that there is much to be learned from this exercise if you keep it ongoing.

CONVERSATIONS WITH THE AGORAPHOBIA

An excellent extension of the letter writing is to have actual spoken dialogues between you and the agoraphobia. We suggest that you sit in a room that is comfortable for you, a place where you feel safe. We then encourage you to imagine what your agoraphobia looks like, to locate it somewhere in the room and to engage it in conversation. In the beginning this, too, may seem strange or even silly. But the purpose of the exercise is to say out loud all the things you are thinking anyway; and the agoraphobia is again given the chance to talk back. These conversations can be scary, exciting and frustrating, but ultimately they are very rewarding. Again let us stress the fact that there is no right or wrong way of visualizing your agoraphobia or of conversing with it.

Some clients have described their agoraphobia as "prison bars" that keep them trapped, others have said it looks like some shapeless thing that simply holds them back. There are those who have described it as "a writhing mass of tentacles" or arms that are always pulling them back every time they try to do something. For still others the agoraphobia has been visualized as "a dark cloud" or as "the color black." The point is that your own individual picture of your agoraphobia is what will work for you in this exercise.

So find your comfortable safe place. Try to relax and not feel too awkward. (This may be hard at first.) Imagine what your agoraphobia looks like; remember, whatever images or pictures you get are okay. If you find yourself feeling anxious, breathe slowly from the diaphragm. It's understandable that you will be afraid when you meet the enemy head-on! Once you have an image or picture, take a few minutes to rehearse what you think you might like to say. When you are confident, start talking to your agoraphobia. You may want to shout at it: "Get out!" "Leave me alone!" "Stop bothering me!" Whatever comes to mind is perfectly okay for you to say. At first you may discover that you have no words at all, that to even address your agoraphobia is too much for you, too overwhelming. This is all right, too. But as you practice, *the words will come!*

EXAMPLES OF DIALOGUES CLIENTS HAVE HAD WITH AGORAPHOBIA

Client (in a tiny voice): "I don't like looking at you, any time. It scares me. I feel like even just talking to you . . . is . . . dangerous. . . . It might make me have a panic attack."

Agoraphobia: "What are you looking at me for? Do you think you can make me go away just by talking to me? Not a chance! I'm bigger than you and stronger. You can't fight me!"

Client (in a loud angry voice): "I HATE YOU! Leave me alone! I am sick and tired of you and of all the problems you cause me. I want to get rid of you forever!"

Agoraphobia: "Look who's over there talking big. You don't scare me, buster! You want a fight, I'll give you one. I just hope you're up to it!"

Client (in a calm, matter-of-fact voice): "We need to talk for a few minutes. At least, that's one of the things suggested in this book I'm reading. I feel kind of silly, but I'd like to make a bargain with you. What do you think we can work out? My husband wants me to accompany him to a business luncheon next month and I'd really like to be able to go. I'm willing to have you make me miserable if you'll leave me alone for that day!"

Agoraphobia: "No one's ever bargained with me before. I usually set all the rules. I'm intrigued, though. I'll need some time to think about it."

* * *

Lisa (age 17, who had to drop out of high school in her senior year): "Because of you I can't date. I can't go to movies, restaurants are scary, amusement parks or wherever the other kids go. What boyfriend would want me?"

Agoraphobia: "You just stay at home . . . you're different from the other kids your age. You don't belong out there. I will be sure to keep you in."

Lisa: "It's not fair—it's not fair! I'm scared. No one else is scared like I am. I don't understand."

Agoraphobia: "Stop trying to figure this out. . . . I have you where I want you."

Lisa: "No, you don't. I'll figure a way out of this. I'm too young to be like this. I don't want to be like this the rest of my life."

It is clear from this dialogue that Lisa was determined to fight this problem. The more she used this exercise and engaged in dialogue, the more she found the determination and motivation within herself.

As with the letter-writing exercises, the types of conversations you can have with your agoraphobia are infinite, and they will vary as you practice them. Usually a common theme emerges after several exchanges: It is the fight about who's going to win the war, you or the agoraphobia. Some days you will have the upper hand and some days it will be the agoraphobia. What is important about pushing yourself to have these conversations is that you will discover that *you can be less fearful* of the agoraphobia. A sense of personal power—an ability to fight back—does lie within you. It's just waiting for you to give it a chance to get out and engage the enemy. So do not delay; begin your conversations today.

FINDING THE PART OF YOU THAT IS NOT SCARED AND TALKING TO THE PART THAT IS

We'd like you to begin this exercise by thinking about a frightened child. If you came across a little girl or boy who was scared, your first instinct probably would be to recognize and acknowledge the fear, then to reassure and comfort the child. It is highly unlikely that you would ever scold or punish.

Unfortunately, scold and punish is precisely what most of our clients do to themselves when they are frightened. They are extremely harsh and severe with themselves and often batter themselves mentally.

The purpose of having a dialogue with the scared part of yourself is to turn your negative attitude into a positive, nurturing one. In practicing this kind of dialogue, you will come to learn that *you can be your own "safe person."* You will learn that whenever you need to travel—on a bus, train, in a car or even on foot for a short walk outside your home—there is always a safe person with you, not your husband, not your daughter, but *you.* Always present and willing to take care of the scared and anxious part of yourself is that safe person in you just waiting to help.

In beginning this exercise, many clients have found it useful to look at a childhood photograph of themselves as they practice talking to and taking care of the frightened child within them. Others prefer to start talking immediately to the scared adult in themselves. Once again we will offer some excerpts from the conversations of previous clients who shared them in the hope that they would prove helpful as you begin to try to change some of your negative thoughts and feelings about yourself. We know from experience that once you've practiced having these conversations they *will* prove beneficial.

Example 1.

Amy, a thirty-four-year-old housewife and mother of two preschool children, brought in a photograph of herself that had been taken when she was six years old. The picture showed a shy and frightened little girl.

Amy: "When I look at you I'm tempted to yell at you. I want to tell you to stand up straight, to stop looking so timid. You look like you're scared of your own shadow! I don't like looking at you. I know I'm supposed to try to turn things around by trying to take care of you. But right now that seems almost impossible. I feel like shaking you!"

When she was asked what the little girl in the photo might say back to her, Amy was silent for a while, looking perplexed. Then, as she stared at the photo, she saw herself as that child. She grew sad as she began to speak.

Amy (as the little girl she was): "Please don't shake me! I'm scared! I don't know what to do! I'm so frightened! What if I pass out or have a heart attack? How can you help me?"

We encouraged Amy to try to respond to the scared little girl in a more positive fashion, even if it felt artificial. Here's an excerpt of that response.

Amy: "What's the matter? Can I help you? Come over here. There's nothing to be afraid of. . . . This is ridiculous. I can't do it! This isn't going to help me!"

Eventually, after a good deal of practice, these conversations with the scared part of herself empowered Amy with the ability to stop the harsh and critical way she treated herself. She developed a more nurturing attitude to herself.

Example 2.

Jack, a forty-two-year-old divorced business executive, conjured up an image of the part of himself that was scared.

Then he spoke in a stern voice:

Jack: "What's the matter with you? Get out there! Toughen up! You've always been too damn sensitive, a big crybaby. I've had enough of you!"

At this point Jack abruptly stopped talking, looking almost shocked. When we asked him what was happening, he said, "That's exactly how my father talked to me when I was growing up. Always scolding, always threatening me. I don't believe it! That's precisely what I'm doing to myself, too, isn't it?"

By talking to the scared part of himself, Jack suddenly became aware of the old tapes in his mind and where they came from. Many people are surprised by such revelations during this exercise. Don't be afraid or alarmed if suddenly awarenesses occur to you. Recognizing negative ways of thinking about oneself and where and how we got them is a key step in the process of replacing them with more positive, nurturing ones.

Example 3.

Phyllis was quite open to change and determined to push herself, as became apparent in her initial words to the scared little girl in her.

Phyllis (a twenty-eight-year-old single social worker): "Hello, there. I can see that you are very frightened. I'd like to be able to take care of you, but I'm afraid I don't know how. I'd like to try, but you're going to have to be very patient with me. This is all so new. I'm just as scared as you are. I'm willing to give it a try if you are. Are you?"

Take time now and start some dialogue with the scared part of you. You may choose the scared adult in yourself, and you may choose the scared child. You may switch back and forth. Whatever is easiest for you is fine. Try to notice what your feelings are as you do this exercise. Is it difficult for you to be positive and encouraging with the frightened part of you? Would you rather not deal with that area of yourself at all? Does seeing this part of you make you angry? sad? scared? Or does it make you just a little bit excited and optimistic? It is excitement and optimism we're looking for, and they are sure to emerge with persistent practice.

WHO AM I UNDERNEATH MY AGORAPHOBIA?

Many clients have found this exercise puzzling initially, but have found it very rewarding in the long run.

Start by giving some thought to the question, "Who am I underneath my agoraphobia?" You may have probably come to identify yourself as someone who is scared of your symptoms, avoidant, unable to travel, and overwhelmed by agoraphobia. But apart from all that, who are you? What attributes do you possess that have nothing to do with agoraphobia? Give this a lot of thought and try to make a list of ten positive statements about yourself, not about you the agoraphobic. If you feel positive about something, jot it down. Try not to worry about what anyone else would think; if it's something you feel good about that's what's important. Nothing is insignificant! Are you a good cook? How's your gardening? Crocheting? Needlepoint? Are you a good listener? Are you pleasant with other people? Good with animals? Do you paint? Sculpt? Sing? How are you with children? Do you work with wood? Repair small appliances? Write letters? What do you like about yourself? Start your list of attributes. Many of you will be surprised to discover that you have more than ten positive statements to make about yourselves; extend your list.

BECOMING AWARE OF YOUR FEELINGS

This exercise is about your feelings; it is about getting in touch with the anger, sadness and joy in your life. Many agoraphobics are so preoccupied with fear that they become unaware of their other emotions and feelings. They learn to be afraid instead of being mad, sad or glad. As uncomfortable as agoraphobic symptoms are, many of you will choose them over the emotions you are really feeling. Sometimes you think, "If I allow myself to feel my sadness I'll never stop crying." Or, "If I give in to my anger there could be real trouble!"

Sometimes we can *feel* our feelings but cannot express them. Sometimes we are not even aware of what we are feeling. Sometimes we're feeling something when we should be feeling something else; we might feel guilty instead of angry, or angry instead of sad. Sometimes our feelings are responses to the present and other times they're "old" feelings from childhood—angers, hurts, frustrations, sadnesses and old fears that we never really dealt with.

This exercise can be done in two ways. In the first, simply take time to think about anger, sadness and joy. Which of those feelings is the easiest for you to experience? Which is the most difficult? Which is the scariest? Which feelings stem from the present? Which are from the past? How do you allow yourself your feelings? How do you cut them off? Ask yourself this important question: Do you ever replace feelings, unconsciously, with anxiety and panic?

In the second approach to this exercise on feelings we want you either to have a conversation with or write letters to the anger, sadness and joy in yourself. That's one conversation or one letter each to the mad you, the sad you, the glad you and the scared you. Become acquainted with each. In the earlier exercise, "Who am I underneath my agoraphobia?" you looked at who you were apart from being agoraphobic. The purpose of this exercise is to examine what you feel apart from feeling scared, who you are as a feeling person.

Another valuable step in this exercise is to give some thought to these questions: When and how did you learn to feel? Can you remember when you stopped feeling? Whom were you with at that time? Who taught you that it was *not* okay to feel?

FACING THE PANIC—RECLAIMING YOUR POWER

Throughout this book we refer to the courage you'll need in the struggle to overcome your fears and the symptoms of your agoraphobia. Among the hardest of these struggles is dealing with the panic attack. Learning how to face the panic attack is one of the major ways in which *you reclaim your power*.

We are well aware of what we are asking when we say it is crucial that you learn to face the panic, even to invite it, and challenge it. Clients have described this prospect as "Going to my death!" "The most terrifying thing I've ever had to do!" "Something I'll *never* be able to do!"

Thankfully, though, as clients affirm, facing panic is never quite as bad as you imagine it to be, for panic arrives, rises, peaks and then passes. In a sense the panic attack is your number-one enemy, and your choices are to run from it forever or to pluck up your courage and face it! There is a power struggle going on. Running from panic gives it power and strength; facing it returns the balance of power to you.

Those of you who have been practicing the anxiety management techniques presented in the preceding chapters already know that you can achieve some control over your symptoms and your anxiety. This is also true for panic attacks. You *will* reach the point where they won't be so terrifying. Of course they will never feel good, but they will be manageable. You do have the wherewithal to deal with them.

This exercise is one that many clients have found helpful in mustering the courage to face the panic. Make a list of the losses you've suffered as a result of agoraphobia—not the obvious ones like riding in public transportation or driving your car, but the more subtle losses stemming from your immobility.

Are you a music lover who can no longer go see your favorite performers? Are you a religious person who is often unable to attend church, or to stay through the service? Are you a bright person who can't finish high school or college? Has your immobility forced you to give up a promising career? Are there beloved relatives that you can't visit anymore?

Try to make a list of at least ten of the more subtle losses you've suffered due to agoraphobia. The purpose of this exercise is not to sadden or depress you but to provide you with a personal list of things you miss. You can then use this list to encourage and motivate yourself. The items on the list will inspire you on those days when it seems your panic might get the better of you despite all your work.

SAFE PERSONS, SAFETY KITS AND TACTICS

Many agoraphobics have strong fears about being alone, because they're afraid they won't be able to take care of themselves if they have a panic attack. This is perfectly understandable. Anyone who has ever experienced panic knows that the horrible feeling that you are going to die or lose control is terrifying. A natural response to this dread is to try to have people around you whom you've come to regard as safe. A safe person is most often a parent, a child, a sibling or a close personal friend. For some clients a dog can offer some of the comfort of a "safe person."

You all know it doesn't make sense that this so-called safe person could be of real aid, but somehow you feel safer and are able to do more things in the company of that person than you can alone.

Many agoraphobics also put together what we call safety kits that they feel will help them get through a panic attack and therefore make travel somewhat more bearable. Typical safety-kit items would include medications and something to drink, such as water, soda or alcohol; a list of phone numbers of safe persons, doctors or therapists; and occasionally a paper bag that can be placed loosely over the nose and mouth to prevent hyperventilation; and a good-luck charm or rosary beads.

We'd like you to take some time now and give some thought to your safe people and to the items that fill your safety kit. List them in their order of importance in terms of how much "safety" they give you. Once your list is complete, try to imagine which items you would be willing to do without. You can begin to decrease the items on your safety list by eliminating those at the bottom of the list.

As an offshoot of their safe persons and safety kits, numerous agoraphobics also develop safety tactics to use when they go out. They note the location of hospitals along routes of travel as well as the availability of public facilities, telephones, highway exits and public transportation stops. In addition many check weather conditions and traffic reports before venturing out. Think about your various tactics and add them to your list of safe people and safe items; then see which tactics you might be willing to stop using.

The purpose of this exercise is not to take away your sources of safety. The idea is to reevaluate what you think helps you and to begin to see that you can be your own safe person without all of the things that you imagined were keeping you "safe." We can't stress enough the fact that part of your recovery depends on your becoming aware that *you* are your best source of safety. Each of us has to learn to rely on ourselves as opposed to things or objects or other people. Wherever you are, you have the resources within yourself to be safe.

We know that asking you to give up some of your individual safety sources may seem counterproductive. But removing some of the safety conditions you've assembled is critical to your reclaiming your own sense of control and independence.

HUGGING AND COMFORTING YOURSELF

This is another exercise that has helped clients find buried strengths within themselves. This one is simple. The most common human response to a frightened individual is to acknowledge his fears, and then to comfort him with gentle words, gentle touches or hugs that reassure him that you are there for him. In this exercise we're asking you to do unto yourself as you would do unto others. Give yourself the same comfort and support. Realize that you have the resources for doing this. If you would comfort a frightened friend by gently stroking his or her hand, why can't you hold your own hand when you feel a little frightened? You can also give yourself words of reassurance and comfort, either silently or aloud if you happen to be alone. You can even give yourself a hug. Just try it. Doesn't that feel good? If you feel silly, do it again and try to feel that part of you underneath the silliness that knows it feels good.

Contact with your own body will lessen your fear of aloneness and will help you learn to be your own safe person. Someone is there for you, and that someone is you. We know that many of you are very good at being supportive of others. There is no reason why you should not offer the same comfort to yourselves.

This will take a lot of practice. Being self-supportive and self-nurturing has not been a way of life for most agoraphobics. If this exercise in self-support and self-comfort seems difficult for you as an adult, you may find it helpful to imagine yourself as a scared child (see exercise, pp. 200, 201) and to offer your comfort to that vulnerable person. It is highly unlikely that you would turn away from a child who is frightened. Please try to give that same care and concern to yourself.

Take time now to make a list of ways you can begin to take better care of yourself, to give yourself comfort when you need it. Once again, there are no right or wrong ways. It is a real acknowledgment of yourself to recognize what it is that you like. Perhaps ordering a bouquet of fresh flowers, taking a hot bubble bath, listening to a favorite piece of music, reading a poem that you enjoy, buying a new blouse or a tie. Whatever appears on your list is important if it is something that will give you pleasure and a sense of self-caring.

HOW WILL YOU DEFEAT YOURSELF?

The overall purpose of this chapter has been to provide you with an armory of tools that have helped other agoraphobics find and use their inner strengths to fuel them to recovery. We expect that much of what we have asked of you has challenged you to think in new ways. This final exercise may be the most challenging of all: We ask you to ponder the question, How will you defeat yourself?

Many of you will react to this question with dismay, disbelief and perhaps even indignation. But working with clients over the years has shown us that motivation, determination and all of the best intentions are not always easy to maintain. Methods of maintaining that motivation and determination are what we are after in this exercise.

We would like you to make a list of ways in which you might undermine yourselves as you strive to recover. We are not doubting your desire to overcome agoraphobia, but in fairness to you we must make you aware of unintentional self-defeating attitudes that tend to crop up. Overcoming agoraphobia is difficult. For example, there will be days when practice will seem too difficult because you feel too tired or you are not well enough physically (a headache, an upset stomach, a heavy cold, menstrual cramps, are common causes for excusing oneself from practice or travel). There will be days when the weather seems too hot or too cold or too wet. All of these subtle avoidances can undermine your progress, so be aware of excuses you might be making.

Another common avoidance technique is to convince yourself that the practice is not effective. Watch out if you find yourself saying: "This isn't working, it's useless" or "This may work for everyone else, but I'm different" or "I'm worse than others, this won't help me."

You have an idea of the kind of undermining frequently practiced by other agoraphobics. Now make up your list. How are you going to defeat yourself, undermine your progress, set yourself back? When you have at least five items on your list, jot them down on one side of a sheet of paper and draw a line down the middle. Then go back and figure out a way to reverse each of your self-defeating statements. Consider the following lists as an example:

SELF–DEFEATING	SELF–SUPPORTING
I'm worse than anyone else with agoraphobia.	I am really just one of many, and I deserve to be better, too.
I can't do this. I'm too scared.	Yes, I know this is scary. But I also know that if I really try I can do this and I'll take care of myself.
It's too hot to do *anything* (practice, venture out) today.	I know weather conditions really have nothing to do with it. Let's go ahead anyway.
I feel sick this morning. My stomach is upset.	I'm learning to understand that this queasiness is just a symptom and doesn't mean I can't practice or travel.
I'm just too busy today. I'll do it tomorrow.	I can do it anyway.
	Stop avoiding. Nothing is more important than getting over agoraphobia.

It was probably easy for you to do the first column and very difficult to do the second column because that kind of positive thinking is foreign to your experience. With practice you will develop positive and optimistic attitudes while also creating a supportive and caring relationship toward yourself.

It is important to remember that you have learned to think, feel and act like an agoraphobic. Anything that is learned can be unlearned, and those self-destructive messages you've been sending yourself can be replaced by new messages. This chapter is designed to help you begin to replace those old habits with new nurturing ones.

But any new behavior requires practice and perseverance. If you were studying a foreign language or learning to play a musical instrument you would have to go over again and again the new words and phrases or the notes and scales you were studying. Overcoming agoraphobia takes just as much patience and practice or more. But you do have it in you to seize control of your existence.

To help you remember to practice we suggest that you make several lists of the exercises and place them on your refrigerator, on your bathroom mirror, on your bedroom mirror and anywhere else that you think will help remind you to practice.

Include the following in your list:

1. Letter to and from my agoraphobia.
2. Conversations with my agoraphobia.
3. Dialogue between the part of me that wants to get better and the part of me that's scared.
4. Who am I underneath the agoraphobia?
5. Becoming aware of my feelings. Or "mad, sad, glad, scared."
6. Facing the panic.
7. Safe persons, safety kits and tactics.
8. Hugging and comforting myself.
9. How will I defeat myself?

In conclusion, we encourage you to ask yourself how important it is for you to overcome agoraphobia. Are you willing to invest an hour or so each day to practice the exercises and suggestions presented in this chapter? You have lived with your fears for a long time. It will be difficult to overcome them, but these exercises do help, as hundreds of former clients can attest. You too can have mobility; you, too, can be free from symptoms and panic. As one agoraphobic client used to tell herself as she pushed toward recovery, "Fear it! Feel it! *Do it!*"

And of course you may not be able to follow through on your own—that is completely understandable. You may just be too debilitated by anxiety and depression to give it the needed energy and concentration, or you may not yet have enough trust in this book or yourself to believe that what you do can make a difference. No doubt it will be much easier for you if you can get outside help, so use the list of resources at the back of this book to find a program that will help you structure what needs to be done. The sooner you begin the sooner you will be enjoying life again.

Beware of Simple Solutions—as Well as Caffeine and Sugar

No one has ever been able to discover a physiological cause for agoraphobia. Many people have tried, but none has succeeded. Yet each new so-called physiological cause of agoraphobia gets a lot of press coverage, and agoraphobics, their friends and families get excited about the prospects of a seemingly simple cure for the disorder. After all, if the problem is physiological in origin, then surely it can be treated medically.

The fact is that we Westerners have been conditioned to believe that modern medical science is the solution to *all* problems, and we readily accept any explanations and solutions that are cloaked in physiological terms. This acceptance not only removes us from responsibility for the problem and hence guilt, but it provides seemingly easy answers without forcing us to have a hard look at how we lead our lives or pressing us to make difficult changes.

But medical science has never offered any solutions for such psychological problems as phobias. Solutions to these problems have come from an understanding and application of the psychological phenomenon related to the acquisition and reversal of the learned fear and from completing what is essentially an incompleted developmental stage. These solutions require the active participation of the person seeking relief from the phobia. However, there are sometimes complicating physiological factors.

Hypoglycemia results from an imbalance between sugar and insulin in the bloodstream. Much of the food we eat is converted to a sugar substance for utilization by the body and when the system is flooded with too much sugar, insulin is produced by the body to neutralize it. When these two substances are in balance all is well. But when there is too much sugar or insulin, symptoms appear. Excess sugar leads to lethargy and sleepiness; excess insulin precipitates anxiety-like symptoms such as agitation, trembling and fearfulness. This imbalance is more pronounced in those who suffer from hypoglycemia, and most of the time the condition is caused not by disease but by poor eating habits. For example, if you skip breakfast and get by on a cup or two of coffee and perhaps something sweet like a doughnut or pastry, then lunch on a white-bread sandwich with a cola drink and in the evening eat a big dinner with dessert and coffee, then you are very likely to have periods in which your bloodstream is overladen with insulin. At those times you will have anxiety symptoms.

By contrast, when protein and complex carbohydrates are consumed, the process of conversion to sugar is slower and sustained over a longer period of time. This allows the body to adjust insulin output more slowly, and insulin dominance does not occur.

About ten years ago it was postulated that hypoglycemia was a major cause of the panic episodes that lead to agoraphobia. This has been demonstrated to be untrue. However, it is quite possible that hypoglycemic episodes complicate agoraphobia and make it more difficult to overcome since the anxiety symptoms of a hypoglycemic episode will not be much affected by coping skills and will continue to occur so long as eating habits are poor. Therefore it is important to correct the problem if it exists. If when feeling panicked you feel much better right after you eat, and if your panics seem to occur at the same time each day, usually late afternoon, then you may have hypogly-cemia. In any case, if you have not recently been evaluated medically you should definitely do so because there are sev-eral diseases that have similar symptoms to agoraphobia.

Mitral valve prolapse (MVP) was also postulated as a cause of agoraphobia. MVP is a common condition regarded by most physicians as benign. It describes the tendency of one of the heart valves that controls the flow of blood through the heart to balloon when closed under the pressure of the blood flow, much as a balloon stretches when filled with water. Usually MVP is not noticed, but sometimes it pro-duces a slight sensation of discomfort in the chest. The speculation that mitral valve prolapse may be involved in agoraphobia arose from early studies suggesting that the in-cidence of MVP was higher among agoraphobics than in the population at large. More recent studies have found no higher incidence.

It may be that once agoraphobia has developed, the chest sensations felt by some people with MVP can add another discomfort that sometimes frightens agoraphobics who are already sensitized to body sensations. Nevertheless it has been shown that those agoraphobics with MVP are not dif-ferent from other agoraphobics in their degree of distress or in their response to treatment. People with untreated MVP get over agoraphobia as readily as those who do not have MVP.

In the last few years inner ear disorders (IED) have been thought to cause agoraphobia. Such problems can produce dizziness, difficulty with balance, noises in the ear and nau-sea. One uncontrolled study reported inner-ear disorders in a surprisingly high number of agoraphobics. But as yet there have been no controlled studies to determine if there is a higher incidence of IED among agoraphobics than among the general population. And these studies are difficult to administer accurately because agoraphobics tend to hyper-ventilate and to experience dizziness; thus the symptoms of their agoraphobia may be recorded as IED.

There are physiological disorders that can cause anxiety symptoms and panic-like episodes, and agoraphobics will have their share of such disorders independently of agoraphobia itself. Dr. Diane Chambless of the American University in Washington, D.C., reports the treatment of a man who developed agoraphobia after a series of seizures related to a brain dysfunction. A physician successfully treated the seizure disorder, but the agoraphobia fears and avoidance remained. These aspects often take on a life of their own even though the problem that precipitated them has been resolved. But it is clear that the man's ultimate successful treatment for agoraphobia would have been seriously hindered if the physiological disease had not been successfully treated.

Given the consistency of psychological findings and the success of purely psychologically based treatment of agoraphobia over the years, it is most unlikely that any physiological disease will prove to be causative for the great majority of agoraphobics.

Physiological problems can, however, add to an agoraphobic's discomforting body sensations and fears. Such problems can result from the food one eats and perhaps from vitamin and mineral deficiencies, and from allergies.

Studies have demonstrated that caffeine increases the anxiety level of someone who is already anxious, so agoraphobics should avoid all foods containing caffeine. It is also clear that caffeine produces body sensations that many agoraphobics fear, such as rapid heartbeat, agitation and trembling. Yet most agoraphobics love caffeine and have a large sweet tooth. Asked about their eating habits they frequently reply that they're not hungry in the morning. They typically start the day with a cup or two of coffee laced with sugar, and a doughnut or sweet roll. This breakfast, they say, gives them a kind of "up" feeling for a while, but the "rush" rapidly falls away, leaving them feeling "down." They try to retrieve the "up" feeling with another cup of coffee or a caffeinated soft drink, some cookies or a candy bar; the second rush is followed by a second down period that leaves them shaky and symptomatic. Then the craving for sugar and/or caffeine resumes.

"It's a vicious cycle," says Laraine Abbey, R.N., M.S., an orthomolecular nutritionist and clinical ecologist in East Windsor, New Jersey, who has treated more than 350 agoraphobics since 1977. "Caffeine stimulates adrenaline that helps in handling stress and releases hormones that help regulate blood sugar and blood pressure. But if the adrenal glands are repeatedly stimulated they get tired; then when stress occurs, they no longer work as efficiently, and blood sugar and blood pressure may drop precipitously. A lot of the agoraphobics I've seen have low blood pressure and low blood sugar. So I recommend that all agoraphobics eliminate sugar and caffeine from their diets immediately.

"I had one woman in Ohio who was housebound from panic attacks and paranoid," Ms. Abbey says. "She was drinking ten cups of coffee daily. I had her cut out all caffeine: A week later she was panic-free and fully mobile."

Laraine Abbey has produced a number of such dramatic recoveries among agoraphobics with nutritional biochemical guidance. Yet she acknowledges the possibility that many agoraphobics may also require psychological counseling to become panic-free and fully mobile. She asks her clients to tell her everything they eat and drink daily.

The typical diet of an agoraphobic client is loaded with caffeine, sugar and white flour, which is full of chemicals and devoid of the bran and germ that contain most of the nutrients of the grain. Here is one woman's daily diet: 8 A.M., tea with milk and sugar; 10 A.M., tea with milk and sugar; 12:30 P.M., ham on white with a Coke; 2 P.M., tea with milk and sugar; 3:30 P.M., a candy bar; 6:30 P.M., baked macaroni and cheese, tomatoes, fish sticks, a glass of milk; 8 P.M., pretzels and a Coke; 10 P.M., hot milk with Ovaltine.

Caffeine, sugar and white flour were eliminated from the diet, and eight weeks later the woman reported that she'd had only one panic attack, had fewer headaches, less nasal stuffiness and her backaches were gone. "Her energy level was worse initially," Ms. Abbey says, "but I often see this in people in bad shape who cut out the caffeine and sugar that had been propping them up. The client told me, 'I definitely see a relationship between anxiety and caffeine.' She had rated her anxiety—on a scale of 10 as high—at 7 on presenting, and now she was a 2. Her mobility at the start was a 6, now it was a 1 when accompanied, about a 3 when unaccompanied. Three months later—all the while continuing her work in the Temple program—she had no panics and full mobility."

The agoraphobics we have treated benefit from giving up caffeine, sugar, cigarettes and all foods containing white flour.

VITAMIN DEFICIENCIES AMONG AGORAPHOBICS

Long-term dietary abuses can result in defective enzyme activity. Enzymes are activated by vitamins. Therefore Ms. Abbey tests her clients for defective cellular vitamin metabolism. She reports that 70 percent of the agoraphobics she has seen have deficient intra-cellular levels of Vitamin B6 and B1 (thiamine); they have difficulty assimilating the Bs. Vitamin B6 is used to treat premenstrual syndrome (PMS), suffered by many agoraphobic women. B6 plays an important role in the nervous system in that it is neeeded to synthesize many hormones and most neurotransmitters that deliver impulses from one nerve cell to another. This activity affects the way one feels and behaves as well as the way organs function. Thus at a time when the body's demand for B6 is highest, there is not enough available and women feel worse. Megavitamin ingestion of B6 usually takes care of this cell deficiency. Since excess vitamins and minerals may be harmful, any megavitamin regimen should be undertaken only with expert guidance.

Many agoraphobics are allergic to certain kinds of food. On the long list of common food-allergy symptoms compiled by Dr. William G. Crook in his book *Tracking Down Hidden Food Allergy* are faintness, dizziness, palpitations, increased heart rate, chronic fatigue, depression, irritability, anxiety and panic attacks.

"I've had people with agoraphobia who were allergic to milk, wheat, potatoes, mushrooms, squash, sugar, and, of course, caffeine," Ms. Abbey says. "They actually became addicted to those foods and craved them because they temporarily felt better after ingesting them." Of course, once the craving was satisfied and the foods digested, the allergy symptoms appeared.

In recent years Ms. Abbey has treated many agoraphobic women for a condition known as chronic polysystemic Candidiasis, a chronic condition resulting from an overgrowth of yeast in the body and often associated with frequent vaginal infection in women. Yeast weakens the immune system and, according to Ms. Abbey, leads women to exhibit such symptoms as anxiety, depression and tension. Americans take a lot of antibiotics these days and antibiotics kill off the bacteria that normally control the growth of yeast. But Ms. Abbey says that a greater contributor to the growth of yeast that produces vaginal infections in agoraphobics is the high-carbohydrate junk-food diets they eat. "If you want to grow yeast in a culture you feed it sugar," she says. "I treat people with vaginal infections by taking them off sugar and putting them on a low-carbohydrate diet, very similar to the way I treat a person with hypoglycemia."

A case study that Ms. Abbey reported in *The Journal of Orthomolecular Psychiatry* reveals how a nutritional-biochemical approach to agoraphobia can dramatically reduce symptomology in some clients:

On December 17, 1979, a thirty-year-old agoraphobic woman I'll call Lisa, somewhat overweight at 130 pounds, 5′2″, presented with daily headaches, dizziness, fatigue, chest pains and numbness in her left arm. She suffered episodes of "visual blurring," as well as "shakes" (which she referred to as seizures), and stated that rapid movements would provoke them.

Neurological, cardiac and psychiatric evaluations confirmed severe anxiety and agoraphobia. Lisa was in weekly treatment with a psychiatrist for her panic attacks and phobic condition. According to her brother, Lisa's symptoms were so severe that he often carried her into and out of her psychiatrist's office.

In addition to psychological symptoms, Lisa suffered periodontal problems (bleeding and receding gums), muscle spasms, skin problems, and poor hair quality. Her self-image was poor. Her response to the systems-review question "Do you like yourself?" was "No, I always feel ugly and sick."

A detailed three-day record of Lisa's food intake revealed very poor nutritional practices: large-scale consumption of foods high in sugar, fat, salt and caffeine. She was also a smoker.

Nutritional testing established a functional deficiency of vitamins B1 and B6. Hair analysis demonstrated low zinc, chromium and iron. Lisa was also found to be allergic to mushrooms, rice, rye, fructose, brussels sprouts and tobacco, and to have a slight reaction to most foods tested.

Lisa was placed on a nutritional regimen which included a rotational diet (no food repeated more than once in five days). All refined carbohydrates were eliminated, and additives, preservatives and chemicals were avoided as much as possible.

Lisa's nutrition program included vitamins B1, B6, C and E, and the minerals zinc, iron, magnesium and calcium. She was given special low-allergy vitamin brands free of soy, yeast, wheat and corn lactose.

After three months Lisa had improved dramatically. Visual blurring and focusing difficulties were gone, as were her frequent ear infections. Her periodontal symptoms were far less severe. She no longer had muscle spasms, persistent nasal stuffiness, chest pain, headaches, dizziness, light-headedness, trembling hands, numbness or tingling in her extremities. The shakes were gone. Sluggishness and fatigue had disappeared.

Lisa was retested and found to have normal functional adequacy of B1 and B6.

Lisa's phobias and anxiety were almost gone. She still suffered occasional mild episodes in shopping malls or cars. She evaluated herself as 95 percent improved, and her self-image improved right along with the decline in her symptoms.

Ms. Abbey makes one final point about agoraphobics who have impaired thiamine levels. When they consume a great deal of caffeine they often become hypersensitive to their own adrenaline. "A thiamine-impaired agoraphobic who drinks coffee will suffer such physical symptoms as tremblings and speeded-up heartbeat as a reaction to the adrenaline; and that in turn will reinforce the fear of the anxiety. It's almost like being allergic to your own adrenaline."

If you suffer from agoraphobia, it should be apparent by now that it pays large dividends to give up all caffeine and high-carbohydrate junk food in your diet. *Because of the complexity of vitamin and mineral deficiencies as well as food allergies, it is strongly recommended that you do not attempt to self-treat these problems,* but instead seek the help of a knowledgeable professional.

Although there have not yet been any controlled studies to assess scientifically the usefulness of the nutritional approach to the treatment of agoraphobia, our clinical observations are that such an approach combined with psychological treatment seems to be a useful adjunct for some agoraphobics.

For further information about nutritional counseling, please write to Laraine C. Abbey, Health Extension Services, Warren Plaza West, Route 130, East Windsor, New Jersey 08520, enclosing a stamped, self-addressed envelope.

CHAPTER 13

Scientific Evaluation: Sorting Out the Necessary Elements for Effective Treatment

The importance of evaluating treatment programs scientifically cannot be over-emphasized. It has become clear to me that effectiveness is impossible to determine through subjective evaluation. Many times when shown new data on our program at Temple, I have said, "But that can't be right! I know that we are doing better than that. Why, look at how well people did in the last Intensive Program, and the people I have worked with over the years have done better than that!" Such subjectivity is a common error which we all must constantly work to overcome.

We make that error because we tend to remember selectively. That is, those events which support our beliefs are much more likely to be remembered than those that don't. Thus the clients who have done well add more weight to our recollection than the ones who haven't and we remember their successful episodes more than the unsuccessful, so we overestimate progress for most. In addition, we are more influenced by recent experiences, particularly when they are successful ones, than by distant ones. The result is that people doing well now will overshadow less successful, more distant experiences.

Objective data collected in a scientifically sound way help

us to see what is really going on, and this leads to making sound decisions about innovation. For example, through our ongoing evaluation we were able to see that our earlier program, in which we made little effort to help people get off some drugs early in treatment, had problems. People on these drugs were not showing the kind of session-to-session drop in anxiety after exposure to feared places that those people not taking them were achieving. This awareness, which we could not have obtained without systematic data collection, led us to put much heavier emphasis on tapering off these medications very early in treatment.

Apart from the study of drugs which is covered in Chapter Nine, there have been a very large number of published studies of exposure therapies and a few published studies on the outcome of multidimensional treatment, including two from our Agoraphobia and Anxiety Program.

REDUCING SYMPTOMS WITH A BEHAVIOR THERAPY THAT WORKS— EXPOSURE THERAPY

The advent of exposure therapy has been widely regarded as a breakthrough for agoraphobia, for it was the first to be scientifically demonstrated as effective in the reduction of symptoms. Therapy based on exposure has been studied in scores of well-controlled studies, and the findings are consistent. The therapy is most often carried out in departments of psychology, as research, in university settings, and essentially consists of taking people out into situations that are feared and avoided. Measures used in order to determine the effectiveness of the treatment include changes in physical reactions, such as heart rate in the feared situations; behavioral measures, such as determining how far the agoraphobic person can walk toward a feared place such as a store a mile away from home; and the person's report of amount of fear experienced while performing the excursions into previously avoided places.

After such treatment some 65 percent of clients show at least a 50-percent improvement in overcoming phobic avoidance to three to five targeted situations, such as walking a certain distance from home, or riding a bus or shopping, and an improvement of about 35 percent when all situations are considered. In the few studies measuring change in panic, exposure therapy also leads to a significant reduction in the frequency of panics. On the whole about 75 percent of those who finish exposure treatments show some improvement. One strikingly consistent positive finding is that with exposure therapy, there is very little relapse with up to nine years of follow-up inquiries by the investigators.

Keep in mind that these are averages and that some of these people were restored to nearly normal life with this very short treatment, which comprises usually ten to twenty sessions. The advantages, in addition to brevity, are that it is inexpensive and readily available at many university psychology departments where there are likely to be behaviorally trained clinicians. Those who are doing research in agoraphobia often provide treatment for very little or no cost.

On the negative side, however, about one in five people who apply for this kind of treatment either do not begin therapy or drop out before finishing. It has been estimated that only about 2 percent experience complete reversals of agoraphobic symptoms by the end of treatment, while at the end of four years after treatment one study found only about five in one hundred people completely free of symptoms.

COMBINING OTHER THERAPIES WITH EXPOSURE THERAPY GETS BETTER RESULTS

While exposure therapy is necessary and sometimes even sufficient for effective treatment, clearly more is required for maximum benefit in most cases. Recent research supports this assumption.

Drs. Bruce Arnow, C. Barr Taylor, W. Stewart Agras and Michael J. Telch at Stanford University reported in a controlled study that when the usual exposure therapy was combined with behavioral marriage therapy, the resulting changes in agoraphobic symptoms were greater than those in a group of agoraphobic people who received only exposure treatment.

At the Temple program, we combine behavior therapy with psychotherapy, Gestalt therapy and family therapy and have found this to be a much more effective approach than any others reported. In 1985 we completed a study of thirty-five of our clients six months after they began treatment in two-week Intensive Treatment Programs. Ten of these clients were completely free of their avoidance and panic symptoms and were no longer agoraphobic; thirty showed between 25 percent and 100 percent improvement in both of these symptoms, and twenty reported that they no longer experienced panic. Also, six months after completing the two-week intensive treatment only six of the clients continued to require work on avoidance and fear of places. Sixteen were still in psychotherapy; most were working on problems other than agoraphobia, such as difficulties in relationships, self-esteem and expressiveness. These clients had been severely avoidant and disturbed by their phobias and were not taking any medications that might be considered antipanic drugs. (About 25 percent of the clients who enter our program are taking such drugs when they apply to the program and begin treatment while taking them.)

The results of this study indicate that an integrated approach to the treatment of agoraphobia produces improvement over a broad range of measures of functioning. Six months after the Intensive, clients, all of whom were drug free, indicated, on the average, that their phobies were only a bit more than mildly disturbing. Eighty-six percent were improved 25 percent or more on measures of avoidance and panic. The fact that a little over six months after beginning treatment *64 percent reported no panic attacks at all and 29 percent were in the normal range on avoidance when alone as well as being free of panic* is particularly striking when juxtaposed with the claims by biologically oriented professionals that panic attacks *must* be controlled by medication. And our program is not the only one that has demonstrated over the years that panic among agoraphobics can be reduced significantly with psychosocial treatment.

Also notable is the low dropout rate for the Intensive Treatment Program. So far we have analyzed data on the first 158 clients who entered the Intensive Program. Only three (2%) have withdrawn, compared with a dropout rate of some 12 percent for exposure programs and up to 40 percent for those who are treated with medication. The momentum, the support, the involvement of family members and the psychotherapeutic work involved in the Intensive Program at Temple seem to overcome the dropout factor.

In contrast to other programs in which clients with higher levels of pre-treatment depression, trait anxiety, social anxiety and marital dissatisfaction have been reported less likely to improve, these factors have not thwarted improvement among our clients.

While these results are impressive compared to those reported anywhere else, there are still improvements to be made. That is why we are constantly using our research data to reevaluate and upgrade our program.

Our work in this area began almost two decades ago, before there were any agoraphobia treatment centers. Though we take pride in our progress, we still have a long way to go before we can rest assured that all that can be done has been done. While it may never be possible that everyone who suffers from agoraphobia improves 100 percent, that is the goal toward which all our work is aimed.

A Guide to Treatment Programs for Agoraphobia

ABOUT THIS DIRECTORY

Many of the treatment centers, self-help groups and newsletters listed herein have been drawn from a list maintained by the Temple Agoraphobia and Anxiety Program in Bala Cynwyd, Pennsylvania. Others have been obtained in response to a mailing to professional members of the Phobia Society of America (PSA), and in response to ads placed in professional publications.

All treatment centers were asked to fill out a form describing their programs. From this information we chose to list those centers that appear to offer a program that includes at least the minimal elements of what is considered by most phobia specialists to be treatment of choice.

While we have made an effort to screen these listings, we cannot guarantee that they will all furnish appropriate treatment of suitable quality. For this reason and because it makes good sense anyway, it is important for anyone seeking help to be an informed consumer. By way of helping in that pursuit I am including suggestions for things to look for when selecting a treatment program. Keep in mind that phobias can be "cured" but that the traditional talk therapies alone have proved insufficient. You need a recently developed kind of treatment from a program that specializes in the treatment of phobias. For agoraphobia this includes a particular form of behavior therapy.

Until the 1970s behavior therapists, although successful in treating other phobias, did no better than traditional therapists when working with agoraphobia. An effective treatment for other phobias, called systematic desensitization, did not work well for agoraphobia. Therefore, it is important to determine if a potential therapist has kept up with the times rather than using an old technique. What has proved to be indispensable is exposure therapy—that is, exposure to places that elicit fear and are avoided.

One difficulty with exposure treatment is that it is time-consuming. A good length for a session is ninety minutes or more. If your therapist needs to use the standard fifty-minute psychotherapy hour, it becomes very difficult for her or him to provide effective treatment.

Group exposure treatment has been demonstrated to be equal in effectiveness to individual exposure treatment and in addition provides additional benefits such as extended support and opportunity to learn from others with the same problems. However, as an alternative the therapist can instruct the client to carry out her own exposure work, meeting with her weekly to set up assignments, give feedback and encouragement, and give training in coping skills. Research indicates that this approach produces good results for about one-third of agoraphobic clients, compared to the two-thirds who are helped when the client is actually accompanied by a therapist. In the latter situation the therapist can of course provide immediate feedback and suggestions and prevent potential errors. That advantage is also not available for agoraphobics who work on their own with books, manuals, and/or tape-recorded treatment programs. Nevertheless these may provide the only form of exposure-based treatment available in some communities.

As another alternative, some clinics employ paraprofessional therapists to conduct the exposure treatment. These people should have training in exposure work with phobics and ought to be functioning under the supervision of a professional. Often the paraprofessional is a former phobic, who can give the client additional encouragement and the feeling of really being understood. Problems do arise when there is insufficient supervision because of the significant additional problems experienced by agoraphobics. Some caution should be used, therefore, in working with the paraprofessional who has set up an independent practice.

A professionally trained therapist—a licensed psychologist, psychiatrist or clinical social worker—should be available to provide adjunct psychotherapy since there are often psychological problems that interact with phobias. Not every agoraphobic will require the services of a therapist, but one should be available when needed.

The counselors that you work with should be experienced. You can check on them by asking for the names and telephone numbers of several people who have been through their program. Of course, the program will need to get permission from each before you call, but any competent center will have no trouble providing plenty of references.

If there is no appropriate help in your area, there are centers in addition to ours that offer intensive programs for out-of-town people. Since you are unlikely to complete all of your work in a short, concentrated period, it is helpful to have someone locally who will be willing to continue the work begun in intensive treatment. Many people completing our two-week program do not require additional travel work and may be in a position to benefit at that time from more traditional therapy.

I have personally reviewed and found to be excellent the tape programs distributed by CHAANGE and Outgrowing Agoraphobia (see listings under CORRESPONDENCE/TAPE PROGRAMS). They are both very well-organized programs that are sound technically and offer a great deal of information. I believe they both do as good a job as can be done, given the limitations inherent in self-help formats.

The list is constantly being updated. If you would like current information about programs in your area, please send your request and a self-addressed stamped envelope to the Temple Agoraphobia & Anxiety Program, 112 Bala Avenue, Bala Cynwyd, Pennsylvania 19004. There is no charge for this service.

For a constantly updated listing of programs throughout the world you may contact The Phobia Society of America at 133 Rollins Avenue, Suite 4B, Rockville, Maryland 20852-4004. Telephone (301) 231-9350. For information about other offerings of the Society, please see the PSA listing at the end of this chapter.

TREATMENT PROGRAMS LISTED BY STATE
ALABAMA

SOUTHEASTERN PSYCHOLOGICAL AND COUNSELING SERVICES
1707 MONTGOMERY HWY., SUITE 203
DOTHAN, ALABAMA 36303
205-793-1820   WALTER JACOBS, PH.D.
Treatment programs are cognitive behavioral and include systematic desensitization, in vivo desensitization and a variety of cognitive restructuring techniques.

WEST MOBILE PSYCHOLOGY CENTER
4325 MIDMOST DRIVE, SUITE B
MOBILE, ALABAMA 36609
205-344-1482   MICHAEL S. ROSENBAUM, PH.D.
Individual therapy for phobias and agoraphobia, including fieldwork. TERRAP group program for individuals with agoraphobia.

THE FAMILY TRANSITION CENTER
1124 E. FAIRVIEW AVE.
MONTGOMERY, ALABAMA 36106
205-263-7388   SAMUEL D. COLLIER, M.ED.

Individual therapy using systematic desensitization, gradual exposure and paradoxical techniques.

ARIZONA

LIVING GROWTH PHOBIA CENTER
2000 IDYLWILD
PRESCOTT, ARIZONA 86301
602-778-3627   CHARLOTTE RUDEAU, M.A.
Therapy is based on techniques from the TERRAP and Weekes programs and includes fieldwork, relaxation and nutrition. Seven-day live-in residence program available.

TERRAP PHOENIX
2111 E. BASELINE, SUITE F-1
TEMPE, ARIZONA 85283
602-897-9059   CINDY GLICK
Twelve-week group TERRAP self-help educational program.

PSYCHOLOGY AND REHABILITATION ASSOCIATES
19 NORTH NORRIS
TUCSON, ARIZONA 85719
602-792-3070   GEORGE MAYO, PH.D.
Individual psychotherapy, systematic desensitization and educational lectures offered for the treatment of agoraphobia.

CALIFORNIA

BEVERLY PSYCHIATRIC & PSYCHOLOGICAL CENTER
416 N. BEDFORD DRIVE, SUITE 205
BEVERLY HILLS, CALIFORNIA 90210
213-278-6342   DENNIS J. MUNJACK, M.D.
In vivo exposure, desensitization, behavioral, dynamic and pharmacological treatments are offered in either individual and/or group settings.

MARALYN L. TEARE, M.S., M.F.C.C.
383 SOUTH ROBERTSON BLVD., SUITE A
BEVERLY HILLS, CALIFORNIA 90211
213-659-6440   MARALYN L. TEARE, M.S.

Individual in vivo exposure using a behavioral/perceptual model to teach phobic symptom reduction in the treatment of agoraphobia, panic disorders and specific phobias.

FRANCES F. KING, M.A., M.F.C.C.
314 N. CORDOVA STREET
BURBANK, CALIFORNIA 91505
818-848-1432   FRANCES F. KING, M.A.
Private practice treating phobias and compulsive behavior using neurolinguistic programming, desensitization, behavior modification, relaxation, visual imagery, breathing exercises and assertiveness training.

AGORAPHOBIA TREATMENT PROGRAM
1355 STRATFORD COURT
DEL MAR, CALIFORNIA 92014
619-755-0515/453-6543   DOUGLAS S. HYMAN, PH.D.
Individual and group therapy, travel/exposure work (in vivo), multimodal treatment orientation including cognitive/behavioral, psychoanalytic and family therapy.

THE CALIFORNIA CLINIC
7988 CALIFORNIA AVE.
FAIR OAKS, CALIFORNIA 95628
916-965-4606   TERENCE J. SANDBEK, PH.D.
Individual and group therapy is available with emphasis on cognitive/behavioral techniques including in vivo desensitization.

TERRAP OF FRESNO
6771 N. LAFAYETTE AVENUE
FRESNO, CALIFORNIA 93711
209-435-8181   MARLENE BISSELL
Sixteen-week course, 1½ hours per week, includes two sessions of fieldwork.

TERRAP, N.E. LOS ANGELES CENTER FOR PHOBIAS
2505 CANADA BLVD., SUITE 3-C
GLENDALE, CALIFORNIA 91208
818-244-2465   JOANNE BRUCKNER

Behavior modification techniques combined with cognitive therapy. The TERRAP courses are time-limited and focus on relaxation, in vivo desensitization, behavioral rehearsal, assertiveness and cognitive restructuring.

TERRAP, EAST BAY PHOBIA TREATMENT CENTER
22300 FOOTHILL BLVD., SUITE M-14
HAYWARD, CALIFORNIA 94541
415-881-5992   CHARLES WICKSTRAND
Individual and group therapy available for phobias and agoraphobia.

SAUL LASSOFF, PH.D.
225 W. WINTON AVE. #209
HAYWARD, CALIFORNIA 94707
415-785-3200   SAUL LASSOFF, PH.D.
Individual and in vivo therapy is available for agoraphobia and other phobias, including fears of flying and water.

TERRAP PHOBIA TREATMENT CENTER
3688 MT. DIABLO BLVD.
LAFAYETTE, CALIFORNIA 94549
415-376-5530   JOYCE E. KAPLAN
Individual and group therapy available for phobias and agoraphobia.

DR. PATRICIA J. ROSE
9404 GENESEE AVE., SUITE 271
LA JOLLA, CALIFORNIA 92037
619-458-9154   PATRICIA ROSE, PH.D.
Individual therapy with emphasis on exposure and skill training, combined with insight-oriented psychotherapy.

ANXIETY DISORDERS CLINIC
U.S.C. MEDICAL CENTER
DEPARTMENT OF PSYCHIATRY
1937 HOSPITAL PLACE
LOS ANGELES, CALIFORNIA 90033
213-226-5329   DENNIS J. MUNJACK, M.D.

All modalities of treatment are available: individual, group, behavioral, eclectic, pharmacologic, and in vivo.

LOS ANGELES MEDICAL PSYCHOLOGY GROUP
8425 W. 3RD STREET, SUITE 407
LOS ANGELES, CALIFORNIA 90048
213-653-0733   OLUJIMI BAMGBOSE, PH.D.
Individual, group and travel therapy are available.

PHOBIA PROGRAM OF SOUTHERN CALIFORNIA TERRAP
9510 BOLTON ROAD
LOS ANGELES, CALIFORNIA 90034
213-836-6445   MARLENE SCHENTER
Treatment for agoraphobia consists of a sixteen-session self-help/educational program with in vivo exposure. Individual therapy with in vivo exposure is available for other phobias. Program for fear of flying.

ALAN RAPPOPORT, PH.D.
1010 DOYLE STREET
MENLO PARK, CALIFORNIA 94025
415-329-1233   ALAN RAPPOPORT, PH.D.
Individual therapy and exposure for phobias and agoraphobia.

TERRAP MENLO PARK
1010 DOYLE STREET
MENLO PARK, CALIFORNIA 94025
415-327-1312   ARTHUR B. HARDY, M.D.
Group and individual therapy, telephone therapy, in vivo desensitization, time-limited programs and a correspondence course are available.

SUSAN GRUSS ODEKERKEN, M.A., M.F.C.C.
21137 PLACERITA CANYON ROAD
NEWHALL, CALIFORNIA 91321
805-259-2614   SUSAN GRUSS ODEKERKEN
Individual and group therapy are available for general phobias and agoraphobia. Use of behavioral techniques is prominent, i.e., training in desensitization, progressive relaxation, etc.

GLADMAN MEMORIAL HOSPITAL
2633 E. 27TH STREET
OAKLAND, CALIFORNIA 94601
415-536-8111   CHRISTOPHER MCCULLOUGH, PH.D.
Inpatient treatment program for agoraphobia. Extension of the
San Francisco Phobia Recovery Center. Treatment is holistic and
includes attention to nutrition and exercise as well as psychotherapy with emphasis on desensitization and exposure.

INSTITUTE FOR PHOBIC AWARENESS
1472 SAN JACINTO WAY
PALM SPRINGS, CALIFORNIA 92263
619-327-2184   MARILYN GELLIS, PH.D.
Weekly self-help group; individual desensitization sessions and
fieldwork; individual therapy as needed.

PHILIP E. BERGHAUSEN, JR., PH.D.
3455 RAMBOW DRIVE
PALO ALTO, CALIFORNIA 94306
415-493-3552   PHILIP BERGHAUSEN, PH.D.
Individual psychotherapy available stressing in vivo and imaginal
desensitization; group work available through the Terrap program.

ALAN RINGOLD, M.D.
900 WELCH ROAD #400
PALO ALTO, CALIFORNIA 94304
415-327-5795   ALAN RINGOLD, M.D.
Behavioral and cognitive approach including in vivo desensitization used in group and individual therapy. Medication and stress
management available when indicated.

MERRILL D. DARLINGTON, PH.D.
6859 MAGNOLIA AVENUE, SUITE 3
RIVERSIDE, CALIFORNIA 92506
714-686-6200   MERRILL DARLINGTON, PH.D.
Individual cognitive/behavioral therapy; TERRAP groups; fieldwork and exposure therapy and local home visits are available.

TERRAP SACRAMENTO
1116 24TH STREET
SACRAMENTO, CALIFORNIA 95816
916-442-1902   JOHN E. LEMAN, PH.D.
Sixteen-week structured group program which includes exposure
therapy; individual behavioral or psychodynamic therapy; home
visits and telephone consultations are also available.

BIOFEEDBACK INSTITUTE OF SAN DIEGO
2850 6TH AVENUE, SUITE #508
SAN DIEGO, CALIFORNIA 92103
619-298-3464   DAVID W. JACOBS, PH.D.
Biofeedback-assisted relaxation training, followed by systematic
desensitization and, as needed, assertion training, marital counseling, travel planning and psychotherapy are available.

JOHN A. GRABEL, PH.D.
4295 GESNER STREET, SUITE 1-C
SAN DIEGO, CALIFORNIA 92117
619-275-4050   JOHN A. GRABEL, PH.D.
Treatment is individual and behaviorally oriented and includes in
vivo sessions, usually several times per week.

SUSAN JASIN, PH.D.
9636 TIERRE GRANDE #102
SAN DIEGO, CALIFORNIA 92126
619-271-9393   SUSAN JASIN, PH.D.
Group and individual therapy is available with emphasis on cog-
nitive/behavioral techniques including in vivo exposure.

TERRAP SAN DIEGO
9601 AERO DRIVE, SUITE 280
SAN DIEGO, CALIFORNIA 92123
619-565-8921   CLAUDETTE DECOURLEY
Individual psychotherapy and group program available for agoraphobia and other phobias with emphasis on desensitization and
behavioral change. Home visits and support groups also available.

SAN FRANCISCO INSTITUTE OF BEHAVIORAL MEDICINE & THERAPY
2750 GEARY BOULEVARD
SAN FRANCISCO, CALIFORNIA 94118
415-921-6171, x213; 775-2533   MICHAEL J. CORLEY, PH.D.
Small groups of three to five individuals; individualized exposure
programs; other programs available on request.

MALCOLM KUSHNER, PH.D.
415 SPRUCE STREET
SAN FRANCISCO, CALIFORNIA 94118
415-589-7161   MALCOLM KUSHNER, PH.D.
Treatment is individual and utilizes desensitization and in vivo exposure as well as an intensive behavioral analysis.

OUTGROWING AGORAPHOBIA
P.O. BOX 40308
SAN FRANCISCO, CALIFORNIA 94110
Correspondence/tape program for combating agoraphobia.

SAN FRANCISCO PHOBIA RECOVERY CENTER
85 LIBERTY STREET, SUITE 200
SAN FRANCISCO, CALIFORNIA 94110
415-441-2583   CHRISTOPHER J. MCCULLOUGH, PH.D.
Emphasis is on individual psychotherapy and desensitization techniques. Treatment is holistic and includes attention to nutrition
and exercise as well as psychotherapeutic dimensions.

JACQUELINE B. PERSONS, PH.D.
399 LAUREL STREET
SAN FRANCISCO, CALIFORNIA 94118
415-922-6657   JACQUELINE B. PERSONS, PH.D.
Behavioral therapy with emphasis on obsessive/compulsive disorders.

PHOBIA COUNSELING CENTER
1745 SARATOGA AVE.
SAN JOSE, CALIFORNIA 95129
408-255-6911   BERNARD M. SJOBERG, PH.D.
Behavioral/cognitive therapy orientation for all types of phobias,

including agoraphobia and school phobia. Emphasis on in vivo exposure therapy.

PHOBIA CARE TREATMENT CENTER
550 N. PARKCENTER DRIVE, SUITE 206
SANTA ANA, CALIFORNIA 92705
714-547-2400   JERRY A. KASDORF, PH.D.
All treatment is individual and includes assessment, medication as needed, self-help coping techniques, cognitive restructuring and desensitization.

BENJAMIN CROCKER, M.D.
1000 FREMONT AVE., SUITE A
SOUTH PASADENA, CALIFORNIA 91030
818-441-0550   BENJAMIN CROCKER, M.D.
Individual and group treatment of panic disorder and phobias, especially agoraphobia. Emphasis is on autogenic and cognitive approaches, including exposure work; medication is available.

TERRAP—ORANGE COUNTY
14140 BEACH BLVD., SUITE 204
WESTMINSTER, CALIFORNIA 92683
714-891-4446   HARRIET GYOR
Group programs for agoraphobia include a sixteen-week program and a one-week intensive; individual therapy, fieldwork, biofeedback and hypnotherapy also available.

PHOBIA PROGRAM OF SOUTHERN CALIFORNIA
5301 COMERCIO LANE
WOODLAND HILLS, CALIFORNIA 91364
818-347-0191   RONALD M. DOCTOR, PH.D.
Offers a variety of programs for treatment of phobic and agoraphobic disorders. TERRAP serves as program for agoraphobia. Freedom to fly course and fear of driving course available.

COLORADO

RICHARD M. BABBITTS, PH.D., COLORADO TERRAP
3100 N. ACADEMY BLVD., SUITE 117
COLORADO SPRINGS, COLORADO 80907
303-574-7077   RICHARD BABBITTS, PH.D.

Treatment program includes individual, group and marital therapy with emphasis on behavioral/cognitive techniques including field exposure.

BEHAVIOR THERAPY INSTITUTE OF COLORADO
1562 SOUTH PARKER ROAD
PARKER BUILDING SUITE 112
DENVER, COLORADO 80231
303-337-9588   THOMAS R. GILES, PSY.D.
Individual behavioral therapy including travel/exposure, paradoxical intention, marital treatment, antidepressants and cognitive restructuring.

STRESS MANAGEMENT CENTER
2141 N. 7TH STREET
GRAND JUNCTION, COLORADO 81501
303-243-3001   CAROLYNN NELSON, M.A.
Individual counseling including insight therapy, relaxation techniques, biofeedback, desensitization and behavioral contracting.

PHOBIA TREATMENT CENTER
777 SOUTH WADSWORTH BLVD., SUITE 120
LAKEWOOD, COLORADO 80227
303-988-5706   COLLEEN STEPHENS
Group and individual treatment for phobias including agoraphobia. Treatment is behavioral in nature; focus is on skill acquisition.

CONNECTICUT

BEHAVIORAL MEDICINE COMMUNITY ASSOCIATES
645 BIRCH MOUNTAIN ROAD
MANCHESTER, CONNECTICUT 06040
203-646-4233   DONALD PET, M.D.
Individual, group and contextual therapy are offered.

TERRAP NEW HAVEN
35 MARLIN DRIVE
NEW HAVEN, CONNECTICUT 06515
203-389-2919
                                               JANE MILLER, M.S.

Twelve-week group program with follow-up fieldwork and individual treatment is available.

Vincent A. Covino, Ph.D.
p.o. box 2468
vernon professional building
vernon, connecticut 06066
203-872-1037   vincent a. covino, ph.d.
Cognitive/behavioral therapy, individual and group, in vivo desensitization, relaxation and biofeedback are available.

Pain Management and Behavior Therapy Center
567 vauxhall street extension, suite 319
waterford, connecticut 06385
203-443-4343   o. desiderato, ph.d.
Primarily individual treatment; approach is cognitive-behavioral (exposure, cognitive restructuring).

S.O.A.R., Inc. (Seminars on Aeroanxiety Relief)
p.o. box 747
westport, connecticut 06881
203-259-0087   tom bunn
Seminars offered in several East Coast cities for people who want to overcome fear of flying. Program is an outgrowth of those started at Pan Am.

Marianne H. Lewis, M.S.N.
47 sturges ridge road
wilton, connecticut 06897
203-762-2601   marianne h. lewis, m.s.n.
Individual and group therapy and travel/exposure therapy are available.

FLORIDA

Family Centered Counseling
2828 south seacrest blvd., suite 212
boynton beach, florida 33435
305-736-1340   john skow, m.s.w., a.c.s.w.
Individual, group, support groups and home-visit formats are available. The agoraphobic treatment groups are time-limited.

AGORAPHOBIA RESOURCE CENTER
2699 SOUTH BAYSHORE DRIVE
COCONUT GROVE, FLORIDA 33133
305-854-0652   PAULA LEVINE, PH.D.
Group, individual (including exposure) and family approaches are available for the treatment of agoraphobia.   Five-to-ten-day intensive programs available.

PHOBIA CENTER OF VOLUSIA COUNTY
403 N. WILD OLIVE AVE.
DAYTONA BEACH, FLORIDA 32018
904-761-0093   WILLIAM P. FRIEDENBERG, PH.D.
Individual therapy, including in vivo exposure; didactic and support groups available.

DR. KAREN GROSS-GLENN
650 ROYAL PLAZA DRIVE
FORT LAUDERDALE, FLORIDA 33301
305-463-2673; 547-5741   KAREN GROSS-GLENN, PH.D.
Individual therapy includes the use of both imaginal and in vivo techniques for dealing with fears as well as cognitive therapy and assertiveness training.

TERRAP—MIAMI
6905 WEST 16TH DRIVE
HIALEAH, FLORIDA 33014
305-823-8885   GERALD A. KURTZ, PH.D.
Individual and group psychoanalysis, psychotherapy, family therapy, behavior therapy and in vivo fieldwork training to overcome phobias and agoraphobia.

PHOBIA TREATMENT CENTER OF NORTH FLORIDA
3716 UNIVERSITY BOULEVARD S., SUITE 6B
JACKSONVILLE, FLORIDA 32216
904-739-3688   ALAN J. HARRIS, PH.D.
Individual, group and homebound therapy using a cognitive/behavioral approach.   Group treatment is time-limited.   In vivo desensitization and cognitive desensitization using imagery are incorporated into the program.

UNIVERSITY OF MIAMI PHOBIA AND ANXIETIES CLINIC
1550 N.W. 10TH AVE.
MIAMI, FLORIDA 33136
305-547-6755   AMBER E. GOLDSTEIN, M.S.W.
Individual and group therapy available using Ericksonian treatment approaches, NLP techniques for removal of phobias, practice learning with exposure and medication when necessary.

FLORIDA STRESS SERVICES
9055 S.W. 87TH AVENUE, SUITE 307
S. MIAMI, FLORIDA 33176
305-939-7648   GARY E. MINERVINI, PH.D., C.M.D.
Hypnotherapy, systematic progressive desensitization, biofeedback, autogenics and psychotherapy are available in both individual and group therapy.

ORLANDO REGIONAL MEDICAL CENTER AGORAPHOBIA CLINIC
1414 SOUTH KUHL AVENUE
ORLANDO, FLORIDA 32806
305-841-5111   DEIRDRE BRIGHAM, M.S.
Groups run for ten sessions and include cognitive restructuring, relaxation training, behavioral principles and graded exposure to feared situations.

SUNCOAST PSYCHOLOGICAL SERVICES
3302 ALTERNATE 19 NORTH
PALM HARBOR, FLORIDA 33563
813-786-1329   TRICIA B. WILMOTH, PH.D.
Hypnosis, self-hypnosis, relaxation training, systematic desensitization and humor are the treatment techniques used in both individual and group sessions.

THE CENTER FOR COUNSELING SERVICES
140 S. UNIVERSITY DRIVE
PLANTATION, FLORIDA 33324
305-475-1371   WILLIAM PENZER, PH.D.
Individual psychotherapy, including home visits, using a combination of behavioral, cognitive and dynamic techniques.

COMMUNITY BEHAVIORAL SERVICES
7402 NORTH 56TH STREET, SUITE 890
TAMPA, FLORIDA 33617
813-985-9593   MARK BARRY LEFKOWITZ, PH.D.
The program is based on the CHAANGE Program, a sixteen-week audiocassette program developed in Charlotte, N.C. The tapes are used in conjunction with either group or individual therapy.

GEORGIA

ATLANTA PHOBIA CLINIC
960 JOHNSON FERRY ROAD, SUITE 215
ATLANTA, GEORGIA 30342
404-256-0802   STEPHEN W. GARBER, PH.D.
Individual and group therapy for all types of phobias and agoraphobia, includes both exposure in vivo and imaginal.

GRANDVIEW THERAPY CLINIC
2996 GRANDVIEW AVE., N.E., SUITE 307
ATLANTA, GEORGIA 30305
404-266-0962   CHARLES MELVILLE, PH.D.
Individual, group and couples therapy available for phobics, including behavior therapy and guided exposure fieldwork.

PSYCHOTHERAPY CENTER OF ATLANTA
1145 SHERIDAN ROAD, N.E.
ATLANTA, GEORGIA 30324
404-325-8512   EDWARD W. L. SMITH, PH.D.
Individual and group therapy using a Gestalt approach with emphasis on awareness and graded exposure is available.

WOODLAKE PSYCHOTHERAPY ASSOCIATES/TERRAP ATLANTA
2531 BRIARCLIFF ROAD, SUITE 116
ATLANTA, GEORGIA 30329
404-325-9602   REBECCA BOONE, PH.D.
Individual therapy, including in vivo desensitization, is available.

ILLINOIS

COMMUNITY COUNSELING CENTER
2615 EDWARDS STREET
ALTON, ILLINOIS 62002
618-462-2331   DONNA R. SCHMIDT, A.C.S.W.

A six-week group program is offered which includes cognitive restructuring, anxiety reduction techniques and self-hypnosis training. Individual travel therapy is available as needed.

MERCY CENTER FOR HEALTH CARE SERVICES
1325 NORTH HIGHLAND AVE.
AURORA, ILLINOIS 60506
312-859-2222   GARY R. DEC, PSY. D.

Services for agoraphobia include a twelve-week group sequence offering travel/exposure therapy and groups for family members. Biofeedback-assisted relaxation training and systematic desensitization are available for simple phobias and anxiety disorders.

JERRY PORZEMSKY, PH.D., P.C.
2909 W. FARGO AVE.
CHICAGO, ILLINOIS 60645
312-262-5757   JERRY PROZEMSKY, PH.D.

Individual treatment utilizing Neurolinguistic programming, hypnosis and supportive counseling which frequently includes family members.

COPE, LTD. (CENTER OF PHOBIC ENCOUNTERS)
940 PINE STREET
GLENVIEW, ILLINOIS 60025
312-724-3450   LARRY J. KROLL, PH.D.

Individual and group (sixteen-week sessions) therapy. Systematic desensitization includes both imagery and in vivo exposures.

NEUROPSYCHIATRIC ASSOCIATES OF ILLINOIS, P.C.
1117 S. MILWAUKEE AVE.
LIBERTYVILLE, ILLINOIS 60048
312-367-1611   JOHN K. LARSON, M.D.

Individual counseling and ongoing support groups utilizing in vivo and in vitro approaches are offered. Conservative use of medication if indicated.

HUMAN DEVELOPMENT CENTER, INC.—AGORAPHOBIA CLINIC
4306 F. WEST CRYSTAL LAKE ROAD
MCHENRY, ILLINOIS 60050
815-385-6524   MARLEEN LORENZ, R.N., M.A.
Twelve-week structured group which includes relaxation and assertiveness training, in vivo exposure and goal setting.

CENTRUM COUNSELING AND PHOBIA CLINIC
461 N. HARLEM AVE.
OAK PARK, ILLINOIS 60302
312-386-7974   MARVIN COHEN, PSY. D.
A combination of behavioral and psychodynamic techniques is available individually, with families or in groups. Systematic desensitization in vivo is combined with insight-oriented therapy.

FAMILY STRESS AND PHOBIA CENTER
3526 N. CALIFORNIA, SUITE 205
PEORIA, ILLINOIS 61603
309-682-7900   SHELDON N. BERGER, PH.D.
Treatment includes desensitization, in vivo work, gradual approximations and traditional insight-oriented psychotherapy.

LIFE ENRICHMENT SERVICES, INC.
2238 APPLEBY DRIVE
WHEATON, ILLINOIS 60187
312-653-1923   THOMAS L. POWER, M.A.
Twelve-week travel group for agoraphobia and individual and couples therapy are available.

INDIANA

PARK CENTER
909 E. STATE BLVD.
FORT WAYNE, INDIANA 46804
219-482-9111   JUDY TERRILL SANDERS, M.S.
Two-week intensive clinic and ongoing weekly group include travel work and psychotherapy; individual sessions are also available.

INDIANA COUNSELING AND PHOBIA CENTER
9302 NORTH MERIDIAN STREET, SUITE 102
INDIANAPOLIS, INDIANA 46260
317-844-6489   PATRICIA FOSTER
TERRAP program—time-limited structured group therapy, individual therapy and travel/exposure therapy are offered by a recovered phobic with three years' experience.

MICHIANA PSYCHOLOGICAL ASSOCIATES
828 E. COLFAX
SOUTH BEND, INDIANA 46617
219-233-3003   JAMES F. BROGLE, PH.D.
Individual and group therapy based on the TERRAP program is offered.

IOWA

THE TEAM
BOX 4645
DES MOINES, IOWA 50306
515-243-5224   SASCHA WAGNER
Contextual-therapy approach combined with psychotherapy and support groups. In-home program available.

KANSAS

MEMORIAL HOSPITAL PSYCHIATRIC SERVICES
600 MADISON
TOPEKA, KANSAS 66607
913-354-5373   JACK KNOPS, PH.D.
Individual treatment using medication and behavior therapy including exposure. Group psychotherapy, phobia support groups and assertiveness training are also available.

KENTUCKY

ANXIETY MANAGEMENT CENTER
135 EAST MAXWELL SUITE 302
LEXINGTON, KENTUCKY 40508
606-259-0396   DAVID A. MEYER, M.D.

A combined medical and psychological approach is available through individual, group and family therapy.

LOUISIANA

TERRAP NEW ORLEANS
2716 ATHANIA PARKWAY
METAIRIE, LOUISIANA 70002
504-835-5819   JANE STENNETT, PH.D.
Sixteen-week self-help group program—includes in vivo desensitization; individual sessions and biofeedback as well as follow-up groups are also available.

MAINE

ANXIETY DISORDERS RESEARCH PROGRAM
PSYCHOLOGY DEPARTMENT, 301 LITTLE HALL
UNIVERSITY OF MAINE AT ORONO
ORONO, MAINE 04469
207-581-2055   GEOFFREY L. THORPE, PH.D.
Various behavioral and cognitive/behavioral treatments implemented in a research context. Procedures include graduated exposure in vivo, stress-inoculation training, imaginal exposure, etc.

MARYLAND

PSYCHOLOGICAL SERVICES INCORPORATED
111 ANNAPOLIS STREET
ANNAPOLIS, MARYLAND 21401
301-263-8255   JON WILLIAMS, PH.D.
Ongoing group, individual and family psychotherapy program combining contextual exposure with cognitive/behavioral multimodal therapy and biofeedback-assisted desensitization, and medication as needed.

ANXIETY AND DEPRESSION ACTION GROUP
704 OLD CROSSING DRIVE
BALTIMORE, MARYLAND 21208
301-484-8826   ROSLYN DIAMOND, L.C.S.W., PH.D.
Individual and group psychotherapy using a cognitive-behavioral approach and in vivo exposure. Home visits are also available.

PHOBIA PROGRAM OF BALTIMORE
7238 T PARK HEIGHTS AVENUE
BALTIMORE, MARYLAND 21208
301-764-7462   ROBERT L. DUPONT, M.D.
Sixteen-week program combining group psychotherapy and individual travel therapy, each on a weekly basis.

PHOBIA CLINIC OF EDWARD L. ANSEL, PH.D.
THE REGENCY
3643 GLENGYLE AVENUE
BALTIMORE, MARYLAND 21215
301-358-3977   EDWARD L. ANSEL, PH.D.
Agoraphobia is primarily treated in group psychotherapy and in vivo exposure sessions. Other phobias treated in individual therapy and with in vivo exposure sessions.

VINCENZA P. BOWLES ASSOCIATES
6017 ROSSMORE DRIVE
BETHESDA, MARYLAND 20814
301-530-0632   VINCENZA BOWLES, M.S.W.
Concurrent group plus individual therapy. Groups focus on education and support, using cognitive/behavioral models, while individual therapy is geared to exposure therapy.

NEW VENTURES, INC.
BOWIE CITY HALL
KENHILL DRIVE
BOWIE, MARYLAND 20715
301-464-2622   BETTY SILON, PH.D.
Individual, group, in vivo desensitization, and hypnosis for agoraphobia, social phobias, fear of public speaking and stage fright.

THOMAS JOSEPH HUNT, PH.D.
10784 HICKORY RIDGE ROAD
COLUMBIA, MARYLAND 21044
301-730-0100   THOMAS J. HUNT, PH.D.
Individual, marital, family treatments for phobic children, adolescents and adults with a special emphasis on the use of hypnobehavioral therapy.

PSYCHOLOGICAL HEALTH SERVICES, INC.
10774 HICKORY RIDGE ROAD
COLUMBIA, MARYLAND 21044
301-730-3130; 730-8149   JOHN R. MAY, PH.D.
Individual treatment including systematic desensitization, relaxation exercises, auditory and visual stimuli and travel/exposure therapy.

BEHAVIOR SERVICE CONSULTANTS, INC.
133 CENTERWAY, BOX 97
GREENBELT, MARYLAND 20770
301-474-2146   LINDA J. CIMARUSTI, PH.D.
Offers special programs for phobias, which include cognitive/behaviorally oriented and psychodynamic psychotherapy with individuals, couples, families and groups.

PHOBIA PROGRAM OF WASHINGTON
6191 EXECUTIVE BLVD.
ROCKVILLE, MARYLAND 20852
301-468-8980   ROBERT L. DUPONT, M.D.
Sixteen-week program combining group psychotherapy and individual travel therapy, each on a weekly basis.

SHEPPARD-PRATT HOSPITAL
TOWSON, MARYLAND 21204
301-823-8200   SALLY WINSTON, PSY.D.
Weekly group psychotherapy and in vivo exposure sessions as well as individual psychotherapy and marital therapy are available.

MASSACHUSETTS

ANDOVER PHOBIA CLINIC
166 NORTH MAIN STREET
ANDOVER, MASSACHUSETTS 01810
617-475-7249   JORGE H. DENAPOLI, M.D.
Group and individual psychotherapy, psychopharmacotherapy, behavior modification and relaxation techniques. Systematic desensitization and in vivo exposure.

AGORAPHOBIA TREATMENT CLINIC
MCLEAN HOSPITAL
115 MILL STREET
BELMONT, MASSACHUSETTS 02178
617-855-2991   PERRY L. BELFER, PH.D.
Full range of treatment modalities available, including individual,
couples, family and group treatment, as well as in vivo exposure
and psychopharmacological intervention as needed.

AGORAPHOBIA TREATMENT AND RESEARCH CENTER
264 BEACON STREET
BOSTON, MASSACHUSETTS 02120
617-262-5223   STEVE FISCHER, PSY.D.
Pharmacotherapy, individual therapy and individual and group
exposure therapy are available.

BEHAVIOR ASSOCIATES
45 NEWBURY STREET
BOSTON, MASSACHUSETTS 02116
617-262-9116   JOEL L. BECKER, PH.D.
Individual psychotherapy and in vivo travel/exposure groups are
available for the treatment of agoraphobia, using a cognitive-
behavioral approach.

CROSSROADS COUNSELING CENTER, INC.
670 WASHINGTON STREET
BRAINTREE, MASSACHUSETTS 02184
617-843-7550   RICHARD C. RAYNARD, PH.D.
Phobia program consists of four to twelve sessions of individual
therapy using behavioral methods, including desensitization in situ.
Home visits are available.

LAHEY CLINIC MEDICAL CENTER
DEPARTMENT OF BEHAVIORAL MEDICINE
41 MALL ROAD
BURLINGTON, MASSACHUSETTS 01805
617-273-8610   LYLE KANTOR, PH.D.
Individual cognitive/behavioral treatment including imaginal and
in vivo desensitization is offered as well as a group for agoraphobia.

DR. TOKARZ AND ASSOCIATES
290 MAIN STREET
COTUIT, MASSACHUSETTS 02635
617-428-5772   THOMAS P. TOKARZ, PH.D.
Individual psychotherapy and travel/exposure therapy are available for the treatment of phobias, including agoraphobia. Home visits are available.

FRANKLIN COUNTY MENTAL HEALTH CENTER
13 PROSPECT STREET
GREENFIELD, MASSACHUSETTS 01301
413-774-4313   HARRIET E. STERNBERG, M.S.W.
Weekly individual sessions and a monthly agoraphobic group are offered using Claire Weekes's techniques.

VALLEY CLINICAL ASSOCIATES
474 MAIN STREET
GREENFIELD, MASSACHUSETTS 01301
413-773-8530; 744-3580   HARRIET E. STERNBERG, M.S.W.
Supportive groups meet twice monthly in various surrounding areas; individual sessions are available using Claire Weekes's techniques.

ACTION THERAPIES COUNSELING CENTER
24 MASON STREET
LEXINGTON, MASSACHUSETTS 02173
617-862-4419   SHIRLEY BABIOR, ACSW
Individual psychotherapy, couples and family therapy, and travel/exposure therapy are offered.

ALAN C. TURIN, PH.D., AND ASSOCIATES, P.C.
19 MUZZEY STREET
LEXINGTON, MASSACHUSETTS 02173
617-862-4844   ALAN C. TURIN, PH.D.
Individual therapy utilizing systematic desensitization in imagery and in real-life situations, stress management and relaxation training, and hypnosis are available.

ADULT AND CHILD CONSULTATION CENTER
ZERO GOVERNORS AVE. #23
MEDFORD, MASSACHUSETTS 02155
617-391-3266   LIONEL S. LYON, PSY.D.
Individual sessions using behavioral therapy in the office and in vivo.

TERRAP, BOSTON
30 LINCOLN STREET
NEWTON HIGHLANDS, MASSACHUSETTS 02161
617-965-4949; 965-1322   RANDIE HARMON HENDRICK, M.A.
Thirteen-week group programs using systematic desensitization and behavioral techniques, including fieldwork. Individual sessions are also offered.

WALTER MITCHELL, PSY.D.
122 SCHOOL STREET
SPRINGFIELD, MASSACHUSETTS 01105
413-788-7838   WALTER MITCHELL, PSY.D.
Individual and family therapy is available for the treatment of panic-related disorders.

STEVEN C. FISCHER, PSY.D.
24 WILDWOOD LANE
SUDBURY, MASSACHUSETTS 01776
617-443-5747   STEVEN C. FISCHER, PSY.D.
Individual therapy using behavioral techniques is offered.

MICHIGAN

UNIVERSITY OF MICHIGAN ANXIETY DISORDERS PROGRAM
DEPARTMENT OF PSYCHIATRY—UNIVERSITY HOSPITAL
ANN ARBOR, MICHIGAN 48109
313-764-5348   GEORGE CURTIS, M.D.
Individual therapy using behavioral techniques, medication and supportive psychotherapy is offered.

TERRAP, MICHIGAN, INC.
111 SOUTH WOODWARD, SUITE 205
BIRMINGHAM, MICHIGAN 48011
313-642-7764   LAWRENCE A. CANTOW, M.D.

Group, time-limited program includes relaxation, desensitization, gradual approximation or graded exposure. Individual therapy is available as needed.

DAVID J. WARTEL, PH.D.
6346 ORCHARD LAKE ROAD, SUITE 108
WEST BLOOMFIELD, MICHIGAN 48033
313-626-1330   DAVID J. WARTEL, PH.D.
Group and individual therapy available using cognitive therapy, hypnotherapy, systematic desensitization and in vivo exposure.

MINNESOTA

METROPOLITAN ACHIEVEMENT CENTERS, INC.
606 24TH AVENUE, SUITE 602
MINNEAPOLIS, MINNESOTA 55454
612-332-1503   ROBERT E. CRONIN, JR., PH.D.
Individual and group therapy, therapist-assisted exposure therapy and biofeedback-assisted deep-relaxation therapy are offered.

PHOBIA PROGRAM
BEHAVIORAL MEDICINE CLINIC
ABBOTT NORTHWESTERN HOSPITAL
800 E. 28TH STREET AT CHICAGO AVE.
MINNEAPOLIS, MINNESOTA 55407
612-874-5369   DOUGLAS A. HEDLUND, M.D.
Focused group therapy, in vivo "practice," group exposure therapy and a time-limited intensive program are available, as well as individual cognitive behavioral therapy and psychiatric evaluations.

HUMAN EFFECTIVENESS INSTITUTE
350 MARTIN BUILDING
MANKATO, MINNESOTA 56001
507-345-4679   GEORGE V. KOMARIDIS, PH.D.
Group therapy and individual desensitization therapy are offered for phobias and agoraphobia; social assertion training is offered for social phobias.

MISSISSIPPI

ACUTE ANXIETY/AGORAPHOBIA RECOVERY CONCERN
SUITE 234, HIGHLAND VILLAGE
JACKSON, MISSISSIPPI 39211
601-982-8531   ROBIN D. KING, PSY.D.
Program affiliated with CHAANGE, using the fifteen-week time-limited cognitive behavioral training.

MISSOURI

ADULT/CHILD CENTER FOR BEHAVIORAL DEVELOPMENT
411 MICHOLS ROAD, SUITE 217
KANSAS CITY, MISSOURI 64112
816-931-9912   JACK R. ALVORD, PH.D.
Individual and group therapy using a behavioral orientation, including travel/exposure therapy, is available.

DONNA R. SCHMIDT, A.C.S.W.
3020 EHLMANN ROAD
ST. CHARLES, MISSOURI 63301
314-946-3958   DONNA R. SCHMIDT, A.C.S.W.
The six-week group program includes cognitive restructuring, anxiety-reduction techniques, etc. Individualized travel sessions, counseling and family therapy as needed.

ST. LOUIS UNIVERSITY MEDICAL CENTER
1221 S. GRAND BLVD.
ST. LOUIS, MISSOURI 63104
314-771-6400, x202   C. ALEC POLLARD, PH.D.
The primary focus is in vivo exposure, as well as other behavioral interventions. Individual, group and family therapies are available, as well as outpatient, inpatient and home visits.

MONTANA

BILLINGS MENTAL HEALTH CENTER
1245 NORTH 29TH STREET
BILLINGS, MONTANA 59102
406-252-5658   DAVID PIERCE, M.S.W.
Individual, group and in vivo therapy are available.

H.E.L.P. (HUMANE, EFFECTIVE, LIBERATING PROBLEM-SOLVING)
P.O. BOX 4862
MISSOULA, MONTANA 59807
406-721-6061   MADGIE M. HUNT, ED.D.
For agoraphobia, individual therapy, including travel/exposure and stress-management techniques, is offered. For other phobias, individual therapy, including desensitization and an eclectic approach, is offered.

NEW JERSEY

CARRIER FOUNDATION—BEHAVIORAL MEDICINE PROGRAM
P.O. BOX 147
BELLE MEAD, NEW JERSEY 08502
201-874-4000   E. S. PAUL WEBER, M.D.
The program is a total-push program including active intervention and exposure to the feared situations as well as family interviews, relaxation training and adjunctive therapies.

PHOBIA RELEASE EDUCATION PROGRAM
15 ALDEN STREET, SUITE 11-12
CRANFORD, NEW JERSEY
201-272-0303   NANCYMARIE BRIDE, M.A.
Program includes mutual-help treatment group, individual therapy and exposure treatment.

BARRY G. DALE, D.M.D., F.A.G.D.
151 ENGLE STREET
ENGLEWOOD, NEW JERSEY 07631
201-569-7361   BARRY G. DALE, D.M.D.
General dentist treating dental phobia including agoraphobics with same. Treatment involves systematic desensitization and progressive relaxation.

HACKENSACK MEDICAL CENTER
ADULT OUTPATIENT MENTAL HEALTH SERVICES
50 SECOND STREET
HACKENSACK, NEW JERSEY 07601
201-441-2150   VIRGINIA WASSERMAN
Individual and group psychotherapy and medication with a multidiscipline approach are offered.

PSYCHOLOGICAL SERVICE ASSOCIATES
49 GROVE STREET
HADDONFIELD, NEW JERSEY 08033
609-428-6640   DAVID M. CORDIER, PH.D.
Simple phobias are treated with systematic desensitization; treatment for agoraphobia includes individual, family and couples
therapy as well as travel/exposure group.

TERRAP—SOUTH JERSEY
406 MAIN STREET, ROOM 10
METUCHEN, NEW JERSEY 08840
201-574-9866   ROCIO C. DAY, A.C.S.W.
Individual and group treatment with in vivo desensitization and
disinhibition, as well as family and marital therapy and psychotherapy, are available.

PHOBIA PROGRAM OF NORTH JERSEY
31 S. FULLERTON AVE.
MONTCLAIR, NEW JERSEY 07042
201-744-6914   LIBBY HOFMANN, M.S.W.
Group, individual, travel/exposure and home visits are offered,
using a behavioral/cognitive approach.

COLUMBIA CONSULTATION CENTER
25 EGBERT HILL ROAD
MORRISTOWN, NEW JERSEY 07960
201-267-9566   CHARLOTTE LEITNER
Individual and group therapy available utilizing in vivo exposure,
hypnotherapy, desensitization, imagery, behavior modification and
adjunct therapies.

SUSAN K. ARBEITER, PSY.D.
1835 ROUTE 130
NORTH BRUNSWICK, NEW JERSEY 08902
201-297-7946   SUSAN K. ARBEITER, PSY.D.
Individual psychotherapy, group therapy, in vivo therapy with
the aide of a recovered phobic, and support groups are available.

GERALD GROVES, M.D.
654 STATE ROAD
PRINCETON, NEW JERSEY 08540
609-924-5757   GERALD GROVES, M.D.
Individual behavior therapy. Pharmacotherapy, when indicated.
Small-group therapy. Group and individual exposure therapy.

DEBORAH PHILLIPS, D.S.C.
211 N. HARRISON STREET
PRINCETON, NEW JERSEY
609-924-1212   DEBORAH PHILLIPS, D.S.C.
Individual Behavior Therapy treatment for agoraphobia and other
phobias. Exposure, flooding, desensitization and pharmacological consultation available.

PHOBIA PROGRAM OF NORTH JERSEY
2 W. HANOVER AVE., SUITE 203
RANDOLPH, NEW JERSEY 07869
201-895-4840   HERMAN HUBER, PH.D.
Individual treatment, behavioral therapy, graduated exposure and
psychotherapy are offered.

PHOBIA THERAPY CENTER AT RANDOLPH
20 CLOVER LANE
RANDOLPH, NEW JERSEY 07869
201-895-2081   STANLEY HOROWITZ, PH.D.
Individual and sometimes group therapy is offered. Approach
is eclectic but can include some behavioral techniques, i.e.,
travel/exposure or directive psychotherapy.

NEW JERSEY CENTER FOR COUNSELING AND PSYCHOTHERAPY
95 WATCHUNG AVE.
ROSELLE PARK, NEW JERSEY 07204
201-241-4692; 757-3410   ANTHONY TODARO, PH.D.
Individual and group treatment are available, including travel and
exposure work.

IMPACT
14 HOMESTEAD ROAD
TENAFLY, NEW JERSEY 07670
201-569-7678   ILSE NATHAN, M.A.

Individual and group therapy are available, using progressive desensitization and in vivo/travel/exposure when appropriate.

St. Francis Pain and Stress Center
601 hamilton avenue
trenton, new jersey 08629
609-599-2533   william j. o'connor, ed.d.
Individual, group and family psychotherapy are offered, utilizing biofeedback, mental rehearsal and in vivo desensitization.

TERRAP—North Jersey
117 edgemont road
upper montclair, new jersey 07043
201-783-5588   karen a. levy, m.s.w.
Individual treatment is offered in office, home and field settings, using guided exposure, cognitive restructuring, and communication and relaxation training.   Ongoing biweekly support group is available for agoraphobics.

Wayne Psychological Group
330 ratzer road, suite 25
wayne, new jersey 07470
201-696-6656   emile b. gurstelle, ph.d.
Treatment may include one or all of the following: relaxation training, biofeedback, systematic desensitization, stress management, self-hypnosis and psychotherapy.

NEW YORK

Focus: A Private Mental Health Center
346 quail street
albany, new york 12208
518-482-8331   samuel press, m.d.
Provides a goal-oriented, session-limited therapy approach using some cognitive/behavioral elements.

Phobia and Anxiety Disorders Clinic
state university of new york at albany, draper 107
1535 western avenue
albany, new york 12222
518-456-4127   david h. barlow, ph.d.

For agoraphobia, group therapy, self-directed in vivo exposure, couples therapy and cognitive modification are offered. For social phobia, group therapy is available and focuses on social skills, cognitive modification and exposure assignments.

BABYLON CONSULTATION CENTER
534 DEER PARK AVE.
BABYLON, NEW YORK 11702
516-587-1924   MICHAEL J. BECK, PH.D.
Individual and group therapy focus on desensitization using guided imagery and hypnotherapy.

INSTITUTE FOR BEHAVIOR THERAPY—WESTCHESTER DIVISION
83 RYDER ROAD
BRIARCLIFF MANOR, NEW YORK 10510
914-762-2986   WILLIAM GOLDEN, PH.D.
Group and individual therapy are available and emphasize desensitization, exposure therapy, hypnosis, biofeedback and cognitive/behavioral therapy.

ROBERT ACKERMAN, M.S.W.
33 PROSPECT PLACE
BROOKLYN, NEW YORK 11217
718-857-3297   ROBERT ACKERMAN, M.S.W.
Specific, goal-oriented individual treatment using a cognitive/behavioral approach and often supplemented with family therapy. Supported exposure is utilized and home visits are available.

BROOKLYN PHOBIA CENTER OF NEW YORK PSYCHOLOGICAL CENTER
2634 OCEAN AVENUE
BROOKLYN, NEW YORK 11229
718-743-1100   CAROL LINDEMANN, PH.D.
Short-term symptom-focused treatment, individually or in groups, with in vivo where helpful.

PASS—GROUP, INC.
1042 EAST 105TH STREET
BROOKLYN, NEW YORK 11236
718-763-0190   SEYMOUR S. JAFFE, M.D.

Individual and group program based on the work of Dr. Claire Weekes, emphasizing education, diet modification and relaxation techniques.

PHOBIA CLINIC
DEPARTMENT OF PSYCHIATRY, BOX 1203
DOWNSTATE MEDICAL CENTER
450 CLARKSON AVENUE
BROOKLYN, NEW YORK 11203
718-270-1000   STEVEN FRIEDMAN, PH.D.
Behaviorally oriented individual and group treatment are offered with emphasis on exposure, and frequently supplemented with family therapy. Home visits are available on a limited basis.

THE PHOBIA LIFE LINE
20 PLAZA STREET
BROOKLYN, NEW YORK 11238
718-638-1190   PAUL SCHULMAN, PH.D.
Individual and group psychotherapy are available for the treatment of phobias. Home visits can be arranged.

DR. JACOB GOLDSTEIN
207 OCEAN PARKWAY
BROOKLYN, NEW YORK 11218
718-643-8972; 871-8256   JACOB GOLDSTEIN, D.S.SO.
Psychoanalytically oriented psychotherapy supplemented by desensitization, travel/exposure, etc.

PHOBIA CENTER OF FOREST HILLS (a division of the New York Psychological Center)
110-50 71ST ROAD (1 G)
FOREST HILLS, NEW YORK 11375
718-861-6841   CAROL LINDEMANN, PH.D.
Short-term symptom-focused treatment, individually or in groups, with travel/exposure when appropriate.

FOREST HILLS CONSULTATION CENTER
110-50 71 ROAD
FOREST HILLS, NEW YORK 11375
718-261-6868
                                          S. PAPPALARDO, PH.D.

Individual and group psychotherapy using behavior modification are offered.

PHOBIA CLINIC
LONG ISLAND JEWISH—HILLSIDE MEDICAL CENTER
P.O. BOX 38
GLEN OAKS, NEW YORK 11004
718-470-4556   CHARLOTTE M. ZITRIN, M.D.
Desensitization in fantasy and in vivo.   Both group and individual treatment are available.   All forms of phobias are treated.

PHOBIA CENTER OF GREAT NECK (a division of the New York Psychological Center)
51 HILL PARK
GREAT NECK, NEW YORK 11023
516-861-6841   CAROL LINDEMANN, PH.D.
Short-term symptom-focused treatment, individually or in groups, with travel/exposure when appropriate.

BIO-BEHAVIORAL PSYCHIATRY
560 NORTHERN BLVD.
GREAT NECK, NEW YORK 11021
516-487-7116   FUGEN NEZIROGLU, PH.D.
Three-week intensive exposure and response prevention program for obsessive/compulsives.   Three-week intensive for agoraphobics.   Individual and group therapy are also available, including assertiveness training groups.

TERRAP NEW YORK
356 NEW YORK AVE.
HUNTINGTON, NEW YORK 11743
516-754-3246; 549-8867   JULIAN HERSKOWITZ, PH.D.
Encompasses behavioral, cognitive/behavioral and allied treatment strategies in a sixteen-week group treatment program or in individual therapy.   In vivo desensitization is an important part of the program.

PHOBIA WORKSHOP, INC.
66 ROLLING WAY
NEW ROCHELLE, NEW YORK 10804
914-636-5816   ROBERT L. SHRIRO, M.D.

Ten-week group program consists of one group meeting per week in addition to one individual session in the phobic situation per week.

DENTAL PHOBIA CLINIC—DEPARTMENT OF DENTISTRY
MT. SINAI HOSPITAL
100TH STREET AND MADISON AVE.
NEW YORK, NEW YORK 10029
212-650-7681   ANDREW S. KAPLAN, D.M.D.
This program is for patients with specific dental phobia, or dental phobia as a component of agoraphobia. Behavioral and psychodynamic approaches are used.

TED GOLDSTEIN, D.D.S. (DENTAL PHOBIAS)
133 EAST 58TH STREET
NEW YORK, NEW YORK 10022
212-755-7040   TED GOLDSTEIN, D.D.S.
Group and/or individual treatment ranges from interview conferences through dental treatment and can include Gestalt work, relaxation training, progressive desensitization, hypnosis, etc. Patients can be treated by their own dentists or by program dentists.

ANXIETY CLINIC
16 EAST 79TH STREET
NEW YORK, NEW YORK 10021
212-861-9052   JACK SCHMERTZ, PH.D.
Individual and group psychotherapy: support, ventilation and insight therapy are offered.

RAEANN DUMONT
61 SULLIVAN STREET
NEW YORK, NEW YORK 10012
212-868-3330   RAEANN DUMONT
Individual, group and family counseling using contextual/cognitive therapy is available for the treatment of phobias and obsessive/compulsive disorders.

MARVIN L. ARONSON, PH.D.
124 EAST 28TH STREET
NEW YORK, NEW YORK 10016
212-532-2135   MARVIN L. ARONSON, PH.D.

Specialty is the treatment of fear of flying in individual or group sessions.

FLY WITHOUT FEAR
310 MADISON AVENUE
NEW YORK, NEW YORK 10017
212-697-7666   CAROL GROSS
Group program for aviaphobics which combines education, desensitization, relaxation techniques and group support.

DIANE GOLDKOPF, PH.D.
250 WEST 57TH STREET, SUITE 2128
NEW YORK, NEW YORK 10019
212-874-3911   DIANE GOLDKOPF, PH.D.
Treatment is tailored to the individual and could include relaxation training, desensitization (imaginal and in vivo), modeling and bibliotherapy.

GROUP FOR PSYCHOLOGICAL COUNSELING
230 EAST 48TH STREET
NEW YORK, NEW YORK 10017
212-421-3019; 535-7830   DON SACO, PH.D.
Behavioral/cognitive therapy emphasizes anxiety management through imaginal and in vivo exposure. Social skills and assertiveness training as well as marriage and family counseling are also offered.

ROGER L. MARCH, M.S.W., C.S.W.
580-16 MAIN STREET
ROOSEVELT ISLAND
NEW YORK, NEW YORK 10044
212-355-0839   ROGER L. MARCH, M.S.W., C.S.W.
Individual cognitive and in vivo psychotherapy as well as insight-oriented therapy are available. Home visits can be arranged.

NEW YORK PSYCHOLOGICAL CENTER
245 EAST 87TH STREET
NEW YORK, NEW YORK 10128
212-860-5560   CAROL LINDEMANN, PH.D.
Short-term, symptom-focused treatment, individually or in groups, with travel/exposure when appropriate.

PHOBIA ASSOCIATES, INC.
81 GRAND STREET
NEW YORK, NEW YORK 10013
212-226-6804   ROGER L. MARCH, M.S.W., C.S.W.
Cognitive/contextual therapy offered for all types of phobias and
obsessive/compulsive problems in both group and individual sessions. Outreach program available for those who are unable to
travel.

ST. LUKE'S ROOSEVELT HOSPITAL CENTER—PHOBIA CLINIC
36 WEST 60TH STREET
NEW YORK, NEW YORK 10023
212-554-7172   NATALIE SCHOR
Cognitive/behavioral, supported exposure and/or insight-oriented
psychotherapy. Individual, group, outreach and in vivo modalities utilized.

PEEKSKILL COMMUNITY SERVICE CENTER
750 WASHINGTON STREET
PEEKSKILL, NEW YORK 10566
914-739-6500   ALFRED MURPHY, M.D.
Individual and group therapy available with emphasis on contextual therapy.

PHOBIA TREATMENT PROGRAM OF ROCHESTER
3300 MONROE AVENUE, SUITE 309
ROCHESTER, NEW YORK 14618
716-381-9060   HAROLD A. ZIESAT, PH.D.
Twelve-week program includes progressive relaxation training, in
vivo systematic desensitization, cognitive therapy and assertiveness training. Group and individual therapy are available.

ROBERT M. OSWALT, PH.D.
SKIDMORE COLLEGE PSYCHOLOGY DEPARTMENT
SARATOGA, NEW YORK 12866
518-584-5000   ROBERT M. OSWALT, PH.D.
Systematic desensitization used with individuals and with groups
in the office and in vivo.

WESTCHESTER PHOBIA AND COUNSELING CENTER
762 WARREN AVE.
THORNWOOD, NEW YORK 10594
914-769-1503
FRANK MOSCA, PH.D.
Primarily individual therapy focusing on the use of contextual, in vivo, cognitive and option modalities.

WOMEN'S CONSULTATION CENTER
239 GENESEE STREET, SUITE 411
UTICA, NEW YORK 13501
315-733-1090
EILEEN KENT, M.S.
Time-limited individual counseling which can begin with home visits.

PHOBIA CLINIC
WHITE PLAINS HOSPITAL MEDICAL CENTER
DAVIS AVENUE AT EAST POST ROAD
WHITE PLAINS, NEW YORK 10601
914-681-1078
MANUEL D. ZANE, M.D.
Eight-week course combining weekly group and practice sessions to learn to approach phobic situations. One- or two-week intensive program also available.

PENINSULA COUNSELING CENTER
124 FRANKLIN PLACE
WOODMERE, NEW YORK 11598
516-239-1945
SHIRLEY SMITH, C.S.W.
Twelve-week group program includes both group and individual therapy and exposure therapy. Individual therapy and home visits are also available.

NORTH CAROLINA

HEALTH PSYCHOLOGY CENTER
P.O. BOX 269
CHAPEL HILL, NORTH CAROLINA 27514
919-942-3300
REID WILSON, PH.D.
For agoraphobia, group and individual therapy are offered and include travel/exposure, medication consultation and hypnosis. Individual behavioral treatment is offered for other phobias.

CHAANGE—THE CENTER FOR HELP FOR AGORAPHOBIA/ANXIETY
THROUGH NEW GROWTH EXPERIENCES
2915 PROVIDENCE ROAD, SUITE 310
CHARLOTTE, NORTH CAROLINA 28211
704-365-0140   JAMES SELBY, PH.D.
Individual and group therapy and an in-home therapeutic process
on cassette tapes are available.

JIM SCHERER ASSOCIATES, INC.
604 GREEN VALLEY ROAD, SUITE 405
GREENSBORO, NORTH CAROLINA 27408
919-292-6947   KEN FRAZIER, M.S.
Group work is based on the TERRAP program. Individual treatment is based on cognitive processing and includes relaxation and
assertiveness training, etc.

TERRAP—NORTH CAROLINA
1212 HUNTING RIDGE ROAD
RALEIGH, NORTH CAROLINA 27609
919-847-6333   RONALD D. FRANKLIN, M.A.
Sixteen-week time-limited groups include in vivo desensitization,
individual therapy and home visits.

PHOBIA PROGRAM OF RALEIGH
2321 BLUE RIDGE BLVD.
RALEIGH, NORTH CAROLINA 27607
919-781-1707   ROBERT L. DUPONT, M.D.
Sixteen-week group program includes group therapy, individual
therapy and in vivo (travel) therapy.

OHIO

TERRAP CLEVELAND—FREEDMAN AND ASSOCIATES
24300 CHAGRIN BLVD., #110
BEACHWOOD, OHIO 44122
216-831-3100   MICHAEL L. FREEDMAN, PH.D.
Group treatment for agoraphobia using TERRAP program.
Twenty-four weekly group meetings include education, behavior
therapy, desensitization, in vivo practice, etc. Individual therapy
also available.

DONALD JAY WEINSTEIN, PH.D., INC.
24100 CHAGRIN BLVD., SUITE 400
BEACHWOOD, OHIO 44122
216-831-1040   DONALD JAY WEINSTEIN, PH.D.
Individual and group treatment is available with emphasis on a
cognitive/behavioral approach with forced exposure.

PHOBIA CLINIC OF UNIVERSITY HOSPITALS OF CLEVELAND
HANNA PAVILION
2040 ABINGTON ROAD
CLEVELAND, OHIO 44106
216-844-3557   BARBARA FLEMING, PH.D.
Treatments include mainly cognitive/behavioral therapy in either
individual, group, couple or family modes. In vivo exposure is
often included, and medication and traditional psychotherapy are
also available.

RIVERSIDE METHODIST HOSPITAL PHOBIA PROGRAM
OUTPATIENT PSYCHIATRY
3535 OLENTANGY RIVER ROAD
COLUMBUS, OHIO 43214
614-261-4710   JAN BAKER, PH.D.
Group and individual therapy plus in vivo exposure are offered
primarily for the treatment of agoraphobia, but also for social
phobias, simple phobias and obsessive/compulsive behaviors.

PHOBIA SERVICES & FLY FREE OF FEAR
EASTLAND PSYCHOLOGICAL CENTER
4480 REFUGEE ROAD, SUITE 300
COLUMBUS, OHIO 43227
614-864-1844   JAN BAKER, PH.D.
Individual and ongoing group therapy with considerable in vivo
treatment as well as home visitation. Fear-of-flying treatment includes airport trips, lectures and a flight.

TERRAP SOUTHWESTERN OHIO
1077 KENBROOK DRIVE
DAYTON, OHIO 45430
513-426-3871   V. H. THALER, PH.D.
Sixteen-week self-help education and training group program; individual or couple counseling and fieldwork are offered.

FAMILY SERVICE OF HANCOCK COUNTY
401 W. SANDUSKY STREET
FINDLAY, OHIO 45840
419-423-6991   JOHN A. MALACOS, PH.D.
Eighteen-week TERRAP program which includes group counseling, in vivo, etc. Agoraphobia and simple phobias are also treated individually, using behavioral techniques.

PHOBIA PLUS
P.O. BOX 30767
GAHANNA, OHIO 43230
614-888-2105   DONNA BARTON, M.A.
Individual, group, marital and family counseling are available, as well as home visits and support groups.

RICHARD BROMBERG, PH.D.
5450 FAR HILLS AVE., SUITE 103
KETTERING, OHIO 45429
513-439-1224   RICHARD BROMBERG, PH.D.
Individual treatment is available, using desensitization, in vivo and imaginal; relaxation training; cognitive restructuring and fieldwork.

TERRAP–NORTH CENTRAL OHIO
NORWALK PSYCHOLOGICAL SERVICES
153 EAST MAIN STREET
NORWALK, OHIO 44857
419-668-5914   DONALD A. LEAKE, M.A.
Multimodal treatment approach including behavioral techniques. TERRAP group program is offered for the treatment of agoraphobia.

TERRAP TOLEDO
5800 MONROE STREET, BUILDING B
SYLVANIA, OHIO 43560
419-882-7189   JOEL M. KESTENBAUM, PH.D.
TERRAP group for agoraphobia; individual and group therapy available for other phobias; travel/exposure treatment available. Treatment approach is cognitive/behavioral.

SIVA P. KURUP, M.D., INC.
2000 EAST MARKET STREET
WARREN, OHIO 44483
216-393-5566
                                                    SIVA P. KURUP, M.D.
Individual therapy using behavioral techniques is offered either in
the office or in a hospital setting. Desensitization and flooding
techniques are used with imaginal stimuli or in vivo.

OREGON

PORTLAND AGORAPHOBIA CENTER
2104 N.W. EVERETT
PORTLAND, OREGON 97210
503-281-4846
                                                    DON F. PAGANO, PH.D.
Twenty-four-week group program for agoraphobia using TERRAP
format and flooding, bioenergetic and breathing exercises. Individual therapy in the office or in vivo.

HELEN TUGGY, PH.D.
2035 S.W. 58TH #201
PORTLAND, OREGON 97221
503-297-3224
                                                    HELEN TUGGY, PH.D.
Individual, group, travel/exposure and time-limited therapy contracts are available.

RICK WARREN, PH.D.
10175 S.W. BARBUR BLVD., SUITE 300B
PORTLAND, OREGON 97219
503-245-8937
                                                    RICK WARREN, PH.D.
Exposure and response prevention and cognitive restructuring are
offered for obsessive/compulsives; anxiety management, flooding,
focusing, breathing, assertive training and cognitive restructuring
are offered for phobias.

PENNSYLVANIA

NORTHWEST PSYCHOTHERAPY ASSOCIATES
813 BRUSHTOWN ROAD
AMBLER, PENNSYLVANIA 19002
215-628-0177
                                                    JAY K. CHERNEY, PH.D.

Individual psychotherapy, exposure therapy, travel group and a support group are offered for agoraphobics. Treatment programs for school phobia and driving phobia are also offered on an individual basis.

FRANK M. DATTILIO, M.ED.
1251 SOUTH CEDAR CREST BLVD., SUITE 211-D
ALLENTOWN, PENNSYLVANIA 18103
215-432-5066   FRANK M. DATTILIO, M.ED.
Treatment of simple and social phobias and agoraphobia is available on an individual and small-group basis. Treatment may include exposure therapy, biofeedback or medication.

AGORAPHOBIA & ANXIETY PROGRAM
DEPARTMENT OF PSYCHIATRY
TEMPLE UNIVERSITY MEDICAL SCHOOL
112 BALA AVENUE
BALA CYNWYD, PENNSYLVANIA 19004   LINDA WELSH, ED.D.
215-667-6490   ALAN GOLDSTEIN, PH.D.
Multilevel treatment approach including individual and/or group psychotherapy, exposure and couples therapy is offered for the treatment of agoraphobia, simple phobias, social anxiety and chronic anxiety. Two-week intensive-treatment program for agoraphobia is offered approximately eight times per year and a two-day program for building anxiety-coping skills is offered about six times per year. There are also periodic flying-fear and public-speaking anxiety workshops. Audiotapes to be used in conjunction with this book, *Overcoming Agoraphobia*, are available.

CARY S. ROTHSTEIN, PH.D.
1 HIGHLAND DRIVE
CHALFONT, PENNSYLVANIA 18914
215-822-7829   CARY S. ROTHSTEIN, PH.D.
Individual therapy using a behavioral approach is offered to individuals with panic disorders and agoraphobia.

TERRAP OF NORTHWESTERN PENNSYLVANIA
P.O. BOX 207, GRISWOLD PLAZA STATION
ERIE, PENNSYLVANIA 16501
814-454-4806   ANTHONY F. CILLUFFO, PH.D.

Twenty-week TERRAP program is offered for the treatment of agoraphobia and includes lectures, fieldwork and support groups.

TERRAP OF HERSHEY
BOX 19
HERSHEY, PENNSYLVANIA 17033
717-534-1451; 534-3652   JOSEPH A. LAFRANCE, M.A.
A systematic desensitizing behavioral training program is offered for groups and includes education, assertiveness and communication training and fieldwork. Individual therapy including home visits is also available.

PHOBIA TREATMENT SERVICES/GROWTH OPPORTUNITY CENTER
570 WELSH ROAD
HUNTINGDON VALLEY, PENNSYLVANIA 19006
215-947-8654   MICHAEL LAYNE, PH.D.
Cognitive/behavioral treatment of phobias is offered on an individual or group basis and includes in vivo exposure work.

SPENCER KREGER, M.D.
929 MENOHER BLVD.
JOHNSTOWN, PENNSYLVANIA 15905
814-255-1054   SPENCER KREGER, M.D.
TERRAP program is offered for groups; individual and medication therapy also available.

TERRAP OF PENNSYLVANIA
918 PARK AVENUE
PITTSBURGH, PENNSYLVANIA 15234
412-341-1162   RAYMOND A. HORNYAK, PH.D.
Individual and group behavior therapy are available for simple phobias and obsessive/compulsive disorders. For agoraphobia, a twenty-week cognitive/behavioral group program is offered.

PETER A. BOLTZ, M.S., ED.
1804 W. MARKET STREET
POTTSVILLE, PENNSYLVANIA 17901
717-628-5241   PETER A. BOLTZ, M.S.
Individual therapy can include psychoanalysis utilizing hypnosis, relaxation training, desensitization and biofeedback.

RHODE ISLAND

COMMUNITY COUNSELING CENTER
160 BEECHWOOD AVENUE
PAWTUCKET, RHODE ISLAND 02861
401-722-7855   JANE K. THOMPSON, A.C.S.W.
Individual and family therapy are available as well as a "Fears
Group" which provides a structured ten-week, goal-directed program of education, support and travel/exposure therapy.

SOUTH CAROLINA

BEHAVIORAL CONSULTANTS, INC.
722 EAST MCBEE AVENUE
GREENVILLE, SOUTH CAROLINA 29601
803-232-8542   VIRGINIA D. WHEELAN, A.C.S.W.
Program for agoraphobia includes cognitive/behavioral therapy,
relaxation training, in vivo exposure and family counseling on an
individual basis.

SUMTER SHOW MENTAL HEALTH ASSOCIATES
449 CHIPPEWA CIRCLE
SUMTER, SOUTH CAROLINA 29150
803-469-2100   GENE H. WOOD, JR., PH.D.
Individual treatment is available using a cognitive/behavioral approach and includes travel/exposure.

TENNESSEE

TERRAP—MEMPHIS
3000 A WALNUT GROVE ROAD
MEMPHIS, TENNESSEE 38111
901-324-2980   GILBERT KATZ, M.D.
Group program includes in vivo desensitization. Two-week intensive program with an emphasis on fieldwork is also offered.

TEXAS

AUSTIN CENTER FOR HUMAN RESOURCES
1000 EAST 32ND STREET, SUITE 3
AUSTIN, TEXAS 78705
512-476-4208   LESTER HARRELL, PH.D.

Individual therapy emphasizing a cognitive/behavioral approach and including relaxation training, cognitive coping skills and in vivo experience is offered. Group therapy and support groups are also available.

PSYCHOLOGICAL SERVICE CENTER
5333 EVERHART ROAD, SUITE 265 C
CORPUS CHRISTI, TEXAS 78411
512–855–6914   GEORGE H. KRAMER, JR., PH.D.
Individual and group therapy are available and can include desensitization, travel/exposure and biofeedback training.

PHOBIA CENTER OF THE SOUTHWEST
12860 HILLCREST #119
DALLAS, TEXAS 75230
214–386–6327   JAMES O. WILSON, M.A.
Group, individual, in vivo, time-limited and medication programs are available.

PHOBIA CENTER OF THE SOUTHWEST
29 CENTRE WEST
FORT WORTH, TEXAS 76107
817–332–1307   CLARK VINSEN, M.S.W.
Group, individual, in vivo, time-limited and medication programs are available.

PHOBIA CENTER OF THE SOUTHWEST
14139 HEATHERFIELD DRIVE
HOUSTON, TEXAS 77079
713–497–2310   ARLENE BAKER
Group, individual, travel/exposure and medication programs are available.

ROBERTA COHEN AND ASSOCIATES
11777 KATY FREEWAY,
NORTH BUILDING, SUITE 155
HOUSTON, TEXAS 77079
713-556-0555   ROBERTA COHEN, M.S.W.
Individual and group treatment are available on both time-limited and longer-term basis. CHAANGE tape program is also available.

MINIRTH-MEIER CLINIC
2071 NORTH COLLINS BLVD.
RICHARDSON, TEXAS 75080
214-669-1733   RICHARD L. FLOURNOY, PH.D.
Individual and group therapy include relaxation training, systematic desensitization, hypnotherapy, biofeedback and psychopharmacology.

SAN ANTONIO PHOBIA CLINIC
7711 LOUIS PASTEUR, SUITE 814
SAN ANTONIO, TEXAS 78229
512-696-4041   HABIB NATHAN, M.D.
A multidisciplinary approach which includes in vivo desensitization, travel/exposure, group therapy and use of medication. Three-month course followed by a self-help group.

UTAH

TERRAP
167 EAST 6100 SOUTH
SALT LAKE CITY, UTAH 84107
801-262-1441   JOANN JONES
TERRAP program directed by a recovered agoraphobic.

CLINIC FOR PHOBIAS AND ANXIETY DISORDERS
DEPARTMENT OF PSYCHIATRY
UNIVERSITY OF UTAH MEDICAL CENTER
SALT LAKE CITY, UTAH 84132
801-581-5811   MARK E. OWENS, PH.D.
Group, individual and couples therapy are available with focus on education, exposure and supportive therapy.

VIRGINIA

ROUNDHOUSE SQUARE PSYCHIATRIC CENTER/PHOBIA TREATMENT
1444 DUKE STREET
ALEXANDRIA, VIRGINIA 22314
703-836-7130   DAVID L. CHARNEY, M.D.
Group, individual, family and marital therapy using a psychopharmacological, hypnotic or behavioral approach are available for

the treatment of shyness, social phobias, agoraphobia and fear of public speaking.

CENTER FOR BEHAVIORAL MEDICINE/PHOBIA PROGRAM
2817 PARHAM ROAD
RICHMOND, VIRGINIA 23229
804–270–4111   RONNA SAUNDERS, M.S.W.
Sixteen-week program includes group sessions and individual in vivo sessions.   Self-help follow-up group is available.

PHOBIA CLINIC OF SOUTHWEST VIRGINIA
THE COUNSELING CENTER
3144 BRAMBLETON AVENUE, S.W.
ROANOKE, VIRGINIA 24018
703–774–4211   KATHLEEN A. BREHONY, PH.D.
Behavioral treatment program includes group and individual therapy and a support group.   Program features educational components, panic management techniques, in vivo and imaginal exposure, couples counseling, etc.

CENTER FOR BEHAVIORAL MEDICINE
PEMBROKE II, SUITE 135
VIRGINIA BEACH, VIRGINIA 23462
804–490–8806   LISA ZOCCO, PSY.D.
This center is one of Dr. DuPont's programs and offers individual, group and in vivo sessions for all types of phobics.   Sixteen-week program is available.

WASHINGTON, D.C.

AGORAPHOBIA PROGRAM, THE AMERICAN UNIVERSITY
C/O DEPARTMENT OF PSYCHOLOGY
4400 MASSACHUSETTS, N.W.
WASHINGTON, D.C. 20016
202–885–1715   DIANNE L. CHAMBLESS, PH.D.
Individual in vivo exposure for agoraphobia and behavior therapy for other anxiety disorders are available.

WASHINGTON STATE

TERRAP—SEATTLE
16414 S.E. 22ND STREET
BELLEVUE, WASHINGTON 98008
206-746-3006   DIANE STOUFFER
Sixteen-week group therapy program includes relaxation training,
systematic desensitization, assertiveness training, stress management and in vivo fieldwork.

SEATTLE PHOBIA CLINIC
CABRINI MEDICAL TOWER, SUITE 1910
901 BOREN AVENUE
SEATTLE, WASHINGTON 98104
206-343-9474   GERALD M. ROSEN, PH.D.
Behavior therapy for phobias include self-administered and therapist-assisted practice.   Additional psychotherapy or marital therapy for agoraphobia is offered.

ART PESKIND, PH.D.
ALLENMORE MEDICAL CENTER, SUITE A-115
SO. 19TH AND UNION
TACOMA, WASHINGTON 98405
206-572-2411   ART PESKIND, PH.D.
Individual cognitive/behavioral treatment includes education about
agoraphobia, physical and cognitive anxiety-control techniques, in
vivo practice and desensitization guidance, dealing with emotions,
and assertiveness training.

WISCONSIN

JOHN RAUCH, A.C.S.W.
2300 N. MAYFAIR ROAD
MILWAUKEE, WISCONSIN 53226
414-259-0240   JOHN RAUCH, A.C.S.W.
Treatment for agoraphobia is offered using supported exposure,
antidepressant medication or a combination as well as psychotherapy.

COLUMBIA HOSPITAL ANXIETY DISORDERS PROGRAM
2025 E. NEWPORT AVE.
MILWAUKEE, WISCONSIN 53211
414-961-4602   K. KWANG SOO, M.D.
Treatment is individualized and may include psychotherapy, group
psychotherapy, medication therapy, desensitization, flooding, relaxation techniques, biofeedback and couples counseling.

MENTAL HEALTH CARE ASSOCIATES
7929 NORTH PORT WASHINGTON AVE.
MILWAUKEE, WISCONSIN 53217
414-351-4747   BELLA H. SELAN, M.S.
Individual treatment for all types of phobias is available. The main
emphasis is on exposure, cognitive restructuring and other behavioral interventions but sometimes is combined with traditional
therapy.

MOUNT SINAI MEDICAL CENTER
DEPARTMENT OF PSYCHIATRY
950 NORTH 12TH STREET
MILWAUKEE, WISCONSIN 53233
414-289-8150; 289-8620   BELLA H. SELAN, M.S.
Eight-week travel/exposure groups and individual psychotherapy
including exposure are offered.

INTERNATIONAL CENTERS

FLINDERS MEDICAL CENTRE
BEDFORD PARK
SOUTH AUSTRALIA 5042
08-275-9911   R. J. HAFNER, M.D.
Individual and group exposure in vivo combined with spouse-aided
therapy where appropriate.

DR. OMER VANDEN BERGHE
FACULTY PSYCHOLOGY
TIENNESTRAAT 102
B3000 LEUVEN
BELGIUM

PERSONAL GROWTH CENTRES
11323 BRAESIDE DRIVE S.W.
CALGARY, ALBERTA T2W 2V6, CANADA
403-281-6937   MARY WARR
Group and individual counseling emphasizing behavioral and insight-therapy techniques.

S. RACHMAN, PH.D.
PSYCHOLOGY
UNIVERSITY OF BRITISH COLUMBIA
#154-2053 MAIN
VANCOUVER, BRITISH COLUMBIA, CANADA

VICTORIA HOSPITAL
SOUTH STREET
LONDON, ONTARIO, CANADA
519-432-5241   G. M. WEISZ, PH.D.
Cognitive/behavioral approach utilized in both group and individual therapy, including travel/exposure.   Individual psychotherapy available as needed.

GERALD D. PULVERMACHER, PH.D., AND ASSOCIATES
1704 CARLING AVE., SUITE 200
OTTAWA, ONTARIO, CANADA K2A 1L7
613-728-5837   GERALD D. PULVERMACHER, PH.D.
Individual and couples therapy utilizing a cognitive/behavioral approach and including in vivo desensitization, relaxation and assertiveness training.

DONALD H. MEICHENBAUM, PH.D.
PSYCHOLOGY DEPARTMENT
UNIVERSITY OF WATERLOO
WATERLOO, ONTARIO
CANADA N2L 3G1

HÔPITAL LOUIS H. LAFONTAINE
MODULE DE THERAPIE BEHAVIORALE,
7401 HOCHELAGA
MONTREAL, QUEBEC, CANADA H1N 3M7
514-253-1113   JEAN-MARIE BOISVERT, D.PS.

Ten-week group program, including exposure and individual psychotherapy, is offered.

BEHAVIOR THERAPY SERVICE—ROYAL VICTORIA HOSPITAL
687 PINE AVENUE WEST
MONTREAL, QUEBEC, CANADA H3A 1A1
514-842-1231, x.741   IAN F. BRADLEY, PH.D.
Treatment is offered on an individual basis with access to an exposure-based group.

UNIVERSITY HOSPITAL ANXIETY/AGORAPHOBIA PROGRAM
DEPARTMENT OF PSYCHIATRY
UNIVERSITY HOSPITAL
SASHATOON, SASK., CANADA
306-343-5141   R. C. BOWEN, M.D.C.M.
Open group, individual travel/exposure and behavioral therapy are offered.

ACADEMIC DEPARTMENT OF PSYCHIATRY
MEDICAL SCHOOL MIDDLESEX HOSPITAL
MORTIMER STREET
LONDON, W1, ENGLAND
01-636-8333   VICTOR MEYER, PH.D.
Individual treatment programs available, using behavioral techniques.

ISAAC MARKS, M.D.
INSTITUTE OF PSYCHIATRY
DECRESPIGNY PARK
LONDON SE5 8AF, ENGLAND

ANDREW MATHEWS, PH.D.
ST. GEORGE'S HOSPITAL MEDICAL SCHOOL
CRANMER TERRACE
LONDON SW17 ORE, ENGLAND

MICHAEL G. GELDER, M.D.
DEPT. OF PSYCHIATRY
UNIVERSITY OF OXFORD
THE WARNEFORD HOSPITAL
OXFORD OX3 7JX, ENGLAND

ROCHDALE HEALTH AUTHORITY
DEPARTMENT OF CLINICAL PSYCHOLOGY
BIRCH HILL HOSPITAL
ROCHDALE, ENGLAND
0706-77777   L. E. BURNS, PH.D.
A full range of behavioral treatments, including flooding, desensitization, individual and group exposure, cognitive restructuring, etc., is offered.

IVER HAND, M.D.
PSYCHIATRIC UNIVERSITY CLINIC
MARTINISTR. 52
D-2000 HAMBURG 20, WEST GERMANY

DR. JOERN J. BAMBECK & DR. ANTJE WOLTERS
INSTITUT FÜR VERHALTENSMODIFIKATION
JAKOB-KLAR-STRABE 9
D-8000 MUNCHEN 40, WEST GERMANY

JOHN C. BOULOURGOURIS, M.D.
DEPARTMENT OF PSYCHIATRY
UNIVERSITY OF ATHENS
EGNITION HOSPITAL
VASSILISSIS SOPHIAS 74
ATHENS, GREECE

DR. GIOVANNI LIOTTI
INSTITUTE OF PSYCHIATRY
UNIVERSITY LA SAPIENZA
VIA DEGLI SCIPION, 245
00192 ROMA, ITALY

DR. ROGER BAKER
DEPARTMENT OF PSYCHOLOGY
ROYAL CORNHILL HOSPITAL
ABERDEEN, SCOTLAND

LARS GORAN OST, PH.D.
PSYCHIATRIC RESEARCH CENTER
ULLERAKER HOSPITAL
S-75017 UPPSALA, SWEDEN

Dr. Sahika Yukosel
DEPARTMENT OF PSYCHIATRY
TA KAPA HOSPITAL
ISTANBUL, TURKEY

Paul M. G. Emmelkamp, Ph.D.
ACADEMIC HOSPITAL
DEPARTMENT OF CLINICAL PSYCHOLOGY
OOSTERSINGEL 59
GRONINGEN, THE NETHERLANDS

SELF-HELP SUPPORT GROUPS

C.A.L.L. (Concerned Agoraphobics Learning to Live)
380 TOLOSA WAY
SAN LUIS OBISPO, CALIFORNIA 93401
805-543-3764   DARYL M. WOODS
Self-help group of agoraphobics who meet once weekly. Extensive telephone and mail contact throughout the U.S.

Greenwich-Norwalk Support Group
101 D LEWIS STREET
GREENWICH, CONNECTICUT 06830
203-869-5178; 838-1041   MARY NADIG
Support groups, daily intensive course, and phone therapy.

New Beginnings—Phobia Support Groups
8905 COPENHAVER DRIVE
POTOMAC, MARYLAND 20854
301-424-2386   WANDA FALCI
Program includes reinforcement of skills and information for the phobic through discussions and readings. Led by a recovered agoraphobic.

Agoraphobics Inspiring Each Other
LOWELL COMMUNITY HEALTH CENTER
597 MERRIMACK STREET
LOWELL, MASSACHUSETTS 01854
617-458-8633   IRENE KNOX

Self-help support group for agoraphobics. Weekly meetings consist of group discussion, professional speakers, field trips, lending library, relaxation tapes, hot-line, educational handouts, etc.

A.I.M.—AGORAPHOBICS IN MOTION
2911 E. TEN MILE ROAD
WARREN, MICHIGAN 48089
313-755-4545   MARY ANN MILLER
Support group, telephone counseling and support, recovery through ten tools. Led by a recovered agoraphobic.

A.I.M.—AGORAPHOBICS IN MOTION
BOX 459
ROCKAWAY, NEW JERSEY 07866
201-627-2014   ESTELLE JULIAN
Informational newsletter for those people who will not go out of their homes. $2.50 per copy.

NEW JERSEY SELF-HELP CLEARINGHOUSE
ST. CLARE'S HOSPITAL COMMUNITY MENTAL HEALTH CENTER
POCONO ROAD
DENVILLE, NEW JERSEY 07834
800-FOR-MASH IN N.J.
201-625-7026 OUTSIDE   EDWARD J. MADARA
Free service that maintains a comprehensive computerized listing of self-help mutual aid groups. Also has information on how to start a self-help group.

GROUP BY MAIL
154 CHATFIELD ROAD
BRONXVILLE, NEW YORK 10708
914-337-3220   D. JEAN ESTERBROOK
Mail program which emphasizes caring and supportive help from the other members of the group.

PHOBAID
525 NORTH BROADWAY
UPPER NYACK, NEW YORK 10960
914-358-0063   MIRIAM CAVIN
Self-help group meets weekly and is led by a paraprofessional trained by Dr. Zane.

AGORAPHOBICS MEETING CHALLENGES
C/O YWCA
WEST CHESTER, PENNSYLVANIA
215-696-4181   MARION MICHAEL
Weekly program consists of setting goals; discussing topics such
as anxiety, depression, nutrition, etc.; visiting lectures by professionals; and outings.   Consulting psychologist available.

PHOBICS ANONYMOUS
C/O JOHN RAUCH, A.C.S.W.
2300 N. MAYFAIR ROAD
MILWAUKEE, WISCONSIN 53226
414-259-0240   JOHN RAUCH, A.C.S.W.
Co-founded by two social workers, Phobics Anonymous will
sponsor support groups for agoraphobia sufferers and other phobia sufferers with focus on self-help education, sharing of experiences, coping methods and support.

F.L.O.A.T. (FREEDOM, LIFE OF AGORAPHOBICS TOGETHER)
C/O DOUG MACLEAY
6 GLACIER CRESCENT
SHERWOOD PARK
ALBERTA, CANADA T8A 2Y2
403-464-2377   DOUG MACLEAY
Source of information for agoraphobics in Canada.   Self-help
group.

PROGRAMS BY CATEGORY

The following programs have been cross-referenced:

CORRESPONDENCE/TAPE PROGRAMS

TERRAP-MENLO PARK, MENLO PARK, CALIF.
CHAANGE, CHARLOTTE, N.C.
PHOBIA WORKSHOP AND AGORAPHOBIA CENTER, GRANTVILLE, PA.
OUTGROWING AGORAPHOBIA, P.O. BOX 40308, SAN FRANCISCO, CALIF.

DENTAL PHOBIA PROGRAMS

BARRY G. DALE, D.M.D., ENGLEWOOD, N.J.
DENTAL PHOBIA CLINIC, NEW YORK, N.Y.
TED GOLDSTEIN, D.D.S., NEW YORK, N.Y.

FLYING PROGRAMS

PHOBIA PROGRAM OF SOUTHERN CALIFORNIA, LOS ANGELES, CALIF.
S.O.A.R., INC., WESTPORT, CONN.
MARVIN L. ARONSON, PH.D., NEW YORK, N.Y.
FLY WITHOUT FEAR, NEW YORK, N.Y.
PHOBIA SERVICES & FLY FREE OF FEAR, COLUMBUS, OH.
TEMPLE AGORAPHOBIA & ANXIETY PROGRAM, BALA CYNWYD, PA.

INTENSIVE TREATMENT PROGRAMS

TERRAP-ORANGE COUNTY, WESTMINSTER, CALIF.
AGORAPHOBIA RESOURCE CENTER, COCONUT GROVE, FLA.
PARK CENTER, FORT WAYNE, IND.
ABBOTT NORTHWESTERN HOSPITAL, MINNEAPOLIS, MINN.
BIOBEHAVIORAL PSYCHIATRY, GREAT NECK, N.Y.
PHOBIA CLINIC, WHITE PLAINS, N.Y.
TEMPLE AGORAPHOBIA AND ANXIETY PROGRAM, BALA CYNWYD, PA.
TERRAP-MEMPHIS, MEMPHIS, TENN.

RESIDENT PROGRAMS (INPATIENT)

LIVING GROWTH PHOBIA CENTER, PRESCOTT, ARIZ.
GLADMAN MEMORIAL HOSPITAL, OAKLAND, CALIF.
CARRIER FOUNDATION, BELLE MEAD, N.J.

ORGANIZATIONS

PHOBIA SOCIETY OF AMERICA
133 ROLLINS AVENUE, SUITE 4B
ROCKVILLE, MARYLAND 20852-4004
This organization is dedicated primarily to functioning as a clearinghouse for information about phobic disorders. It was slow

getting off the ground and erratic in performance in the beginning, but is now staffed with competent and dedicated people and is doing a fine job. Its dues-paying members include agoraphobics, paraprofessionals and professionals interested in phobias. Members receive a very informative newsletter and the society also offers for sale an updated listing of treatment facilities. The society sponsors an annual conference with excellent presentations geared toward both the professional and lay audience.

Index